Language, culture and identity in app linguistics

British Studies in Applied Linguistics

Published in collaboration with British Association for Applied Linguistics (BAAL)

Each volume in the series consists of a selection of peer-reviewed papers on a theme of general interest, based on presentations at the BAAL Annual General Meetings. In covering state-of-the-art research in the UK and elsewhere, the series aims to broaden the scope of applied linguistics to include areas as diverse as sociolinguistics, discourse analysis, communication studies and language education.

Volumes 1-15 in this series were published by Multilingual Matters; volumes 16-18 were published by Continuum.

For more information about BAAL visit their website: www.baal.org.uk

Previously published
Applied Linguistics at the Interface
Edited by Mike Baynham, Alice Deignan and Goodith White
(Volume 19)

Reconfiguring Europe: the contribution of applied linguistics
Edited by Constant Leung and Jennifer Jenkins
(Volume 20)

British Studies in Applied Linguistics: Volume 21

Language, culture and identity in applied linguistics

Selected papers from the
Annual Meeting of the British Association for Applied Linguistics
University of Bristol, September 2005

Edited by
Richard Kiely, Pauline Rea-Dickins,
Helen Woodfield and Gerald Clibbon

BRITISH ASSOCIATION FOR APPLIED LINGUISTICS
in association with

LONDON   OAKVILLE

Published by

Equinox Publishing Ltd.
UK: Unit 6, The Village, 101 Amies Street, London, SW11 2JW
USA: DBBC, 28 Main Street, Oakville, CT 06779
www.equinoxpub.com

First published 2006

British Library Cataloguing-in-Publication Data

A catalogue record for this book is available from the British Library.

ISBN-13: 978-1-84553-219-2 (paperback)
ISBN-10: 1-84553-219-8 (paperback)

Library of Congress Cataloging-in-Publication Data
British Association for Applied Linguistics. Meeting (38th : 2005 :
University of Bristol)
  Language, culture and identity in applied linguistics / edited by
Richard Kiely ... [et al.].
     p. cm. -- (British studies in applied linguistics ; v. 21)
  Papers from the 38th annual BAAL Conference held at the University of
Bristol in Sept. 2005.
  Includes bibliographical references.
  ISBN-13: 978-1-84553-219-2 (pbk.)
  ISBN-10: 1-84553-219-8 (pbk.)
  1. Language and culture--Congresses. 2. Identity
(Psychology)--Congresses. I. Kiely, Richard, 1955- II. Title.
  P35.B64 2005
  306.44--dc22
                                        2006020074

Typeset by Catchline, Milton Keynes (www.catchline.com)
Printed and bound in Great Britain by Antony Rowe Ltd.,
Chippenham, Wiltshire

Contents

Introduction

Richard Kiely, Pauline Rea-Dickins,
Helen Woodfield and Gerald Clibbon

This volume is a collection of papers from the 38th Annual BAAL Conference held at the University of Bristol in September 2005. The *Call for Papers* illustrates the thematic framing of the conference:

> The theme for the conference – Language, Culture and Identity in Applied Linguistics – reflects different aspects of knowledge-building across the field. The notion of language and culture represents the communities and institutions which house and frame both language learning and language use. The notion of language and identity focuses on the relationships each individual has with communities and institutions, and which are evidenced in interactions in work, social and learning contexts. The theme of the meeting, then, provides opportunities for engagement with issues of language use, language form, language learning, language pedagogy and language assessment which inform on the construction of identity and on the social and cultural contexts where identity is profiled.

The papers in this volume reflect this theme in a range of ways. Each contribution represents a performance, that is, a use of language for a specific purpose in a defined social setting. Each was initially performed in the social context of the conference, then revised and reframed as a written paper. The processes of adaptation and tuning which have generated these texts illustrate some of the complexities inherent in language use. Understanding language use, spoken and written, as performance has always been important in applied linguistics. Hymes, in 1972, signalled that what is important as a focus for enquiry in applied linguistics is 'what is done' in language rather than what is correct, mandated or ideal. An important strand of research in applied linguistics has since then, explored language performance as a means of theorising language use and social context in order to understand how language both shapes and reflects the ways we think and act. This approach has facilitated the development of applied linguistics research to address issues of learning, access to learning, ethics, opportunity, marginalisation and discrimination, providing a critical angle on aspects of the social world which are so often taken for granted. The twin themes of the BAAL 2005 conference – Culture and Identity – build on understanding language as 'performance'.

Culture in applied linguistics is typically viewed as a dynamic rather than a static, a small 'c' account of how people live their lives (Kramsch, 1993; Holliday, 1999), rather than a big 'C' collage of the highest achievements in artistic and social enterprises. Street (1993) characterises this dynamic perspective on culture:

> In fact there is not much point in trying to say what culture is … What can be done, however, is to say what culture does. For what culture does is precisely the work of defining words ideas, things and groups … We all live our lives in terms of definitions, names, and categories that culture creates. The job of studying culture is not finding and then accepting its definitions but of discovering how and what definitions are made, under what circumstances, and for what reasons. These definitions are used, change, and sometimes fall into disuse. Indeed the very term culture itself, like these other ideas and definitions, changes its meanings and serves different and often competing purposes at different times. Culture is an active process of meaning making and contest over definition, including its own definition. This then, is what I mean by arguing that *Culture is a verb.* (Street, 1993: 25)

Identity is also a process of constant, performed meaning-making, whether for groups, communities, or individuals. Identity is increasingly viewed not as a fixed label, but as a means of articulating the relationship we have with the world around us. Wenger captures this fluid, evolving notion of identity and identification processes in a way which makes language a key node in researching and understanding it:

> Building an identity consists of negotiating the meanings of our experience of membership in social communities. The concept of identity serves as a pivot between the social and the individual, so that each can be talked about in terms of the other. It avoids a simplistic individual-social dichotomy without doing away with the distinction. The resulting perspective is neither individualistic nor absolutely institutional or societal. It does justice to the lived experience of identity while recognizing its social character – it is the social, the cultural, the historical with a human face. (Wenger, 1998: 145)

All the papers and other contributions at BAAL 2005 were performances: *doing* culture and identity regardless of what the subject matter was. The process of submitting and selecting the papers that ultimately appeared on the programme reflects a culture, in Street's terms, of discovering what a suitable paper for a BAAL conference involves, and why. And participating in the conference is in a sense a negotiating of identity with BAAL, whether as a central or peripheral member, enacting a facet of identity performed many times before, or establishing a new or ephemeral connection with the organisation and conference.

The papers in this collection relate more directly to the concepts of culture and identity in applied linguistics. Ivanič, in a plenary lecture, explores the relationship between 'identity work' and learning. Drawing on the experience of Logan, a learner developing literacy skills as part of his professional education, she shows how research into the fine weave of identity work can reveal learning opportunities and experiences. She uses concepts from activity theory to illustrate the connectedness of context and action, of potential and actual achievements on the one hand, and constraints and barriers on the other.

The papers of Conrick and Duvfa and Pietikäinen explore language and identity issues in contexts which have traditionally been cultures of language conflict. In Quebec in Canada, the perceived balances and imbalances of French and English have become the focus of legislative attention: the fluidity of identity in the rigid packaging of legal statute. Conrick examines recent developments in the sociolinguistic drama of Loi 101, the law which affords protection for French in Quebec. Her analysis shows how the resolution in the courts is, like the law itself, a matter of interpretation which depends on the identity lens it is viewed through. In relation to gender and identity, she also shows how Canadian French is challenging the 'fixedness' of the convention which privileges grammatical gender over actual gender. Dufva and Pietikäinen provide a rich account of developments over decades in Sami language use and identity in Finland. The picture is complex, with patterns of growth, stability and decline evident in the accounts of Sami speakers of different ages, and in different family and community language contexts. While the goal of maintaining culture and identity through language may reflect established themes, the novelty and contemporary media contexts of language use evidenced in their data and discussion may challenge what we see as heritage and as the focus and means of preservation.

Sophocleou and Fraser examine attitudes to languages and the ways these shape language change and achievements in language learning. Sophocleou describes a research study into attitudes towards different forms of the Greek-Cypriot Dialect in Cyprus. The research, using a Matched Guise technique shows the conventional divide in attitudes – the more formal and high status the dialect form, the more educated, prosperous and distant the speakers are assumed to be. The study also suggests that the increasingly wide use in the media of traditionally informal dialect forms may be adding a complexity to the picture, as high status users such as politicians and media figures make greater use of informal forms. Fraser, researching language attitudes in an English as a Foreign Language (EFL) and English as an International Language (EIL) context explores attitudes of Japanese students to different accents in English. The study confirms the preference for American native-speaker accents. A particularly interesting aspect of this study is the comprehension check gathered as data: the accents which afforded greatest ease of comprehension were Asian (including Japanese) speakers of English. These, however, were not considered desirable as learning models, a finding which prompts Fraser to call for a review of the position of dominant native-speaker accents, and consideration of learning models within an EIL framework.

There are four papers which examine different aspects of culture and identity in academic writing. The first two – Nesi and Gardner, and Petrić – use data from interviews with student writers' readers (academic tutors) and the student writers themselves. The next two use the written texts as data, with Griffin using a metadiscoursal framework for analysing undergraduate assignments, and Charles a corpus approach to analyse patterns of identity construction in doctoral theses. Nesi and Gardner present the findings of research into the growing range of genres used for assessment and learning in higher education contexts. Drawing on data from interviews with academic staff in a wide range of disciplines, they set out an inventory of genres, which mesh in a complex way with shared views of what constitutes good academic writing on the one hand, and differing expectations of student voice and text structure in the different disciplines and subject areas on the other. Petrić takes disciplinary affiliation as her focus. Her research examines the identities formed and re-formed as a result of completing an interdisciplinary postgraduate programme. Her findings evidence the extent to which we write as members of a writing community, and in our writing we locate ourselves somewhere between its centre and periphery. Whereas Petrić examines the factors affecting the identity construction of the writer, Griffin looks at the construction of audience identity. She examines the strategies used to establish a relationship with the reader as member of a discipline community, and concludes that tutors, programmes and institutions could provide better guidance for novice writers who are developing their own voice and reader relationships through the construction of audience. Charles' paper illustrates that those students who get to write a doctoral thesis achieve commendable sophistication in voice and identity. Her corpus study of five grammatical patterns in science and social science theses illustrates the writers' capacity to obscure or reveal their identity in a manner appropriate in each case to the claim being made and quality of the evidence used to support it. These studies on identity issues in academic writing illustrate the need for clear guidance from programmes and tutors, especially for novice writers (Nesi and Gardner and Griffin) on the one hand, and the capacity of writers who are becoming increasingly skilled to ultimately find their own academic identity and subtleties of voice (Petrić and Charles) on the other.

The next two papers are from the language classroom, exploring culture and identity in the alignment of teaching and learning. Dippold looks at identity construction in interactive language learning tasks from the perspective of intercultural pragmatics. She analyses how learners of German as a Foreign Language do 'facework', and illustrates that they attend to the pragmatic demands of interactions as far as attentional resources permit. Benati investigates different pedagogic strategies in the Italian as a Foreign language classroom from a processing instruction perspective. His focus is on input on and learning of grammatical patterns, and he develops a research technique using computer-based learning materials. This innovation excludes the possibility of learners benefiting from the responses and suggestions of other students in classroom interaction, and thus achieves a precise focus on the controlled input.

The final paper of this collection is the Pit Corder lecture. In his contribution, Sarangi explores the emergent field of professional discourse studies, and the questions that arise as this field establishes itself both within applied linguistics and the professions it informs, and is informed by. He draws on research into language use in healthcare sites but engages with issues which affect all Applied Linguists: how research into language and communication can achieve its goals when these are just one part of professional action. Sarangi revisits the limitations of applied linguistics set out by Pit Corder, and reframes these as an opportunity for Applied Linguists in all professional fields to achieve greater understanding, relevance and impact.

Sarangi and Ivanič in the papers as in their conference performances, emphasise the importance of embedding *context* in the analysis, and both use *activity* as a concept and metaphor to capture the significance of context in understanding both how language is used, and the consequences of such use. These themes are reflected in the other topics in this collection. In language learning, academic writing, language maintenance, and literacy development, applied linguistics can be a context for research into these fields as subject areas, and their construction in and as discourse. Sarangi's conclusion on the need for a dialogue between communication researchers and professional practitioners, reflects a wider theme for applied linguistics. In many ways this dialogue is just beginning: as we work with the uniqueness of each language performance and the complex contributions of identity and culture in each case, we get a sense in these papers of the journey ahead.

References

Holliday, A. (1999) Small cultures. *Applied Linguistics* 20(2): 237–64.

Hymes, D. (1972) On communicative competence. In J. B. Pride and J. Holmes (eds) *Sociolinguistics*. Harmondsworth: Penguin Books.

Kramsch, C. (1993) *Context and Culture in Language Teaching*. Oxford: Oxford University Press.

Street, B. (1993) Culture is a verb. In D. Graddol, L. Thompson, and M. Byram (eds) *Language and Culture*. Clevedon: BAAL and Multilingual Matters.

Wenger, E. (1998) *Communities of Practice: learning, meaning and identity*. Cambridge: Cambridge University Press.

1 Language, learning and identification

Roz Ivanič

Introduction

My interest in 'identity' started with a fascination for how writers construct their identity at the moment of writing: 'at the point of the pen' or, more realistically these days, at the touch of the keyboard (Ivanič, 1998, 2005; Clark and Ivanič, 1997: Chapter 6). While retaining this focus, in what follows I pay more attention to the sociocultural and historical context within which this discoursal construction of identity happens, locating it within more recent developments in sociocultural perspectives on action, learning and identity, and drawing on my more recent involvement in New Literacy Studies, and my current research on the *Literacies for Learning in Further Education* project.[1] In particular, I pinpoint a common element in the work of Hall (1996), Gee (2003 and 2005), Kress (1997), Lave and Wenger (1991) and Wenger (1998), and propose that 'identification' is the key factor in learning, in language learning and in transformation of practices across contexts.

I am using the word 'language' in the title of this paper as a shorthand to signal all forms of communication, encompassing the full range of semiotic resources and practices. Most of what I say about 'language' can, I suggest, be applied to multimodal, intersemiotic communication in its broadest possible sense (as proposed by, e.g. Cope and Kalantzis, 2000; Kress and van Leeuwen, 2001). I will continue to use the word 'identity' because it is the everyday word for people's sense of who they are, but using it to stand for the often multiple, sometimes contradictory identities which can coexist. The term 'subjectivity' is also useful for indicating that 'identity' is constructed through subject positioning: a process of making the self the subject (Kress, 1996, and Scott, 2000; see also Ivanič, 1998: 10–11, for further discussion of ways of talking about 'identity'). One of the main arguments of this paper, however, is that the noun 'identity' is misleadingly static, and in thinking about the relationship between language, learning and identity it is more productive to think about identity as a continuous process of identification.

In the first section of the paper I use Activity Theory as a heuristic for identifying the key elements of sociocultural perspectives on language and learning. I then introduce the research context on which I draw to exemplify the main argument in the paper: a Food and Drink Service course at a College of Further Education, and one of the students enrolled on it. In the main part of the paper I propose five aspects of identity which concern language and learning: the relational nature of identity, the discoursal construction of identity, identification, the way in which identity is networked, and the way in which identity is continuously reconstructed. I conclude by outlining the implications of these aspects of identity for learning and for language learning.

Sociocultural perspectives on language and learning

This section provides a 'prequel', as it were, to my previous focus on the discoursal construction of identity in academic writing (Ivanič 1998, 2005; Clark and Ivanič 1997; Ivanič and Camps 2001). In that research I treated students' written texts as my primary data, and identified the discourses which the writers were drawing upon. However, I am now suggesting that a more nuanced definition of 'context' needs to be part of the examination of the relationships among language, learning and identity. Educational researchers are working towards an understanding of context which eschews the sense of context as a container, especially as a 'container' of learning (see e.g. McDermott, 1996; Edwards, 2005). Context has more recently been conceptualised rather as a relational phenomenon, in which the 'text' – what is going on – cannot be separated from the 'con' – what accompanies it. The 'texture' of an event changes moment by moment as the elements which constitute it co-emerge: identities, relationships, actions, semiotic resources, the significance and use of space and time, all of which have historical trajectories, are networked to others, and are culturally shaped. Identities and learning are always a part of this networked set of co-emerging factors. It is perhaps more useful to think of the participants in activities as being engaged in a constant process of contextualising, rather than to try to think of 'context' as a separately describable entity.

To examine what this view of context might mean, I am using the basic representation of human activity in Activity Theory (AT), not because I want to espouse the tenets and terminology of AT as an exclusive framing, but because I find it a useful heuristic.[2] Of the various terms used in different theories, 'context', 'community of practice', 'event', activity', I find 'activity' has the advantage that it doesn't suggest the context-as-container metaphor, and doesn't separate action from space or time. Figure 1 presents a simple version of this. I am using the basic AT triangle as a framework on which to hang other insights about communicative resources and practices, doing, learning, and being, drawn from other sociocultural theories of action, learning and/or identity (e.g. Barton and Hamilton, 2005; Clarke, 2002; Gee, 1996; 2000–2001,

2003; Holland et al., 1998; Lave and Wenger, 1991; Pahl and Rowsell, 2005; Wenger, 1998; Wertsch, 1991).

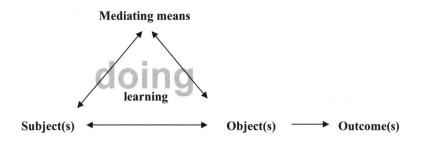

Figure 1: Learning as an integral part of participation in activity

Figure 1 represents the totality of an observable social activity. It is intended to capture diagrammatically the following points:

1. There is no separate 'con' and 'text': the elements of an activity co-emerge and are dynamically interrelated. This is represented by the word 'doing' as a kind of watermark encompassing all the other elements in the diagram.
2. Human activities are purposeful, motivated, goal-directed. In terms of AT, they have one or more 'Object(s)' which may or may not result in one or more 'Outcome(s)'.
3. 'Mediating means', including semiotic systems and artefacts, are fundamental elements of human activities. This emphasises their role as actants, shaping the actions for which they are used.
4. As a corollary of (1), (2) and (3) semiotic artefacts in all media and modes are not decontextualised objects of study, but situated in purposeful human action; their semiotic systems for representing the world are not just sets of rules and patterns to be studied in isolation from their purposeful use.
5. Most (perhaps all) meaningful activity involves learning through participation – conscious or subconscious, intentional or unintentional. This is represented in Figure 1 by the way in which the word 'learning' is almost embedded in the word 'doing'.

So far I have not used the term 'practices', because this implies regularly occurring, culturally recognised ways of doing things, rather than the actual observable actions and texts in a specific event. However, theory and research should not stop with the observable. AT charges the analyst with the challenge of identifying 'activity systems': regularly occurring configurations of Subjects, Objects and Mediating means, and of considering the historical trajectory and (socio-) cultural shapings of the elements observed in an activity.[3] Figure 2 represents the way in which any observable activity draws upon the practices, genres and discourses which are socioculturally available to its Subjects, and how these in turn are shaped by power relations, values and beliefs in the sociocultural context.

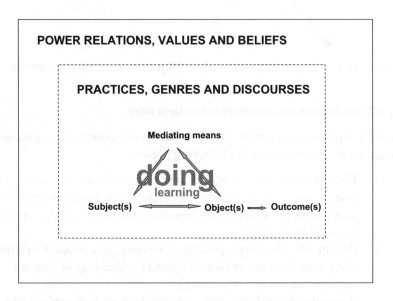

Figure 1.2: The elements of a social activity located in a sociocultural-historical context

The way any element plays out in an observable activity will also project into the future, contributing to the reshaping of socioculturally available practices and communicative resources for future events in the same or similar contexts. This implies that each of the semiotic artefacts (which are the types of mediating means in which I am interested) is likely to have some sort of actual provenance: a place where it was made; people who have literally or metaphorically read it before, and also a cultural shaping, in terms of the genres and discourses on which it is drawing. Each of the actions, too, is an instantiation of practices which make a commonality between this particular event and others like it – others, at least, which share some of its characteristics. And, in due course, I will be focusing on the way in which the people involved, the 'Subjects' of the activity, come to it with a socioculturally shaped history. Each of those observable people, mediating means, actions, and 'objects' of actions has been shaped by its history, by patterns of privileging, and by powerful social, political and economic forces in the cultural and institutional context which has produced it. The term 'context' is perhaps best reserved for this sociocultural-historical shaping.

The value of a sociocultural theory of action and learning such as AT is that subjects, and learning, are firmly located in the context of their participation in social practice, as described above: a subject's 'being' is inextricable from their 'doing'. The AT representation of human activity does not use the word 'identity', but it specifies 'Subjects' as one of the three main elements in an activity system: people – the participants, the social actors in the activity. People are 'subjects' in two senses: the sense of being 'subject' to the social affordances and constraints exerted on them by the activity; and the sense of being the 'subject' performing the action: actors, with agency. A focus on identity involves examining the subject(s) of activities in both these senses. In what follows I distinguish five dimensions of identity through participation: identity is relational; identity is discoursally constructed; identity is not so much a state as a process of identification; identity is networked; and identity is continuously reconstructed. Although my analysis is of the discoursal construction of identity through writing, it is an example of the much wider social process of the discoursal construction of identity through the full range of semiotic resources.

Introducing Logan and the training restaurant

The examples are taken from a case-study which is part of on-going research on the Literacies for Learning in Further Education (LfLFE) project. Logan[4] was at the time a 20-year old student on an NVQ Level 2 course in Food and Drink Service which was one of the focal units for the LfLFE project. Here is how Logan describes himself:

Interview Extract 1

Logan: Well I've been working in, I started working in The Broadway when I was 15, and I worked there for 5 years, and then I moved to The Elms, just six months ago, and it's just like, every other job I've done, I've had no interest for. Everything my mum says, oh get a job in an office or something, I just, it's not me, I'm more of a hands-on person, and I like, I like making people happy, and stuff, do you know what I mean

Interviewer: Right, yeah

Logan: I like the feeling it gives me when I see someone's happy with the meal they've got and they've got a smile on their face, and the whole restaurant's talking and there's a happy atmosphere

A substantial part of the course takes place in the real work environment of the training restaurant at the FE College: it is within an educational institution, but having many characteristics of a workplace. It is thus a hybrid activity, doubling as the provision of food and drink service in a restaurant, and a Level 2 vocational class, neatly embedding learning in doing. Figure 3 represents the hybrid nature of the activity by specifying dual 'Objects' and 'Outcomes' for it. I will come back to the significance of this hybridity for learning in the final section of this paper.

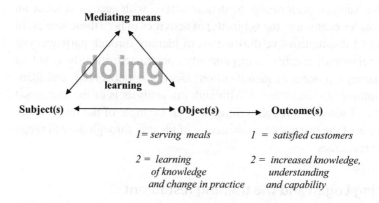

Figure 1.3: The training restaurant as a hybrid activity system

Identity is relational

A person's identity does not have an independent existence, but is co-emergent with other aspects of social activity: relationships, learning, which spaces are relevant, and how time is used. In particular, identity is constructed in the context of social relations. In terms of the AT representation of human activity, this aspect of identity is signalled by the way that the 'Subject' component of human activity is usually pluralised: 'Subject(s)'. Social relations are always also relations of power, and so the workings of status, prestige and hierarchy will shape how identity is constructed.

A person might construct a quite different impression of him/ herself in the company of one set of people from the impression s/he would construct in the company of another group of people. This relational aspect of identity is captured in Goffman's observation of the behaviour of Shetland Islanders in *The Representation of Self in Everyday Life* (1959). He described the way that Shetland Islanders modulated their participation in activities by consciously or subconsciously anticipating the impression others will form of them. Goffman did not distinguish linguistic behaviour from other types of behaviour, nor did he foreground the tensions and power relations with which such representations of self might be fraught. He did, however, put on the agenda the notion that identity is something which is constructed in interaction, rather than an individual state of being.

In one of the restaurants we have visited as part of this research we noticed a sign above the door between the kitchen and the restaurant, saying 'You are going on stage': restaurant managers are very aware of the way in which every aspect of behaviour constructs identity in the eyes of others. The other people involved shape a person's identity at two stages in the process of identity construction. First, the person himself acts, speaks and writes in a certain way according to how he anticipates people will react. But he may not have anticipated correctly. His identity will be constructed by others at the moment of 'uptake' – the observers, listeners and readers may take away a different impression from the one he intended. In both these ways identity is not pre-existing, not even constructed by an individual for himself, but is a product of the social relations between people.

Logan's identity is located within his relationship with others in the training restaurant: other students, the staff, the restaurant manager, the teachers on the course, and the customers. He creates an impression of himself which is dependent upon these people seeing his actions and, in the specific example below, reading his words. In the company of others, his identity would be different. It is essential to locate an analysis of the discoursal construction of identity in the context of a relational view of identity.

The discoursal construction of identity

Using the term 'discourse' in the focused linguistic and semiotic sense of 'the use of communicative practices', it is useful to distinguish three ways in which people are discoursally constructed, both to themselves and to other people:[5]

- by 'address' – the way we are talked to by others;
- by 'attribution' – the way we are talked about by others;
- by 'affiliation' – the way we talk like others;

    (here 'talk' stands for 'communicate using the full range of semiotic resources').

These three means by which identity is discoursally constructed are likely to be operating simultaneously within any communicative event. As Person

A addresses Person B, the identity of Person B may be constructed both by address and by attribution, while the identity of Person A is simultaneously being constructed by affiliation. And in the next utterance the processes may operate in the opposite direction. I will explain each of these processes in more detail, using the construction of Logan's identity in the training restaurant to provide examples, and focusing particularly on the discoursal construction of identity by 'affiliation'.

(i)   The discoursal construction of identity by address

Logan's identity is discoursally constructed by 'address' – by being spoken to, or written to, in one way or another. He may be excluded from conversation; he may be given orders; he may be asked his opinion; he may be thanked; he may be spoken to politely or otherwise: all these communicative acts will position him, will assign a particular identity to him. Taking some examples from written communication, receiving a memo about a change in restaurant opening hours will position Logan as in need of information in order to do the job; written feedback on his performance on the course will position him as a student whose success is in the hands of his tutor-assessors. The discoursal construction of identity by 'address' is, of the three, the most intrinsically relational in that it is the communicative practice itself that constructs identity, whereas in the other two types, social relations provide the context for the discoursally constructive acts.

(ii)   The discoursal construction of identity by attribution

Logan's identity is also discoursally constructed by 'attribution' – by other people's representations of his role, his appearance, his attributes and his actions. If Logan hears himself referred to as a 'student', this will affect his sense of his role in the activity, but if he hears himself referred to as 'the drinks' waiter' this will give him a different sense of who he is. Hearing people using judgmental expressions such as 'trying hard', 'very effective', or invoking community values through expressions such as 'Logan avoided some trouble for us there' will shape his sense of himself. Other people, too, will form impressions of Logan from reading, hearing or seeing the way in which he is referred to or represented by others. In this way, identity is discoursally constructed through attribution.

(iii)   The discoursal construction of identity by affiliation

The discoursal construction of identity by what I am calling here 'affiliation' depends not on other people's use of semiotic resources, but on the person's own use of semiotic resources to act, talk or, in this case, write like other people, and hence to identify him/herself with those people.

> identity ... is the result of affiliation to particular beliefs and possibilities which are available to [people] in their social context.' (Ivanič 1998: 12)

As I will argue in the rest of the paper, this is a process of identification, in which a person's identity is in a continuous process of reconstruction and realignment, rather than a static entity. This type of 'discoursal construction' of identity is achieved, like the previous two, through social interaction. In addition it involves drawing on 'discourses' in the broader sense of configurations of practices, including multimodal communicative practices, which have inscribed in them a particular view of some aspect of social reality (as argued, e.g. by Gee, 1996, and Fairclough, 2003). The term 'discourse' when used in this way is a count noun.

In most social contexts there are multiple discourses in circulation – discourses about several different aspects of social reality, and often more than one discourse of the same aspect of reality. In the training restaurant where Logan works there are several discourses in circulation. The list which follows summarises those discourses of which I have found evidence in the text discussed below (see Figure 4) and, to provide a point of comparison, some other discourses which, I suggest, are likely to be socially available in the same context, but are not in evidence in this piece of data.

Some discourses potentially in circulation in a training restaurant:

- Discourses of food and drink service
  a 'make people happy' discourse
  a 'control the customers' discourse
  a 'customers are a pain' discourse

- Discourses of eating out
  a special occasion discourse
  a cheap and cheerful discourse

- Discourses of male-female (or other) relationships
  a romantic love discourse
  a 'scoring' discourse

- Discourses of writing
  a 'writing is not cool' discourse
  a 'writing serves a useful purpose' discourse
  a 'writing is a creative process' discourse

Potential discourses of food and drink service include a deferential, customer satisfaction 'make people happy' discourse, a regulatory 'control the customers' discourse, a 'customers are a pain' discourse, and more. From the evidence I discuss later, there is also at least one discourse of male-female (or other) relationships in circulation – a romantic love discourse, and probably others too – a 'scoring' discourse, perhaps. There are also, I suggest, at least three contradictory discourses about writing: a 'not cool' discourse of writing, a 'writing serves a useful purpose' discourse, and a 'writing is a creative process' discourse. This context does not, I suggest, support all possible discourses on these or other aspects of social reality. For example, an exploitative capitalist discourse of food and drink service might be prevalent in other contexts but unlikely to be in circulation in a training restaurant.

Each of these discourses is instantiated by particular practices: ways of doing things, choices of words and grammatical ways of putting things, choices of images and other ways of communicating visually, to name the ones which will be significant in this analysis. Identity is discoursally constructed when people participate in the practices which constitute a discourse, and thereby affiliate themselves with others who engage in the same practices. A person cannot draw upon a discourse to which they have not been exposed: discourses are differentially available to people according to their social circumstances. Writing (or, as I prefer to call it, 'wrighting'[6]) is a significant site for the discoursal construction of identities by affiliation, since it is an embodied and purposive practice: people wright with their whole bodies and have the ultimate veto on what emanates from them in wrighting.

To exemplify this I will take an example of the discoursal construction of Logan's identity through 'wrighting'. One day in January 2005 Logan wrought an information sheet about 'Speciality Evenings', to be placed alongside the menu in the training restaurant. The text itself is reproduced in Figure 4. First I focus on the semiotic artefact itself. By making certain selections of linguistic and visual features, Logan participated in some discourses and not others, and thereby aligned himself with some subject positions and distanced himself from others.

We would like to inform everybody about our future dates for our speciality evenings.

♦   10th February   Valentines Day   Evening Meal

♦   17th March   St. Patrick's Day   Evening Meal

♦   21st April   St. George's Day   Evening Meal

If you would like to book any of these dates then please contact reception. Prices are to be confirmed nearer the date.

We would like to thank everybody who made it to our Christmas Luncheons or Dinners and hope we made it a very enjoyable occasion for you. We would also like to thank everyone who dined last year as it is you that make it all possible. The Coulson Restaurant is a centre of training for the catering profession and if it wasn't for the customers the students couldn't receive the experience they do.

Figure 1.4: Logan's 'Speciality Evenings' information sheet

Several features of the linguistic text carry the 'make people happy' discourse of food and drink service: the high proportion of personal pronouns 'we', 'you', 'everybody' and 'everyone'; the proliferation of politeness markers 'we would like to' (three times) and 'please'; the lexis in the semantic field of pleasure and enjoyment: 'hope' and 'very enjoyable', and the use of the speech act 'thank' (twice). Associated with this is the use of the handwriting font for the phrase 'Speciality Evenings', suggesting a 'personal touch', carrying a friendly, cosy, informal discourse of personal relationships. Together these discoursal resources position Logan as someone keen to serve customers: to 'make people happy'.

Interspersed with this is a slightly different discourse of food and drink service: the one I have called a 'control the customers' discourse, carried by the more regulatory, bureaucratic language in the second paragraph. The imperative 'contact' (albeit softened by the politeness marker 'please'), the nominalisation 'reception', the passive 'to be confirmed' signal this discourse and, by using them in his wrighting, Logan is positioned as an efficient manager in the restaurant.

Other features of the linguistic text carry a consistent discourse of eating out as a special occasion: the lexical items 'Speciality Evenings', Christmas Luncheons', 'Dinners' (with a capital 'D'), 'occasion', and 'dined'. This discourse is carried also by the restaurant logo, not designed by Logan, but a standard feature of all restaurant publicity. Its smart, tidily arranged fonts, the 'designer' use of the small 's' and the 'nestling' apostrophe, the 'cool' grey and duck-egg blue colour scheme, and the 'tasteful' graphic representing a delicious aroma all suggest that this is a stylish restaurant. Different fonts, colour schemes and graphics would have carried different discourses of eating out: cheap and cheerful, or healthy, for example. The use of these semiotic characteristics affiliate Logan to this view of eating out as a special occasion and, it is important to add, the values, beliefs and social relations inscribed in it.

The 'romantic love' discourse of male-female (or other) relationships is carried by the mention of 'Valentines Day', and by the main graphics in the text: a red rose, represented symbolically rather than naturalistically, and a pink heart, the largest image on the page, represented as if hand-painted on a balloon or other smooth, three-dimensional surface. This is one way of thinking about relationships: the one with which Logan is identifying through the wrighting of this text.

In addition to its discoursal hybridity, the text is generically heterogeneous, corresponding with the hybrid nature of the activity. So far, I have not mentioned the final sentence of the information sheet. I suggest that this sentence comes from a different genre from the parts of the text discussed so far. The main part of the text is addressed to customers in the 'restaurant information sheet' genre, with Logan in the role of a member of the restaurant staff publicising the excellent future offerings of the restaurant, giving information about how to book, and appreciating the custom of the clientele. The final sentence, however, is different. I suggest that this is not only on a different topic – the restaurant itself as opposed to the staff's gratitude to the customers, but is also in a different genre: an 'educational publicity' genre, with Logan in the role of a member of the hospitality and catering department staff advertising its educational provision. The restaurant staff are no longer referred to as 'we', but as 'the catering profession', 'the students' and 'they'; the customers are no longer referred to as 'you', but as 'the customers'. This is a change from personalised, specific representation of social actors to generic, categorised, and, in the case of 'profession' objectified representation of social actors.[7] The main part of the text represents material processes in real time such as 'thank', 'inform', 'book', 'made it', 'dined', whereas the final sentence represents relational processes, states of affairs and universal truths: 'is', 'if it wasn't for', 'couldn't receive'.[8] This final sentence is giving impersonal, generalised, objectified information: the language of reports and, dare I suggest, of academic writing? Might Logan have taken his first step towards the sort of writing that is valued by educational institutions – whether he ever wants to participate in this or not?

To summarise, in wrighting the 'Speciality Evenings' information sheet, Logan draws selectively on the socioculturally and historically shaped mediating means – discourses and genres – which are circulating in the activity in which he is participating. He reproduces some and not others, thereby both positioning himself and contributing to the reinforcement and continued circulation of these discourses and genres. He is positioned firstly by the discourses he participates in: the 'making people happy', and 'control the customers' discourses of restaurant service, and the 'romantic love' discourse of male-female relationships. And he is positioned, secondly, by the genres in which he participates: positioned as a restaurant manager by wrighting in the information sheet genre; and positioned as a publicist for the college's education and training facilities by the educational establishment publicity genre which he briefly draws upon in his final sentence. This illustrates what I mean by the discoursal construction of identity by affiliation. By his choice of semiotic resources in the wrighting of this single sheet, Logan does not just convey a message, but also constructs a 'discoursal self' – a representation of his identity: of the views of social reality and the social roles with which he identifies.

These discoursally constructed selves may, of course, be partial, or outright deceptions: Logan may 'in reality', whatever that means, actually identify with quite different world views and roles from those suggested above – that is his prerogative. But the relational nature of identity work is such that a person will don a 'self' which is dependent on those who will 'read' it, as discussed above. This raises the interesting issue of the moment at which identity is actually constructed: the moment of a person's action, or the moment of its reception and interpretation by another? I suggest that it is useful to recognise this second moment at which a person's identity is 'read' as 'the projected self'. This is the version of a person's identity which will contribute to the reinforcement and continued circulation of discourses and genres (especially if he is a person with status).

The discourses on which Logan is drawing should not, of course, be left unquestioned. Isn't the 'make people happy' discourse of restaurant service and the 'special occasion' discourse of eating out contributing to the commercialisation and commodification of food and drink service? And does not the deployment of the romantic love discourse of personal relationships inflate this commodification and further exploit people and trick them into emptying their pockets? To this I would answer 'yes, but no ... .'. Yes, Logan is being colonised by these discourses and contributing to their continued circulation, and hence participating in these social processes, and it would be politically preferable for him and all the students on the courses to develop a critical awareness of the nature and consequences of these belief systems. (I will return to this point in the final section of the paper on pedagogical implications.) But, on the other hand, I suggest that it is not entirely sinister that Logan is constructing his identity through participation in these discourses. Logan is a young man who was disaffected by the whole education system and did not have any future when he left school. I suggest that his finding something to identify with, something which is consonant with his sense of himself who likes to 'make people happy', is a key factor in learning for him, as I discuss further in the section on 'identification' below.

People's identities are constructed not only by their deployment of semiotic resources but also by the practices in which they participate. In wrighting this information sheet Logan engaged in literacy practices which affiliated him with particular discourses of wrighting and not others. Here is his account of wrighting it:

Interview Extract 2

Logan: If you get me into a project which I'm interested in, like I won't be bothered how much time I spend on it, I'll sit there and I'll do it until I'm happy and happy that it is correct

Interviewer: Right

Logan: And I'll start off with something and then the end product will end up different, totally different. Like last night when I was doing the information sheet, it started off with quite a lot of graphics and just little bits of writing, but then it changed to more information, little bit about thank you for coming to the Christmas Luncheons and if it wasn't for the customers then this wouldn't be possible, and all that, and just a couple of graphics

By acting in this way Logan was, I suggest, affiliating himself with people who write (or as I prefer to call it, 'wright').[6] He was taking to himself discourses of writing, reconceptualised as 'wrighting', as serving a useful purpose, and as a creative process – constructing (as I will argue later, reconstructing) his identity as someone who sees wrighting as worth spending time on. And anyone who knew that he had spent that much time working on this sheet, or anyone who heard him talking about it in this way, would have ascribed to him the identity of 'someone who wrights'. His identity is constructed by the practice of wrighting (which is part of a broader definition of a 'discourse'), as well as by the semiotic characteristics of its product.

The examples I have given of the way in which Logan's identity is discoursally constructed by affiliation are taken only from his production of a short information sheet. However, his identity is discoursally constructed by other semiotic practices in which he participates and by the mediating means which he employs within the activity of working in the training restaurant as a whole. He is aligning himself with particular social roles and positions by the way he speaks as well as the way he wrights, by the clothes he wears, by his demeanour and movements, by the way he lays the tables, by his timekeeping practices, by how gently or hard he closes the restaurant door behind him.

Identification

An understanding of identity as relational and discoursally constructed implies identity *work*: the continuous making and remaking of who we are. The default meaning of 'identification' turns 'identity' from a noun to a verb: it treats identity not as a state but as a process (in the same way as Street argues that culture is a verb: Street, 1993). There is also a stronger, more active meaning of 'identification' which is found particularly in Wenger (1998) and Gee (2003, 2005): a desire to identify. Identification in this strong sense is essential to full participation, and is what makes identity work happen. When participating in an activity, it will make a massive difference whether a person does or does not identify with the sort of people who are its 'subjects', and whether they take to themselves its 'object(s)'.

Logan gave insights into the way in which he identified with his role in the training restaurant. When the interviewer asked him whether wrighting the 'Speciality Evenings' information sheet was part of his course requirements, he made it clear that composing this information sheet was his own choice, and thus that he was taking ownership of the activity:

Interview Extract 3

Logan.   It's, it is and it isn't! I mean it's like, you get, you can be asked to do them or
         you might not get asked to do them.

In Interview Extract 2 Logan explained that if he is interested in a project, he does not mind how much time he spends on it. This is not just a bit of homework, to be got through as quickly as possible in order to get on with more enjoyable things: doing it is part of being who Logan wants to be. This is an example of what I am calling the 'strong' meaning of identification: actively identifying with the subject positions held out by a social practice. It is this process of active identification which is essential to 'deep learning', as Gee calls it (2005).

Language is a means of identification, an object of identification and a mark of identification. As shown above, language and other semiotic means are the resources a person draws upon in order to construct their affiliations, in order to become like others with whom they want to identify: they are a means of identification. One of the objectives of a newcomer to a social practice is to learn the language and other ways of communicating which characterise that context: the way of achieving this is by becoming 'one of them' – becoming recognised as a member of that community. And it is by their use of language and other semiotic resources that other people recognise someone as 'belonging'.

In the text of the information sheet Logan's identification with the activity in which he is participating is constructed and marked linguistically. In this short text there are seven first person plural referents 'We' and 'our'. Logan wrote this, but he did not refer to himself as 'I'. This 'we' is an associating representation[9] whereby he identifies himself with the staff of the restaurant as a whole: the other trainee restaurant staff, the tutors, and the restaurant manager. Through this 'we' Logan both constructs himself and demonstrates himself to be a full participant in this community of practice.

Identity is networked

The 'Subjects' in an activity bring identities with them to a communicative context: their up-to-now and on-going experiences and affiliations. I suggest that it is productive to see this aspect of identity as a network of subjectivities sustained by the different activities and affiliations of a person's life. It has always been possible to participate physically in more than one activity at a time, and mentally in others. A person can be simultaneously doing their job, engaging in social relationships, and thinking about their religious community, each of which supports a different facet of their identity. However, this facility for 'multi-identifying' is vastly increased by the existence of the internet and virtual spaces, one or more of which can be inhabited simultaneously with other activities. Figure 5 represents the way in which, while a person is participating in an activity, activity A, their identity is networked to the identities supported by other activities in which they (con)currently participate.

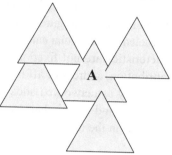

Figure 5: Identity is networked through participation in a range of practices in different domains

For example, while Logan is participating in the training restaurant as a student restaurant manager – as one of the 'Subjects' in activity 'A' in Figure 5, he is also, simultaneously, a person who supports Dundee Football Club, someone who can sit for hours on end playing computer games (some of them with countless other people in virtual space), someone who engages in a wide network of social relationships by texting on his mobile, someone who goes out to play snooker with his friends when he's not in the restaurant. His identity is thus 'networked' in two senses. First, who he is while in the training restaurant is only part of who he is as a whole. His whole identity is a network of discoursal selves across the many activities in which he participates physically, mentally or electronically. Secondly, he as an individual is networked to many people, practices, technologies and artefacts. When he participates in activity A, he is bringing with him all these relationships and connections: they make up the 'autobiographical self' which is both agent and subject in each activity in which he participates, which shapes the way in which he will participate, and hence shapes the identity which he will construct.

Factors in this networked identity are the biological and social categorisations which people bring with them into each activity in which they participate: their gender, race, age, physical characteristics, sexuality, nationality, and socio-economic status. Logan is a slim, able-bodied, 20-year-old heterosexual white British man of a certain class. However, these features do not categorically position him: what they mean depends on the values in each activity in which he participates. They will be more or less foregrounded by the objects, and ideologies (with associated power relations) of the activity, and by the extent to which the activity itself takes precedence over who is involved in it (Gee, 2005). In some contexts these will be extremely salient features of identity, setting people in opposition to each other or establishing hierarchies of privilege and prestige. In others they will be insignificant, with other, more activity-focused aspects of identity coming to the fore. The ongoing interaction can de-emphasise, re-orientate or even reconfigure the unequal power relations that are socioculturally constructed for particular categories of person. People's biological and social characteristics are not fixed aspects of their identity, but given significance by attribution, address or affiliation, as I argued in the previous section. Viewing identity as networked adds further complexity to this picture: a person's biological and social characteristics can simultaneously hold different significations in the different activities in which they are participating.

Identity is continuously reconstructed

In the previous sections I have implied, firstly, that people's identities are in a continual state of flux, co-emergent with the ongoing activity in which they are participating and, secondly, that people bring with them to any activity a history of identifications which are textured into their current sense of self. 'Identity work' is not a one-off thing, but an on-going, continuous process of construction and reconstruction of identity through any form of social action including, as in my example, through wrighting. This continuous reshaping of the self is a characteristic not only of the discoursal construction of identity through participation in an activity, but also of a longer time-scale.

There is a temporal element to the AT representation of an activity as a triangle, which in some sense starts with the people participating on the bottom left, and ends with the 'outcome(s)' (see Figures 1 – 3). During that time-span each participant's identity is in a process of construction and reconstruction, and will be changed as a result of the process. But this is also true over the trajectory of a person's life, as represented in Figure 6. A person's identity will be changed by each activity in which they participate.

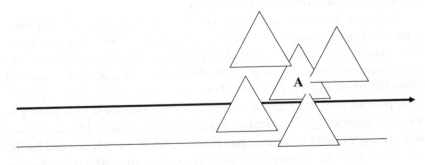

Figure 6: Identity is on a trajectory of continuous reconfiguration and reconstruction

Logan's identity as a wrighter was, I suggest, reconstructed by the experience of wrighting the 'Speciality Evenings' information sheet. He said of his attitude to writing previously:

Interview Extract 4

Logan: And basically, it's not because I didn't want to do the work. It's because I'll sit there and then I'll do my first draft, and I'll get, say, right, yeah, that'll be good but you need to change this bit, and that bit and then I'll come down to do it and again I'll think, I've already done this, it's

Interviewer: Right

Logan: It's the repetitiveness that I don't like, I don't like re-writing things

and

Logan: I think it's the actual, the sitting down and having to concentrate all the time on the piece of paper and the words, that just look so plain on this piece of paper, do you know what I mean? I think it's the very, just how plain things are when you're reading and writing.

But in wrighting the 'Speciality Evenings' information sheet he took on the identity of someone who does wright: someone who was prepared to work for hours and hours to get it right (see Interview Extract 2). When the interviewer asked him about this apparent contradiction between what he said about writing at school and what he said about wrighting the information sheet, he showed a change in his sense of himself as a wrighter – perhaps not a lasting change, but one which is a part of a continuous redefinition of this aspect of his identity:

Interview Extract 5

Interviewer: So, isn't that re-drafting? Isn't that what you hate doing?

Logan: No, because it's different. It's, the information on it changes completely. What I put down first will change completely.

Identity, identification, learning and language learning

The implications of these aspects of language and identity for pedagogic settings have so far been implicit but are, I hope, emerging clearly. Logan was learning by doing – the explicit intention of the way in which the training restaurant was set up. He was also, not quite so explicitly and intentionally, learning in the sense of developing his communicative practices. He is generally thought to be a very successful learner, and the factors which led to his success can, in my view, be generalised to other pedagogic settings.

The picture I have created is of the NVQ Level 2 Food and Drink Service course as a successful educational undertaking, at least for Logan (but it is similarly successful for other students on the course too). Logan's successful learning on this course is mobilised by the way in which he identified strongly with one of the two 'Objects' of the hybrid activity system: he wanted to satisfy customers at the restaurant – to 'make people happy'. He identified with the opportunities for self-hood that were extended to him by the actions and mediating means in this context: the roles, particularly the role of restaurant manager, and the views of the world – the subject positions – inscribed in the preferred discourses in the social context. The course was successful in that it created an environment in which Logan could identify with what he was doing and hence engage in 'deep learning': learning that did not contravene his sense of who he wanted to be.

People's identities are networked across the activities in which they participate and are on a trajectory over time, and this needs to be taken into account both in providing opportunities for participation in educational settings, and in recognising the outcomes from educational provision. People participate in any new activity, including a new educational setting, with a complex configuration of identifications which will shape their sense of themselves and of how they can participate in this new context. One of the outcomes from any social activity is a reconfiguration of participants' subjectivities, both individually and in relation to one another. Learning to feel differently about yourself, even to have a different sense of who you are is in itself a type of learning. In educational contexts 'learning' is not just an increase in knowledge, understanding and capability, but includes the discoursal reconstruction of identity too.

This presents a positive picture of successful learning through identification and innocent participation in discourses. However, discourses are imbued with values, beliefs and social relations, and uncritical participation in them co-opts people to these values, beliefs and social relations. Education should provide not only the opportunity for participation in meaningful social action but also a critical awareness of the ways in which identity is discoursally constructed, and of the concomitants and potential consequences over time of participation in specific discourses. The capacity to examine critically their own processes of identification gives people agency and control over the contribution they are making to the circulation of discourses, and ultimately to the potential transformation of their social world.

Logan learnt because he wanted to BE. He learnt not just table laying and napkin folding, but also wrighting and other communicative practices. Identification not only facilitated the learning which was the intended object of the activity, but language learning too: by engaging in the contributory activity of wrighting the information leaflet, he significantly developed and extended his communicative capabilities. In a classroom, one may ask, what is the identity held out to people? Is it one they want to identify with? If it is just 'student' or 'learner', are they likely to have a role and position from which to speak, wright, interpret, respond? Might it be possible to offer them other subject positions, like Logan's position as a restaurant manager, which might hold out better possibilities for identification, and motivation to communicate in new and desired ways? If 'education' aims to make changes in people's practices and identities, identification is, I suggest, a key to how this can be achieved.

Acknowledgements

The data which provides the example in this paper was collected by Candice Satchwell and Sarah Wilcock and I am particularly grateful to them for their insights and contributions to the analysis.

Notes

1   The 'Literacies for Learning in Further Education' project is investigating the literacy practices on 32 units of study across 11 curriculum areas in FE, and how these interface with students' everyday literacy practices. The project is part of the Teaching and Learning Research Programme (TLRP) in the UK, funded by the Economic and Social Research Council (ESRC), Grant no RES-139-25-0117. The research is being conducted by a team including Angela Brzeski, Candice Satchwell, Richard Edwards, Zoe Fowler, Greg Mannion, Kate Miller, June Smith, Sarah Wilcock and Roz Ivanič (see www.lancs.ac.uk/lflfe).

2   For an introduction to Activity Theory as a heuristic, see Russell (2005).

3   AT is often referred to as Cultural-Historical Activity Theory (CHAT).

4   'Logan' is a pseudonym.

5   I am indebted to Jane Sunderland for the creative experience of team-teaching the Language and Education course at Lancaster University with her, on which we collaboratively developed this 'three a's' typology.

6   From here onwards I use the term 'wrighting' instead of 'writing' when I want to refer to composition which is not just linguistic but also visual. I am using the verb to 'wright', as in the word 'playwright', to mean 'to craft out of a combination of materials'.

7   This analysis uses van Leeuwen's analytical framework for the representation of social actors (van Leeuwen, 1996).

8   This analysis draws broadly on Halliday's Functional Grammar (Halliday and Matthiessen, 2004) and van Leeuwen's analytical framework for the representation of social action (van Leeuwen, 1995).

9   This is a term from van Leeuwen's framework for analysing the representation of social actors (1996).

References

Barton, D. and Hamilton, M. (2005) Literacy, reification and the dynamics of social interaction. In D. Barton and K. Tusting (eds) *Beyond Communities of Practice: language, power and social context*. Cambridge: Cambridge University Press.

Clark, R. and Ivanič, R. (1997) *The Politics of Writing*. London: Routledge.

Clarke, J. (2002) A new kind of symmetry: actor-network theories and the new literacy studies. *Studies in the Education of Adults* 34(2): 107–22.

Cope, B. and Kalantzis, M. (2000) *Multiliteracies: literacy learning and the design of social futures*. London: Routledge.

Edwards, R. (2005) Learning in context – within and across domains. Paper presented at Seminar One in the ESRC Teaching and Learning Research Programme (TLRP) Thematic Seminar Series, 'Contexts, communities, networks: mobilising learners' resources and relationships in different domains'. Glasgow Caledonian University, February. http://crll.gcal.ac.uk/docs/TLRP_ContextSeminars/TLRP_ContxtSem1_Edwards.doc

Fairclough, N. (2003) *Analysing Discourse: text analysis for social research*. London: Routledge.

Gee, J. P. (1996) *Social Linguistics and Literacies: ideology in discourses*. (Second edition. First published in 1990) London: Taylor Francis.

Gee, J. P. (2000–2001) Identity as an analytic lens for research in education. *Review of Research in Education* 25: 99–125.

Gee, J. P. (2003) *What Video Games have to Teach us about Learning and Literacy*. New York: Palgrave Macmillan.

Gee, J. P. (2005) Semiotic social spaces and affinity spaces: from *The Age of Mythology* to today's schools. In D. Barton and K. Tusting (eds) *Beyond Communities of Practice: language, power and social context*. Cambridge: Cambridge University Press.

Goffman, E. [1959] (1969) *The Presentation of Self in Everyday Life*. London: Allen Lane, The Penguin Press.

Hall, S. (1996) Introduction: who needs 'identity'? In S. Hall and P. du Gay (eds) *Questions of Cultural Identity*. London: Sage.

Halliday, M. A. K. and Matthiessen, C. (2004) *An Introduction to Functional Grammar*. (Third edition) London: Oxford University Press / Hodder Arnold.

Holland, D., Lachiotte, W., Skinner, D. and Cain, C. (1998) *Identity and Agency in Cultural Worlds*. Cambridge, MA: Harvard University Press.

Ivanič, R. (1998) *Writing and Identity: the discoursal construction of identity in academic writing*. Amsterdam: John Benjamins.

Ivanič, R. (2005) The discoursal construction of writer identity. In R. Beach, J. Green, M. Kamil and T. Shanahan (eds) *Multidisciplinary Perspectives on Literacy Research*. (Revised edition) Cresskill, NJ: Hampton Press.

Ivanič, R. and Camps, D. (2001) I am how I sound: voice as self-representation in L2 writing. *Journal of Writing in a Second Language* 10(1): 1–31.

Kress, G. (1996) Representational resources and the production of subjectivity. In C. R. Caldas-Coulthard and M. Coulthard (eds) *Texts and Practices: readings in critical discourse analysis*. London: Routledge.

Kress, G. (1997) *Before Writing: rethinking the paths to literacy*. London: Routledge.

Kress, G. and van Leeuwen, T. (2001) *Multimodal Discourse: the modes and media of contemporary communication*. London: Arnold.

Lave, J. and Wenger, E. (1991) *Situated Learning*. Cambridge: Cambridge University Press.

McDermott, R. (1996) The acquisition of a child by a learning disability. In S. Chaiklin and J. Lave (eds) *Understanding Practice: perspectives on activity and context*. Cambridge: Cambridge University Press.

Pahl, K. and Rousell, J. (2005) *Literacy and Education: understanding the new literacy studies in the classroom*. London: Paul Chapman.

Russell, D. (2005) Texts in contexts: theorizing learning by looking at literacies. Paper presented at Seminar Two in the ESRC Teaching and Learning Research Programme (TLRP) Thematic Seminar Series, 'Contexts, communities, networks: mobilising learners' resources and relationships in different domains'. Lancaster, June. http://crll.gcal.ac.uk/docs/TLRP_ContextSeminars/TLRP_ContxtSem2_Russell.doc

Scott, M. (2000) Agency and subjectivity in student writing. In C. Jones, J. Turner and B. Street (eds) *Students Writing in the University: cultural and epistemological issues*. Amsterdam: Benjamins.

Street, B. (1993) Culture is a verb. In D. Graddol (ed.) *Language and Culture* 23–43. Multilingual Matters/BAAL.

van Leeuwen, T. (1995) Representing social action. *Discourse in Society* 6(1): 81–106.

van Leeuwen, T. (1996) The representation of social actors. In C. R. Caldas-Coulthard and M. Coulthard (eds) *Texts and Practices: readings in critical discourse analysis*. London: Routledge.

Wenger, E. (1998) *Communities of Practice: learning, meaning and identity*. Cambridge: Cambridge University Press.

Wertsch, J. (1991) *Voices of the Mind*. Hemel Hempstead: Harvester Wheatsheaf.

2   Identity in a francophone cultural context: issues of language rights and language use in Canada

Maeve Conrick

Introduction

With about seven million francophones recorded in the most recent census in 2001,[1] Canada is a major player in terms of the international standing of French. Francophones[2] represent almost a quarter (22.9 per cent) of the total population of Canada, but their distribution across Canada is very patchy outside the province of Quebec. Francophones are in the majority in Quebec, with a share of over 80 per cent of the population, but in all other provinces and territories, they are a small minority; in most cases the percentage is in single figures, with Ontario for example recording 4.5 per cent. Even in New Brunswick, the province with the second biggest share of francophones after Quebec, the percentage is 33.2 per cent (Statistics Canada, 2002: 26). The current demolinguistic situation presents a significant challenge for francophone communities outside Quebec.

The history of the linguistic landscape in Canada is rich in examples of the cultural and linguistic tension created by the co-existence of various linguistic groups. The conflict stretching over many centuries between speakers of the two dominant languages, English and French, has never reached resolution and opinion continues to be polarised, especially when debate turns to the possibility of constitutional change, as it has done on two occasions during the 1980s and 1990s, when referenda were held in Quebec on the issue of sovereignty. The 'language question' occupies a central position in the consciousness of many Canadians, especially Quebecers, and the fear of a linguistic crisis is never far from the minds of politicians and other interested parties. The role of language in the construction and representation of identity is particularly strong in Quebec, where recent debate on the notion of Quebec citizenship is predicated on the concept of a French-speaking nation, for example in the report of the Commission des États Généraux sur la situation et l'avenir de la langue française au Québec in 2001. In the context of the debate on identity issues in contemporary Quebec, in which language is a central focus, the principal issues discussed in this article concern two important aspects of language rights and language use, firstly, access to English schools in Quebec and, secondly, the modernisation of the French language to reflect the greater participation of women in professional contexts in contemporary Quebec society. These issues have been controversial, as they involve Quebec society confronting the nature of francophone identity, both cultural and linguistic.

Since the introduction of the Canadian Charter of Rights and Freedoms in 1982, provincial provisions on such issues as language rights can be challenged as far as the Canadian Supreme Court. The legal framework in terms of language policy and language planning at federal and provincial levels plays a crucial role in public policy and public debate, with much evidence of tensions resulting from conflicting provisions made at provincial and federal level. This article analyses the outcome of two Supreme Court decisions handed down on 31 March 2005, relating to the controversial issue of access to schooling in English in Quebec, following challenges to restrictions contained in Quebec's *Charte de la langue française* (Charter of the French Language), the infamous Bill 101.

Identity and its linguistic representation are also addressed at the level of gender identity. In this regard, Canada, especially Quebec, has given an international lead because of its widespread use of feminised professional titles in varieties of Canadian French, thus recognising the changed social reality of women's position in and contribution to society. Many public and private bodies, including government departments, companies, universities and publishing houses, have adopted policies on linguistic feminisation. As a result of the demand for increased visibility of women in a professional context, changes have occurred in the lexis and morphology of French in Canada, which distinguish it somewhat from the French of France. This aspect of representation is examined by reference to studies on language use in the francophone print media of Acadia, Quebec and Ontario.

Evolution of the linguistic composition of Canada

Canada is unusual internationally in that it collects and makes available to the public at large a wealth of data on demolinguistic trends. Even Ireland, a country which also has two official languages, seeks very little information on language in its census, beyond the ability to speak and use Irish.[3] By contrast, Statistics Canada collects data every five years on language in four categories: mother tongue, home language, knowledge of official languages and language of work.[4] Consequently, the availability of comparable data facilitates the identification of trends over time, though, obviously, changes have been made in the format and content of the questionnaire.

The evolution of the percentage share of the various linguistic groups in Canada over the last 30 years is illustrated in Table 1.[5]

Year	Anglophones	Francophones	Allophones
1971	60.1%	26.9%	13.0%
2001	59.1%	22.9%	18.0%

Table 1: Canada by mother tongue, share of population, 1971 and 2001

While the share of francophones has declined considerably, the share of anglophones has also decreased, though by a much smaller margin, and the only rise is in the case of the heterogeneous group of allophones (speakers of languages other than English or French).

A striking trend which has been apparent in the results for recent decades is the change in the demographic patterns of francophones across Canada. Since the major social changes which the Quiet Revolution brought in Quebec in the 1960s and the strengthening of Quebec nationalism, there has been a notable evolution in the construction of francophone identity. This was represented linguistically by a change in the term of self reference used by Quebec francophones, who replaced the wider, more generic term *Français canadiens* (French Canadians) with the narrower, provincially-based title *Québécois* (Quebecers). These linguistic, cultural and political changes had an impact not only on how identity was perceived and expressed within Quebec itself, but they also had far-reaching consequences for francophones elsewhere in Canada, who had to redefine themselves differently, both linguistically and symbolically, in relation to the new situation which had become a reality in Quebec. The main consequence was a fragmentation of what had been previously a more country-wide French Canadian identity, into an identity on a provincial basis, with an increased emphasis on more localised terms such as *Franco-Ontariens* (Ontario), *Fransaskois* (Saskatchewan), *Franco-Manitobains* (Manitoba), *Franco-Colombiens* (British Columbia). The increasing concentration of francophones in Quebec is very obvious when the census data are examined. Table 2 details the breakdown of francophone share of population by province and territory, along with the percentage for home language recorded in 2001.

Province/Territory	Mother tongue	Home language
Newfoundland and Labrador	0.5	0.2
Prince Edward Island	4.4	2.1
Nova Scotia	3.9	2.2
New Brunswick	33.2	30.3
Ontario	4.5	2.7
Quebec	81.4	83.1
Manitoba	4.2	1.9
Saskatchewan	1.9	0.5
Alberta	2.1	0.7
British Columbia	1.5	0.4
Yukon Territory	3.3	1.5
Northwest Territories	2.7	1.1
Nunavut	1.5	0.8
Canada less Quebec	4.4	2.7

Table 2: French mother tongue and home language, provinces and territories and Canada less Quebec, 2001

In Quebec, the only province with francophones in the majority, the tendency towards greater concentration is clear when the figures for 2001 are compared with those for the census of ten years before. Percentages for Canada less Quebec declined to 4.4 per cent from 4.8 per cent in 1991. Even New Brunswick,[6] the province with the highest proportion after Quebec, shows a decline to 33.2 per cent, from 34.0 per cent in 1991. In addition, the figures for home language indicate a shift away from French in all provinces and territories except Quebec, where the figures show that allophones are transferring to French in greater numbers than previously. Consequently, the position of French cannot be said to be secure outside Quebec and fears of assimilation are certainly not without foundation. Put another way, there is increasing polarisation between a French-speaking Quebec and a predominantly anglophone rest of Canada.

Analysis of the relationship between geographical concentration and language survival is an issue which has figured for some time in discussion of policy and strategy for the French language in Canada. Many of the studies undertaken in the context of the Royal Commission on Bilingualism and Biculturalism, which carried out its work in the 1960s, were in agreement on the positive correlation between geographical concentration and protection against assimilation. Castonguay concludes as follows:

> *En effet, toutes les études concordaient sur ce point: plus un groupe est nombreux et concentré dans une région, plus il se trouve à l'abri de pertes par voie d'assimilation.* (Castonguay, 1994: 14)

> (In fact, all the studies were in agreement on this point; the more numerous a linguistic group and the more concentrated it is geographically, the more protected it is against assimilation.)

The political redefinition and repositioning of Quebec from the 1970s have had the effect of increasing the marginalisation of the minority French-speaking communities in the rest of Canada, forcing them to seek another focus for the expression of their French identity. The strengthening of francophone Quebec identity may be a significant gain in terms of the survival of a French identity in North America, but it may be at the cost of the francophone communities of the rest of Canada. While the province of Quebec has pursued policies aimed at sustaining and promoting its French character, it has not been exempt from the impact of both positive and negative developments emanating from the federal level.

Official languages legislation and minority language education rights

Language policy at the federal level in Canada since the 1960s, following the report of the Royal Commission on Bilingualism and Biculturalism (1967), has espoused official bilingualism, with the first Official Languages Act passed in 1969. Internationally, Canada has the reputation of being a model of successful official bilingualism, given the comprehensive legislative framework which underpins public policy on language issues. The logic of its language policy has been based firmly on supporting both official languages at the federal level and protecting the rights of minority language communities at the provincial level, i.e. English in Quebec and French in all other provinces. To achieve this objective, various legislative instruments have been put in place, in particular the revised Official Languages Act of 1988 and the sections on Official Languages (16–22) and on Minority Language Educational Rights (23) of the Canadian Charter of Rights and Freedoms (1982). A major feature of the Official Languages Act was the appointment of an Official Languages Commissioner, with responsibility for monitoring the operation of the Act and for dealing with complaints from the public. The current Commissioner, Dr Dyane Adam, has a very high public profile, and is noted for her outspoken comments when she concludes that the federal government has not lived up to its promises on official languages matters. The Commissioner's 2005 *Annual Report* (Commissioner of Official Languages, 2005) criticised the implementation of the federal government's ambitious *Action Plan for Official Languages* (Government of Canada, 2003).

> One of the few turning points in developing linguistic duality was the unveiling of the Action Plan for Official Languages in 2003. While this is no simple achievement, the implementation of the plan does not meet the expectations it created. As was clearly seen in last year's annual report, political leadership is in a downward spiral and is running out of steam; it lacks the strength to properly undertake the renewal of linguistic duality announced in 2003. And, as the report on the last 35 years shows, if this political and governmental leadership does not emerge, Canada may well see its linguistic duality fade. (Commissioner of Official Languages, 2005)

The province of Quebec has pursued a somewhat different path by rejecting bilingualism and adopting instead a policy of French monolingualism, provided for initially by Bill 22 in 1974. More controversially, the *Charte de la langue française*, Bill 101, adopted in 1977, set out measures for the promotion of French in the province, thereby significantly reducing the rights of other linguistic groups. A particular difficulty was the principle that schooling in public and subsidised private kindergarten, elementary and secondary schools in Quebec would be in French, except in certain circumstances where access to education through English would be permitted.

Initially, Bill 101 took a radical approach by restricting access to English schooling to children of parents educated in English in Quebec. However, the introduction of the federal Canadian Charter of Rights and Freedoms in 1982 impacted significantly on language legislation in Quebec, including the fact that the validity of the provisions of Bill 101 could be tested beyond the Quebec Courts, in the Supreme Court of Canada. In 1984, the Supreme Court ruled that the right of access to English schools had to be extended to parents who had received their elementary education in English anywhere in Canada, as provided for by the Canadian Charter.

> Citizens of Canada [...] who have received their primary school instruction in Canada in English or French and reside in a province where the language in which they received that instruction is the language of the English or French linguistic minority population of the province, have the right to have their

children receive primary and secondary school instruction in that language in that province. (Government of Canada, 1982: Section 23. 1.b)

The current position in Quebec is that Bill 101 allows the following children, at the request of one of their parents, to receive instruction in public and subsidised private English-language schools:

(1) The child's father or mother is a Canadian citizen who has received the major part of his or her elementary education in English in Canada.

(2) The child's father or mother is a Canadian citizen and the child has received the major part of his or her elementary instruction in English in Canada.

(3) The child's father and mother are not Canadian citizens but one of them has received the major part of his or her elementary instruction in English in Quebec. (Government of Quebec, 2003: Section 73. 1-3)[7]

The most recent challenges to the educational provisions of Bill 101 were decided on 31 March 2005 by the Supreme Court of Canada, which delivered judgments in three cases, two of which are discussed here.[8] One of the cases, the Gosselin case, was taken by a group of eight francophone families who were refused permission to register their children in English schools. The Court rejected their appeal, holding that their rights under Section 23 of the Canadian Charter of Rights and Freedoms had not been infringed, as 'The appellants are members of the French language majority in Quebec and, as such, their objective in having their children educated in English simply does not fall within the purpose of Section 23' (Roger Gosselin et al. v. Attorney General of Quebec, 2005 SCC 15). The net effect of the judgment is that Bill 101's restrictions on access to English schools remain valid for francophones.

The outcome of the second case, the Casimir case, differed, as the appeal was upheld in part. The main point to be decided was the interpretation of the 'major part' requirement of Bill 101. Mme Casimir had lived in Ontario, where her children were enrolled in a French immersion programme, with half of their instruction in English and half in French. When she moved to Quebec, access to English schools was refused, because 'half' was held not to constitute the 'major part' of instruction in English. The Supreme Court of Canada took the view that the criterion was valid, but that the interpretation of 'major part' should involve a qualitative assessment, rather than being narrowly mathematical. The Court stated that:

All the circumstances of the child must be considered including the time spent in the program, at what stage of education the choice of language of instruction was made, what programmes are or were available and whether learning disabilities or other difficulties exist. (Edwige Casimir v. Attorney General of Quebec, 2005 SCC 14)

In essence, this Supreme Court decision, while reaffirming the fundamental validity of Bill 101, has changed an important element of its application, by requiring Quebec to apply qualitative criteria in assessing conditions for access to English schools. While maintaining the constitutionality of Bill 101, it requires that the interpretation be more liberal. This change may test the delicate linguistic equilibrium in Quebec, by allowing greater numbers to bypass the education through French requirement, thereby undermining a central plank in Quebec's policy of increasing its French character. Political and press reaction to the judgments was swift, if not consistent, in interpreting the significance of this development.

Press and political reaction to the Supreme Court judgments

An analysis of articles published in Canadian newspapers on 1 April 2005, the day following the publication of the Supreme Court judgments, reveals varying interpretations and reactions. In some cases, the relief that the wording of the law will not have to be changed is almost tangible, while others sound the alarm about the liberalisation of its interpretation.[9] Article titles include for example:

> *La loi 101 passe l'examen* (Bill 101 passes the exam)
> Manon Cornellier, *Le Devoir* (Montreal).

> *La loi 101 passe le test suprême* (Bill 101 passes the Supreme test)
> Mylène Moisan, *Le Soleil* (Quebec).

> *La loi 101 est maintenue* (Bill 101 is upheld)
> Stéphane Laporte, *La Presse* (Montreal).

> *L'accès à l'école anglaise ou la sagesse de la Cour suprême*
> (Access to English schools or the wisdom of the Supreme Court)
> Patrice Garant, *Le Soleil* (Quebec).

> Bill 101 survives challenge
> Elizabeth Thompson, *The Gazette* (Montreal).

> Court makes Quebec language law bulletproof
> Chantal Hébert, *Toronto Star*.

> Top court loosens school language laws
> Dave Rogers, *The Ottawa Citizen*.

Une brèche dans la loi 101 (A breach in Bill 101)
Sylvain Larocque, *Le Droit* (Ottawa-Hull).

La Cour suprême affaiblit la disposition scolaire de la loi 101 (The Supreme Court weakens the education measures of Bill 101)
Sylvain Larocque, *L'Acadie Nouvelle* (Caraquet, New Brunswick).[10]

Reaction to the judgments is clearly not divided along purely linguistic lines; rather, individual commentators reach different conclusions, which are not predictable on the basis of the language in which they are expressed. Several editorials, both in English and French, take a measured view, referring to the 'common sense' nature of the judgments:

Le parti du bon sens (The common sense option)
Michel Gauthier, *Le Droit* (Ottawa-Hull).

Court performed a delicate balancing act on language rights
Editorial, *The Vancouver Sun* (Vancouver).

However, the 'Letters to the Editor' pages on the following days reveal the strongly negative opinions on Quebec's language legislation which surface regularly in *The Gazette* (Montreal). Letters on Saturday 2 April are headed: 'Ruling enslaves francophones', 'Bill 101 doomed in the long run', 'Blocked from learning English', 'Immigrants are second class sitizens', and 'Supreme Court needs courage'. Only one letter supports Quebec's language policy ('Quebec is doing something right') and its author points out that she is Welsh.

Quebec Government reaction, as reported in the Canadian press on 1 April 2005, showed considerable relief, as the upholding of the letter of the law meant that a political can of worms had not been opened. The Government had been very fearful of a political crisis if the Gosselin case were upheld, as the reinstatement of freedom of choice would have led to a linguistic crisis. Intergovernmental Affairs Minister Benoît Pelletier breathed a sigh of relief:

Nous sommes soulagés. Si la loi avait été déclarée invalide, nous aurions eu un problème important à résoudre.

(We are relieved. If the Bill had been declared invalid, we would have had a big problem to solve.)

This was followed by a renewal of commitment to the spirit and letter of Bill 101:

Il n'y aura pas une virgule qui sera changée à la loi 101.

(Not even a comma will be changed in Bill 101.) [11]

Parti Québécois (PQ) leader Bernard Landry referred to the judgments as another erosion of Bill 101. His criticism stemmed firstly from his role as leader of the official opposition, but also from the fact that the PQ had originally crafted Bill 101. [12]

Several press commentators remarked on the fact that restrictions on freedom of choice had been relaxed for anglophones, but not for francophones. An article by Jim Brown in the *Winnipeg Free Press* (1 April 2005) put it bluntly: 'Supreme Court rules in favour of anglo parents. But Quebec parents rebuffed'. Several articles argue that Bill 101 treats Quebec's francophones like second-class citizens, because they have fewer choices than anglophones (for example Diane Francis in 'Justice for Quebec's francophones', *National Post*, Ottawa, 31 March 2005, and an editorial in the *Toronto Star*, 'The politics of language', 1 April 2005). While the majority of francophones in Quebec subscribe to the educational provisions of Bill 101, it is clear that for some of them – not least those who took their case to the Supreme Court – their identity as francophones does not necessarily entail schooling in French as a fundamental defining feature. However the views of francophones in Quebec on this issue evolve in the future, the Supreme Court decisions make it clear that debate on possible change will have to take place at a political rather than at a constitutional level. The extent of media coverage (headlines, editorials, articles and letters to the editor) leading up to and following the events in both anglophone and francophone newspapers in Quebec and across Canada indicates that the debate on access to English schools in Quebec continues to be a topic of great social and political controversy. The ongoing challenge for language policy, its makers and interpreters, is to balance the competing rights of all parties and to ensure that all language rights holders at federal and provincial level, are treated with equal consideration. This is a particular challenge for Quebec, given the preamble to Bill 101, which declares:

> *Langue distinctive d'un peuple majoritairement francophone, la langue française permet au people québécois d'exprimer son identité.* (Government of Quebec, 2003: 1) [13]

> (Whereas the French language, the distinctive language of a people that is in the majority francophone, is the instrument by which that people has articulated its identity.)

Aspects of gender representation in a francophone context

While the notion of a 'national' identity as a distinct society in Quebec continues to be debated, with the Commision des États Généraux sur la situation et l'avenir de la langue française (2001) developing the concept of *citoyenneté* (citizenship), other issues of identity have also arisen in the francophone context, not least the identity of women and its linguistic expression. The fact that French is a language with grammatical gender means that morphological matters need to be looked at in light of the new imperatives of referring to women in an increased range of professional roles. Gone are the days when a masculine term only was needed to denote the holder of a post; nowadays a female term of reference is also needed, unless inherently contradictory forms like, '*Je n'aime pas ce professeur, elle n'est pas sympa.*' (I don't like this teacher [masculine], she's not nice.) are to remain the order of the day.

The countries of *la francophonie* – the international francophone community – have not approached this issue with one mind. Rather, there has been a divergence between France itself and policy and practice in the wider francophone context. Quebec adopted a policy on implementing feminisation early on, in the 1970s, and was followed along this path by other francophone regions in Belgium and Switzerland. It can be argued with conviction therefore that francophone countries other than France have paid attention to issues of the representation of female identity by adopting linguistic policies which have considerably increased the visibility of women.

Studies carried out on language use in various francophone communities in Canada (including Acadia and Quebec) have shown that feminisation of professional titles is well established in the media. One such study (Conrick, 2005) examined 381 professional titles collected over a period of about two months in 2004 from the *Carrières et formation* and *Offres d'emploi* (Careers and Appointments) sections of the New Brunswick daily newspaper for francophones, *L'Acadie Nouvelle* (Caraquet) and from the website CareerBeacon. com (http//:www.careerbeacon.com), which advertises itself as:

> *le premier site Web de recrutement […] le plus visité […] le seul à être bilingue du Canada atlantique.*

> (The leading recruitment site […] the most visited […] the only bilingual site of Atlantic Canada).

Table 3 illustrates the breakdown of professional titles collected, by medium and category. Table 4 shows the final results in figures and percentages.

	Non-feminised		Epicenes [14]		Feminised		Total	
L'Acadie Nouvelle	77	26%	61	21%	159	54%	297	100%
CareerBeacon.com	5	6%	39	46%	40	48%	84	100%
Total	**82**	**22%**	**100**	**26%**	**199**	**52%**	**381**	**100%**

Table 3: Data by medium and category of title

Feminised titles	264	69%
Non-feminised titles	117	31%
Total	**381**	**100%**

Table 4: Final results: figures and percentages of feminised and non-feminised titles

The prevalence of feminisation in Canadian varieties is obvious from the results of this study and from those of previous studies carried out on the Montreal newspapers *Le Devoir* and *La Presse* and the Ottawa-Hull newspaper, *Le Droit* (see Conrick, 2002). It contrasts markedly with practice in French newspapers such as *Le Monde*, where the inclusion of women as a target audience in job advertisements is usually limited to a masculine title, followed by the initials 'h/f' in brackets. Consequently, users of French in Canada, led by Quebecers, have been world leaders in adapting their use of the French language to increase the visibility of women in a professional context.

Conclusion

The representation of francophone identity in Canada is indeed a very complex issue, with a multiplicity of factors at play. The last four decades of the twentieth century witnessed considerable shifts in relation to how French Canadians viewed themselves, with the startling changes in self-definition which characterised Quebec leading to the brink of secession from the Canadian state. At another level, the identity of women became an issue in French-speaking Canada, especially Quebec, in the 1970s, when women redefined themselves socially and professionally. Policy makers at many levels, in both the public and private sectors, rose to the challenge of modernising the language accordingly, with the result that evidence of linguistic feminisation is not only prevalent in contemporary Canada, but its influence has spread to other varieties of French on the international stage.

The language question is still central in terms of the representation of Quebec as a 'distinct society' and much attention is paid by the province to the promotion and development of French as the official language, as set out in Bill 101. Many Committees have reported on the state of health of the language (see for example the recent report from the Conseil supérieur de la langue française, 2005) and concerns are voiced continually about the need to protect it from the sea of anglophones surrounding it, not only in Canada, but on the continent of North America. Given the demolinguistic facts, the continuation of the strong position of Quebec is crucial as the locus of francophone identity on the continent. The situation in the rest of Canada is becoming more uncertain, with the spectre of assimilation ever present.

Notwithstanding the age-old tension between the two dominant languages, it is an inescapable fact that Canada has become an increasingly multilingual country, with more than one hundred languages reported as mother tongue in the 2001 census. This fact is sometimes lost sight of in francophone circles, where concerns surrounding the dominance of English are ubiquitous. More than 25 years after the enactment of Bill 101, commentators in Quebec have pointed to the increasing pluralism of French schools in Montreal for example, to which Bill 101 has contributed and which has played a role in the redefinition of group identity. McAndrew makes the following point in that context:

> *La transformation pluraliste de l'école montréalaise de langue française ainsi que ses conséquences à plus long terme sur la création d'une nouvelle identité constituent des exemples d'objectifs non explicitement visés par la loi 101, mais qui n'en sont pas moins des réalités auxquelles elle a fortement contribué. Les enfants de la loi 101, essentiellement des jeunes Montréalais, représentent la première génération de Québécois pour lesquels la langue française est, d'abord et avant tout, une langue de partage intergroupe et non la langue d'un groupe spécifique, étroitement associée à une culture particulière.* (McAndrew, 2002: 73)

(The pluralist transformation of French schools in Montreal and its long-term effects on the creation of a new identity are examples of objectives which were not specifically targeted by Bill 101, but which constitute nonetheless realities to which it has contributed substantially. The children of Bill 101, essentially young Montrealers, are the first generation of Quebecers for whom the French language is, first and foremost, a language of inter-group sharing rather than the language of a specific group, narrowly associated with a particular culture.)

Given the demolinguistic data, there is an obvious need for the issue of plural-ism, linguistic as well as cultural, to occupy the minds of language policy makers in Quebec and on the larger stage in Canada. The tensions between the federal and provincial agendas, particularly in relation to Official Languages policy, seem set to continue, though the Supreme Court has settled some of the issues, at least temporarily. Whatever the ultimate political fate of Quebec, its importance as a major focus of francophone identity outside France is certain to continue. Quebec and Canada will also provide a very useful case study for applied linguists, especially those interested in language policy at various levels, where they may observe and analyse issues such as the evolution of identity in a rapidly changing and internationally important multilingual environment.

Notes

1   The first release of data on language was in December 2002. For full details of Census 2001 data see the Statistics Canada website at http://www.statcan.ca and Statistics Canada (2002).

2   The term 'francophone' is used to refer to a speaker of French as mother tongue. Mother tongue is defined for the purposes of the census as the first language a person learned at home in childhood and still understood at the time of the census.

3   The most recent census was taken in Ireland in 2006, containing a two-part question on the Irish language.

4   All respondents answer the question on mother tongue, while a one-fifth sample answers all four questions.

5   Statistical data for Tables 1 and 2 have been sourced from Statistics Canada; tables have been compiled by the author.

6   New Brunswick is part of the area known as Acadia, which was, along with Quebec, a major area of original settlement of French immigrants from the seventeenth century.

7   These provisions are contained in Section 73 (1) (2) and (3). The section contains several other elements which are not discussed here, including the extension of rights to the child's brothers and sisters and the treatment of instruction in English in unsubsidised private schools.

8   The third case dealt with an administrative matter. For full details of all the judgments and all parties to the cases see 'Recent judgments' available at http://www.lexum.umontreal.ca/csc-scc/en/index.html

9   Some striking illustrations are used to represent opinion, for example *Le Soleil* uses a cartoon which visualises the situation as a 'dam' with a small 'breach', a metaphor which is often used with reference to Bill 101.

10 This is substantially the same article, under a different title, as that published in *Le Droit* by the same author.

11 Pelletier's comments were made at a widely reported press conference (see for example, Robert Dutrisac, *Aucune virgule ne sera changée à la loi, dit Pelletier, Le Devoir*, 1 April 2005, and Norman Delisle, *Le gouvernement du Québec se réjouit, mais le PQ est sur ses gardes, Le Droit*, 1 April 2005).

12 The Bill was introduced by the Parti Québécois government of René Lévesque.

13 The English translation is by the Office québécois de la langue française. Retrieved on 1 May 2006 from http://www.oqlf.gouv.qc.ca

14 The term epicene refers to nouns which have the same morphological form in the masculine and feminine. In French, they usually end in 'e': *juge* (judge), *dentiste* (dentist).

References

Castonguay, C. (1994) *L'assimilation linguistique: mesure et évolution, 1971–1986*. Québec: Les Publications du Québec.

Commission des États Généraux sur la situation et l'avenir de la langue française au Québec (2001) *Le français, une langue pour tout le monde. Une nouvelle approche stratégique et citoyenne*. Québec: Commission des États Généraux sur la situation et l'avenir de la langue française au Québec.

Commissioner of Official Languages (2005) *Annual Report 2004–2005*. Ottawa: Minister of Public Works and Government Service. Retrieved on 26 September 2005 from http://www.ocol-clo.gc.ca

Conrick, M. (2002) Language Policy and Gender Issues in Contemporary French. In K. Salhi (ed.) *French in and out of France: language polices, intercultural antagonisms and dialogue* 205–35. Oxford, Bern: Peter Lang.

Conrick, M. (2005) La modernisation du français en Acadie: les médias et la représentation linguistique et professionnelle des femmes. In G. Clermont and J. Gallant (eds) *La modernité en Acadie* 75–99. Moncton: Chaire d'études acadiennes, Université de Moncton, Collection Mouvange, 12.

Conseil supérieur de la langue française (2005) *Le français, langue normale et habituelle du travail*. Avis à la Ministre responsable de l'application de la Charte de la langue française. Retrieved on 12 September 2005 from http://www.cslf.gouv.qc.ca

Government of Canada (1982) *The Canadian Charter of Rights and Freedoms*. Ottawa: Department of Justice.

Government of Canada (2003) *The Action Plan for Official Languages*. Ottawa: Privy Council Office.

Government of Quebec (2003) *Charte de la langue française*. Quebec: Éditeur officiel du Québec.

McAndrew, M. (2002) La loi 101 en milieu scolaire: impacts et résultats. In P. Bouchard and R. Y. Bourhis (eds) *Revue d'aménagement linguistique* 69–83. Special issue, L'aménagement linguistique au Québec: 25 ans d'application de la Charte de la langue française. Autumn.

Royal Commission on Bilingualism and Biculturalism (1967) *Report, Book 1, The Official Languages*. Ottawa: The Queen's Printer.
Statistics Canada (2002) *Profile of Languages in Canada: English, French and many others*. Ottawa: Statistics Canada, Census Operations Division.

3 Sami languages: between hope and endangerment

Hannele Dufva and Sari Pietikäinen

Introduction

In Spring 2004, the last speaker of Akkala Sami died in Kola Peninsula, Russia (Aikio, 2004). The extinction of the language is one example of endangerment of the Sami languages that are spoken in northernmost Europe. At the same time, a young rap musician, Amoc, uses Inari Sami, a language with less than 500 speakers, in his lyrics that have an audience from the Sami homeland to New York music clubs, thus showing the vitality that is present also in languages that face endangerment.

Below, we will examine some of the manifold practices and experiences that are present in the struggle of the Sami community to maintain their languages. The focus of this paper is to examine forces that may co-exist but work in different, sometimes opposite, directions, thus enhancing either revitalisation or extinction of nine Sami languages. We discuss the Sami language situation from the point of view of applied linguistics, drawing on discussion on linguistic diversity, language revitalisation and language education (see e.g. Hinton and Hale, 2001; Huss, 1999; Magga and Skutnabb-Kangas, 2003). We focus on the situation of the three Sami languages spoken in Finland: Northern Sami that is listed as endangered (c. 30,000 speakers), and Inari Sami (less than 500) and Skolt Sami (less than 500) that are listed as seriously endangered (Salminen, 1993).

The Sami community is estimated as consisting of 50,000–80,000 people, out of whom 7,000–7,500 live in Finland (Aikio-Puoskari, 2001). Sápmi, the traditional Sami homeland, is today split by four nation-states of Norway, Sweden, Finland and Russia which makes the community transnational. The Sami community is also partly diasporic: today, nearly half of the people live outside Sápmi. The region is and has been multicultural and multilingual: the indigenous Sami culture and languages co-exist and interwine with each other and different majority cultures and languages. In addition to different Sami languages, national majority languages and many global foreign languages are used as well as two other regional (minority) languages.

What is the position of the Sami languages then? Exact figures of both ethnicity and mother tongue speakers are difficult to obtain, but it is estimated that today most of the youngest Sami generation learn Sami as a second language (Aikio-Puoskari and Skutnabb-Kangas, forthcoming). This is particularly true for Inari and Skolt Sami. Thus most or all Sami speakers are multilingual to a degree, using at least one Sami language and one majority language (Finnish, Swedish or Norwegian). The individuals' Sami language skills vary much, both in fluency and in how many domains of use, modalities or registers are mastered (e.g. spoken only or literacy in Sami).

The situation of the Sami languages is an example of a context which by its very nature goes beyond the approach typical of much linguistic research where language has been conceptualised in monolithic and monological terms (for criticism, see e.g. Linell, 1998) or, where monolingual bias has been typical (for criticism of monolingually biased SLA research, see Block, 2003). Concepts such as mother tongue/first language/L1 and second/foreign language/L2 that have been questioned before (e.g. Rampton, 1997) may not be wholly adequate for the description of the multilayered, situated and constantly transforming relationship between Sami and other languages.

We suggest that Bakhtin's dialogical notion of language as heteroglossia better describes both the language situation and speakers' experiences. Bakhtin's (1981: 291) conceptualisation of language gives primacy to variation and diversity. Thus, language is seen as a collection of co-existing 'ways of speaking' that evidence different past and present socio-ideological contradictions. This is what happens in the Sami community where languages and ways of speaking intersect in a variety of ways, either intertwining (harmoniously), or, clashing with each other in one language's attempt to win hegemony over others. As different languages have different functions in different situations – ways of speaking are situated – they may also produce situated and hybrid identities.

In this paper, we explore how the practices and experiences that seem to signal further endangerment, and possibly extinction of the languages, intertwine with other practices that speak for their maintenance and revitalisation, in other words, hope. We draw on the data that is being collected in Sari Pietikäinen's research project[1]: interviews of Sami-speaking adults and children complemented with ethnographic data such as drawings, written narratives and on-site observations. We base our comments on actual practices and people's experiences on interviews, on-site observations and particular tasks. In our theoretical and methodological framework (Pietikäinen and Dufva, 2006), we draw on dialogism (the work of the Bakhtin Circle) and CDA (the work of Fairclough). Here, however, a closer theoretical discussion is left aside as is also a detailed discussion of the diverse economical and political issues – such as the unsettled recognition by the Finnish government of the Sami land-owning rights – that have powerful effects on language revitalisation (see e.g. May, 2005; Blommaert, 2005).

Below, we discuss some preliminary observations of the variety and interplay of different forces and tendencies that work on two essential domains of language use (see Fishman, 1964): school and home, either for the Sami languages or against them. Most of our examples below come from interviews (as a translation into English of the original Finnish).[2]

Situational context: the generations of Sami speakers

(1)   At home, we never spoke Finnish at home. Well, sometimes. My mother, she, well, she always felt funny when she spoke Finnish. If you could speak poorly they laughed at you. Then, she told about the time they were evacuated to Kalajoki and she couldn't even ask for some water in Finnish. That was quite … Myself, I learned, my father taught me [Finnish] and then I went to school so it was there I … But it was so and so. Well, the books were strange, and those strange words! One couldn't [learn] them all. Well, one just kept speaking, and then one learned it, kind of. My husband is Finnish, but my daughter does not speak any Sami, and her small son does not speak any Sami. (An elderly female journalist, interview, 2003)

The sequence (Example 1) above may illustrate how – over the last 50 years or so – Sami languages changed from being small but strong community languages into endangered languages known by a few (see also Aikio, 1988; Lehtola, 2000). Below, we will distinguish four generations that are each characterised by different social and cultural circumstances that have transformed the domains of language use (Fishman, 1991) and the significance of the domains themselves (see Lindgren, 2000: 25):

1.   Pre-WW2 period (before 1939): Sami as a mother tongue generation;
2.   After WW2 period (after 1945): language shift generation;
3.   The 1970s: Sami revival generation;
4.   From 2000 on: contemporary Sami generation.

Sami as a mother tongue generation

Before World War Two, Sami languages were regularly learned as a mother tongue and widely used as a primary means of the daily interaction in the community. The community was not monolingual, however. Many people knew different Sami languages but also Finnish and other majority languages were learned as additional languages (Lehtola, 2000: 186–7; Lindgren, 2000).

However, Finnish was both an official language and the language of education and administration in Sápmi. The knowledge of Finnish gradually became more common and ultimately a necessity during the wartime, when many Sami people were evacuated from their traditional habitation as also Example (1) above indicated.

Language shift generation

The post-war years since 1945 and the modernisation process that swept across the world had deep effects on the Finnish society and consequently, on the Sami community. Industrialisation changed the ways they earned their living – one example being reindeer herding – and thus also affected the use of languages that were important carriers of the Sami culture. Education that by the post-war years had become systematised and compulsory to all children aged under 16 was another important factor that changed the traditional Sami society, as – with minor exceptions – it was given in Finnish only. At this time, the language shift from the Sami languages to Finnish truly began (Aikio, 1988). An older journalist recollects (Example 2) how the post-war years homogenised the civic identity as follows:

(2)   I sensed this as a panic situation for many people. There had been a war, people had been killed. Many Finnish-speaking people came here to the homelands of the Sami. The after-war reconstruction was going on and these huge loggings began: this brought more people here and totally turned this society upside down. And also the language became endangered. Mixed marriages increased and the Finnish-speaking schools appeared – and other institutions that 'Finlandised' the Sami. And Inari Sami disappeared almost totally back in the 1950s as a consequence of this. (An elderly male journalist, interview, 2003)

The Finnish-only education played an important role in making a drastic change in the domains of the Sami language use, but also the attitudes of the majority population towards Sami were generally negative. In short, Sami languages became increasingly marginalised and the majority language was spreading to the domains that had been Sami-speaking before. Example (3) below tells a story of being a Sami-speaking child in a majority language school:

(3)   When I was seven and I went to school I did not know any other language than Sami. I went there with no Finnish skills. And sure it was ((pause)). I did not know, for the first half year ... I do not have a very accurate memory [of it], but I feel that I was really lost. Fortunately I was not alone. There were others: tongueless and mindless. We just stood up in the middle of

the lesson and left the room – — – We thought it natural that if you needed to go to toilet you did not report it to anyone else but just stood up and left – — – Our friends scolded us, said 'we were ashamed of you' – — – you don't know how to behave. (A middle-aged male journalist, interview, 2005)

Finnish-speaking school was a cultural shock and trauma to many Sami children in that it forced them to speak Finnish only. But as the children had to leave their Sami-speaking home to live the weekdays in the dormitories – because of the long distances – also their mother tongue skills were disrupted. Education came to be a double-edged sword: it offered an opportunity, but it did so in Finnish only, which meant subtractive bilingualism, a suffocation of one's own language (Aikio, 1988). Many Sami who experienced the stigma of these years started to use Finnish with their own children for the purpose of doing them a favour (Lindgren, 2000). The post-war generation was educated in Finnish and often also trained for jobs and professions in which only the majority language skills were needed. At the same time, during these very years of language shift, also Sami activism started to strengthen and later became manifest, for example, in the rising of the pan-Sami movement.

Sami revival generation

By the 1970s, it was evident that the language issue had to be reconsidered. The Sami community was now working actively for its civil rights and linguistic rights. To take an example, although some teachers had taught Sami or in Sami 'in secrecy', it was not until the comprehensive school reform in the 1970s that the languages were given an official recognition at school (Aikio-Puoskari, 2000). From then on, young people started to demand a right to be educated *in* Sami. A journalist describes her school years as follows (Example 4):

(4) ... (when) I had been for one year in upper secondary school I made a point of requiring instruction in Sami and I managed to achieve that. Mathematics biology geography chemistry, and such, science. And we studied them in Sami. And then I had some difficulties in chemistry and physics and I asked for remedial lessons and the remedial instruction was provided by a Finnish speaking teacher only. (A young female journalist, interview, 2003)

Contemporary Sami generation

Today, the position of the Sami languages within Finnish society is stronger than ever before. Sami languages have regional official status in three northern municipalities. Sami Language Act (1991) along with certain constitutional amendments, acts and laws have made Sami-language services possible in various areas of everyday life (e.g. health care, day care, parishes, libraries, media and education). Now the languages are used in various domains that range from everyday interaction to political life (e.g. Sami Parliament), media usage (e.g. television newsrooms) and diverse areas of popular culture (e.g. Sami-language karaoke, rock, rap or tango). Next we will discuss our data on the domains of school and home in more detail. Has the language shift really been reversed – and has it happened in a similar way with all Sami languages?

Hope and endangerment: two domains of Sami language use

Below, we try to unravel some parts of the truly complex network of factors that characterises language use at home and in education. Choosing these two domains for closer examination we also wished to be able to reflect the elements of hope and endangerment from the point of view of the future generations. What kind of language affordances (van Lier, 2004), or, possibilities to pick up language, there might be for the next generation of potential Sami speakers at home and at school?

Sami languages at home: some observations

In a sense the home is the primary site for language learning: in families mother tongues are transferred from one generation to another, from parents and grandparents to children. The important role of the language use at home is often emphasised in discussing minority language usage and/or language revitalisation (see e.g. Reyhner and Tennant, 1995). As Fishman (1991: 91) points out, intergenerational continuity is of course a key issue in keeping languages alive.

There are several critical factors that make it possible for (any) language to survive as a mother tongue. Leaving the macro-level societal factors aside, an appreciative emotional response towards one's own language is extremely relevant for language maintenance and revitalisation (see e.g. Fishman, 1997). How do Sami speakers characterise their languages and their emotional significance? In the decades of language shift, as our interviewees tell us, Sami speakers were often *ridiculed* because of their language and this resulted in feelings of *shame*. Today the situation seems to be reversed. One of the clearest signals of hope for Sami languages was the positive emotional response that was generally attached to languages. Sami adults spoke about their languages as important personal instruments of *thinking* and *communicating* that *mediate the Sami way of living*. They also saw the languages as a particular *perspective* to the world, as a *bond* between the community, and even a *door* to being a Sami. One example of the importance of language as an instrument of thinking is below:

(5)   Well, sure, Inari Sami is the closest language because I have learned it as
        a first language; these others have become later. And it is so that when one
        starts thinking and reflecting certain things it just seems to happen that one's
        thoughts are in Inari Sami. So that it is only a second choice – depending
        on the subject – that [my thinking] will be in the Finnish language or in
        Northern Sami language. (A middle-aged male journalist, interview, 2003)

Thus for the Sami adults we interviewed, languages were not only alive, but
highly significant and valuable. At an attitudinal level the position of the Sami
language thus seems strong. However, the balance between Sami and Finnish
is far from stable. Despite the highly valued position of the Sami languages,
the interview data shows that the language practices at home still involve
many problems.

One critical point is the presence of several languages in the family: although
family bilingualism can be achieved without any problems, the asymmetrical
position of Finnish and Sami within society may also make it more difficult
to choose Sami as (one) home language. Each couple has to think whether to
raise their children to use both Sami and Finnish, or Finnish only. This is an
acute problem for some young parents who say they spend *many sleepless
nights* over the language question.

Still another warning signal may be that children tend to use Finnish in
their mutual interaction, although they might speak Sami with their parents.
As many families are not only multilingual, but remarriage families as well,
children might have different language backgrounds, which makes it even
easier to use Finnish mutually. One child explains in an interview how different languages are chosen in the family depending on who talks to whom
and ultimately comments: '*well I try to speak Sami with* [my kid brother] *but
somehow it turns into Finnish*'.

Also, the consequences of the decline in the use of Sami languages are still
seen in the everyday life and in the linguistic parenting: there are many who
lost their language either totally or to a degree. Many people would dearly
love to use Sami as their home language, but either the circumstances or their
own language skills seem to be against it. The next example (6) illustrates the
way people may feel about their fluency:

(6)   Even though it's my mother tongue, I … well … I have to, whenever I
        speak, speak my own tongue, I have to work for finding the words. Or, or, I
        cannot manage as natural a conversation as my mother who is eighteen years
        older than I am – – – It's a bit awkward, my language is – – – I have real
        gaps in my language skills – – – As it is not used every day, the language. (A
        middle-aged female journalist, interview, 2005)

The example above is also a comment on how such concepts as mother tongue or L1 are far from being unambiguous in this context. What the woman's words seem to indicate is that Sami is her preferred mother tongue – a result of a conscious, social and political choice. On the other hand, it may not be her natural mother tongue in the sense that she would feel absolutely easy with its use.

Finally, one needs to note that there seem to be significant differences between different Sami languages and domains of use (for Inari Sami, see Olthuis, 2003; for Skolt Sami, see McRobbie-Utasi, 1995). Our data indicates that children who speak Northern Sami are usually able to use their language both at home and at school, whereas Inari Sami children have fewer contacts and may thus tend to associate their Sami language mostly with school, teacher and instruction. Nevertheless, also Inari Sami children expressed confidence about the future of their own language, saying, for example, that they are going to teach Sami to their young relatives.

In all, the data that has been gathered thus far suggests that the use of the Sami languages in the everyday life at home is not unproblematic. Problems derive partly from the past: as a consequence of the language shift, many middle-aged Sami people either lost their language or do not feel comfortable in using it. This causes further problems for the younger generation: the learners may not have that many learning and using opportunities and their language contacts are few. Also, some problems may be due to problems in deciding upon family bilingualism or multilingualism. To compensate, it seems that many, perhaps the majority, in the community itself deeply care and appreciate the languages.

Sami languages at school: practices and experiences

An officially recognised position of the Sami languages in education tells both about their status in the (Finnish) society and the linguistic rights of their speakers. Both indicate that the languages have a future. When Sami-speaking education is considered at a societal level, the situation is better than ever. At the moment, the right to study in any of the Sami languages is ensured by the Sami Language Act and Basic Education Act (1999) which entitles children living in the Sami homeland to have the main part of their education in Sami. Also, there are also positions guaranteed by legislation for Sami-speaking teachers (see also Aikio-Puoskari, 1997).

Above, we showed that those Sami adults we interviewed unanimously appreciated Sami languages. How are Sami languages experienced by the younger generation – and how are they seen as objects of learning? It can be argued that the way children conceptualise and emotionally experience languages is related to their motivation to learn and success in learning and is consequently important for the success of revitalising the languages (see also Hinton and Hale, 2001). We may contrast, for example, the experiences in Ireland where teaching Irish seems to have been less than successful – and where children may express a dislike towards learning it – to the rising figures of Maori speakers in New Zealand that may be related to a language education programme that relies on language nest ideology, native teachers and immersion techniques (Spolsky, 2003).

In a case study of Sami school children's (N=19) conceptualisations of language and language learning, it turned out that children's responses to Sami languages were basically favourable, but not unambiguously so. While most children described the language as *nice, fun, useful* or *easy*, some also said they were *strange* or *difficult*. And although the children felt themselves *happy* when speaking Sami, some also felt *crazy* or *strange*. Thus it seems that children simply seem to have a different relationship and possibly, also a different self-image as language user and language learner and that there might be a difference here between Northern Sami and smaller Sami languages. Growing up as a Sami speaker has many different shades.

During on-site observation it was also possible to look closer at the practices at school and classroom. All children attended Sami-language instruction and were registered as either Sami speakers or Finnish-Sami bilinguals. However, they used a lot of Finnish, both in classroom interaction and in child-child interaction during the breaks. While some children may keep on using only or mostly Sami, it is often Northern Sami. The present domains of Inari Sami being as narrow as they are, we feel that the language may not be experienced as a living mother tongue or a tool of interaction, but rather, as a decontextualised object of study, a second or a foreign language to be learned at school. Our observations seem to support the use of such teaching practices where language is regarded in terms of genuine interaction and/or existing multilingual resources are effectively used in classroom interaction (for a study of Sami language instruction in Sweden, see Hyltenstam and Svonni, 1990).

A sequence from an interview of a child who has participated in Inari Sami 'language nest' – an institution of daycare and/or primary school that works basically as an immersion programme and where children are exposed to Sami – may sum up some of the difficulties of these young speakers:

(7) Int: That's right. Do you remember when you started learning Sami?
    Child: When I was four and I went to the language nest.
             (– — –)
    Int: Mm. Do you remember what language you spoke in?
    Child: Sami, and Finnish with friends.
    Int: Why did you use Finnish with friends?
    Child: We-ell, ((laugh)) we are used to, speaking Finnish whenever we
             have visited each other and
    Int: Yes, with whom do you speak Sami?
    Child: Mm, really only here at school, but, at recess we use Finnish
    Int: Yes. How about the classroom?
    Child: Well, also there we sometimes, use Finnish with the teacher
    Int: Mm mm. Is there anyone at home with whom you speak Sami?
    Child: No. Nobody knows how to speak it.
             (An Inari Sami child, interview, 2005)

Another point that invites discussion is the role of the teacher and teaching methods. First, although there now are qualified teachers, many are also unqualified, particularly in the smaller Sami languages. Also, the teachers' Sami-language skills vary from a fluent native-speaker to a less fluent foreign language user. While a native-speaker teacher may not be a necessity, the literature of indigenous language teaching and language revitalisation seems to suggest that native teachers possess certain qualities that may help children better to understand language as a medium of interaction, thinking and maintaining one's own culture (see e.g. Reyhner and Tennant, 1995). Many experiments have been or are being carried out in Sami language education.

To sum up, although the situation of Sami language at school – and also generally in education – has been made better by various legislative and institutional reforms and there now exists an infrastructure for teaching Sami, the language issue is by no means settled – either from the point of view of institutional efforts or from the point of view of classroom practices.

Conclusion

Looking our observations from the point of view of intergenerational changes, the domains of all Sami languages spoken in Finland have changed radically over the years – for worse but also for better. Before World War II, Sami languages were regularly learned as mother tongues, used at home and were thus also living, albeit mostly oral and unofficial, community languages. Now, at the beginning of the twenty-first century – after facing near-extinction – the languages are reviving as mother tongues but are also used at school both as objects of teaching and mediums of instruction. Sami now exists in written forms and is also fairly widely used in the media (for the role of the media, see Pietikäinen and Dufva, 2005).

In our attempt to track down signals that might speak for a better future to Sami languages, we found many encouraging things. Importantly, own languages seemed to be highly meaningful and significant for the community, adults and children alike. This is important for children's learning of the languages and thus, language revitalisation. In all, it seems justified to imagine a better Sami speaking world. Still, many problems at a concrete level of language use appeared both at home and at school, being often related to the choice of language for spontaneous interaction. Also, the position of the Sami languages was clearly different: Northern Sami is stronger both at home and at school than the other two Sami languages.

As researchers, we have attempted to explore and analyse the situation with means that would both capture the voices of the community and produce such results that could be used to promote the practices of language revitalisation. We therefore link our approach to such critical directions of applied linguistics (Pennycook, 2001) that stress the necessity to examine language use in its social and political context. We feel that increased awareness in developing language education practices for today's multicultural society is needed both within the Sami-language community and within the Finnish community. Linguists can, and should have, a role in this discussion. To add, we attempted at arguing that the multivoiced and situated language use in the community is an argument in itself for a dialogical conceptualisation of language: a vibrant, constantly changing collection of different ways of speaking that co-exist, compete, clash and merge (Bakhtin, 1981; Linell, 1998).

Notes

1   This article was produced as part of Sari Pietikäinen's research project *Empowering Potential of Ethnic Minority Media*, funded by the Academy of Finland.

2   Pauses are marked by a comma (,), authors' clarifications and additions by [ ], omissions by (– – –) and restarts by (…). In some cases, we have summarised our subjects' words: these are given in italics in the text.

References

Aikio, M. (1988) *Saamelaiset kielenvaihdon kierteessä*. Helsinki: SKS.

Aikio, P. (2004) Opening speech in the symposium 'Transnational Communities and ICTs: Citizenship and Participation', 20–22 May, University of Lapland, Rovaniemi, Finland.

Aikio-Puoskari, U. (1997) Sami language in Finnish schools. In E. Kasten (ed.) *Bicultural Education in the North. Ways of Preserving and Enhancing Indigenous People's Languages and Traditional Knowledge* 47–57. Münster, New York, München and Berlin: Waxmann.

Aikio-Puoskari, U. (2000) Tutkimuskohteena saamen kieli koulutuspolitiikassa. Retrieved on 15 January 2006 from http://www.ulapland.fi/home/vies/ ajankohtaista/kide/Kide7_2000/siula.htm

Aikio-Puoskari, U. (2001) About the Saami and the domestic legislation on their language rights. In U. Aikio-Puoskari and M. Pentikäinen (eds) *The Language Rights of the Indigenous Saami in Finland – Under Domestic and International Law* 3–70. Juridica Lapponica 26. Rovaniemi: The Northern Institute for Environmental and Minority Law, University of Lapland, Finland.

Aikio-Puoskari, U. and Skutnabb-Kangas, T. (forthcoming) When few under 50 speak the language as a first language: linguistic (human) rights and linguistic challenges for endangered Saami languages. To appear in N. Ø. Helander (ed.) Guovdageaidnu/Kautokeino: Sámi Instituhhta/Nordic Saami Institute.

Bakhtin, M. M. (1981) *The Dialogic Imagination*. Austin: University of Texas Press.

Block, D. (2003) *The Social Turn in Second Language Acquisition*. Edinburgh: Edinburgh University Press.

Blommaert, J. (2005) Situating language rights: English and Swahili in Tanzania revisited. *Journal of Sociolinguistics* 9(3): 390–417.

Fishman, J. (1964) Language maintenance and language shift as a field of inquiry. *Linguistics* 9: 32–70.

Fishman, J. A. (1991) *Reversing Language Shift: theoretical and empirical foundations of assistance to threatened languages*. Clevedon: Multilingual Matters.

Fishman, J. A. (1997) *In Praise of the Beloved Language. A Comparative View of Positive Ethnolinguistic Consciousness*. Berlin and New York: Mouton de Gruyer.

Hinton, L. and Hale, K. (eds) (2001) *The Green Book of Language Revitalisation in Practice*. New York: Academic Press.

Huss, L. (1999) *Reversing the Language Shift in the far North. Linguistic Revitalization in Northern Scandinavia and Finland*. Studia Uralica Upsaliensis 31. Uppsala University.

Hyltenstam, K. and Svonni, M. (1990) *Forskning om förstaspråksbehärskning hos samiska barn. Språksociologisk situation, teoretiska ramar och en preliminär bedömning*. Rapporter om tvåspråkighet 6: 185–98. Stockholm, Sweden: Centrum för tvåspråkighetsforskning,

Lehtola, V-P. (2000) Kansain välit – monikulttuurisuus ja saamelaishistoria. In I. Seurujärvi-Kari (ed.) *Beaivvi Mánát. Saamelaisten juuret ja nykyaika*. Helsinki, Finland: SKS.

Lindgren, A-R. (2000) *Helsingin saamelaiset ja oma kieli.* Helsinki, Finland: SKS.

Linell, P. (1998) *Approaching Dialogue. Talk, Interaction and Contexts in Dialogical Perspectives.* Amsterdam: John Benjamins.

Magga, O. H. and Skutnabb-Kangas, T. (2003) Life or death for languages and human beings – experiences from Saamiland. In L. Huss, A. Camilleri Grima and K. King (eds) *Transcending Monolingualism: linguistic revitalisation in education. Series Multilingualism and Linguistic Diversity* 35–52. Lisse: Swets and Zeitlinger.

May, S. (2005) Language rights: moving the debate forward. *Journal of Sociolinguistics* 9(3): 319–47.

McRobbie-Utasi, Z. (1995) Language planning, literacy and cultural identity: the Skolt Sami case. *Linguistics. Series A, Studia et Dissertationes 17. Zur Frage der uralischen Schriftsprachen* 31–9. Retrieved on 18 January 2006 from http://www.sfu.ca/~mcrobbie/research.html

Olthuis, M-L. (2003) Uhanalaisen kielen elvytys: Esimerkkinä inarinsaame, *Virittäjä* 107: 568–79.

Pennycook, A. (2001) *Critical Applied Linguistics. A Critical Introduction.* Mahwah, NJ: Lawrence Erlbaum.

Pietikäinen, S. and Dufva, H. (2005) Broadcasting indigenous images: the role of Sami media in identity struggle and language revitalization. Paper read at the conference 'Language in the media: representations, identities, ideologies', 12–14 September, Leeds.

Pietikäinen, S. and Dufva, H. (2006) Voices in discourses: dialogism, critical discourse analysis, and ethnic identity. *Journal of Sociolinguistics* 10(2): 205–24.

Rampton, B. (1997) Second language research in late modernity: response to Firth and Wagner. *Modern Language Journal* 81(3): 329–33.

Reyhner, J. and Tennant, E. (1995) Maintaining and renewing native languages. *Bilingual Research Journal* 19(2): 279–304.

Salminen, T. (1993) *UNESCO Red book of endangered languages. Europe.* Retrieved on 18 January 2006 from http://www.helsinki.fi/~tasalmin/europe_index.html

Spolsky, B. (2003) Reassessing Maori regeneration. *Language in Society* 32(4): 553–78.

van Lier, L. (2004) *The Ecology and Semiotics of Language Learning: a sociocultural perspective.* Boston: Kluwer Academic Publishers.

4 Identity formation and dialect use among young speakers of the Greek-Cypriot community in Cyprus

Andry Sophocleous

Introduction

The two language varieties used in the southern part of Cyprus are Standard Modern Greek (SMG), the official language that is regarded as the prestigious form, and used in educational institutions, in the media, in political gatherings, governmental offices, and in the court of law; and Greek-Cypriot Dialect (GCD) which is used in everyday conversation, amongst family and friends, in folk literature and songs, and in political and cultural satire.

Apart from the obvious distinctions in their functional load, these varieties display marked differences in phonology, morphology, lexis, and syntactic structure. Despite the fact that from a very young age, GCs separate these two varieties and attach distinct values to each one, in practice the relation between SMG and GCD does not seem to be a classic case of diglossia as there is a continuum of usage which ranges from a regional form of SMG to various local forms and subvarieties of the dialect. There is an ongoing debate among GC linguists of whether the relation between a standard form (SMG) and a number of subvarieties of GCD can qualify as a situation of diglossia.

The study of the Greek-Cypriot Dialect has gained much attention the past few years. Numerous studies in the dialect (see Pavlou, 2004; Papapavlou, 2004) revealed that Greek-Cypriots (GCs) rate the official language, SMG, more positively on competence-related traits and characterise its speakers as being more *intelligent*, more *educated* and more *ambitious* than their Greek-Cypriot counterparts who employ GCD. However, Papapavlou (1998) has observed that SMG speakers do not receive higher evaluations than their GCD counterparts on social-attractiveness related traits such as *sincerity*, *kindness*, *friendliness* and *humour*.

The tendency of evaluating speakers of regional dialects or varieties more positively on solidarity/attractiveness-related traits like on *sincerity* or *friendliness*, but less positively on competence/status-related traits, like on *intelligence* and *confidence* is apparent in various empirical studies. For example, Giles and Coupland (1991) refer to a study carried out in 1990 in Kentucky, where local students were asked to evaluate Kentucky accented speakers and standard American speakers. It was observed that the ingroup speakers – Kentucky speakers – were rated high on solidarity and low on status, whereas American speakers scored low on solidarity and high on status. A similar pattern of results was also apparent in one of the studies carried out by Garrett et al. (2003) who observed in a narratives study the language attitudes of Welsh students towards regional speakers. They observed that on the social attractiveness scale of *good laugh*[1] regional speakers received the highest evaluations in relation to RP speakers who received the lowest evaluations on this trait. However, the *good at school*[2] ratings were quite different to the results from the social-attractiveness traits, as RP speakers scored the highest points on this scale (150–51).

Tendencies such as these result from typically-held stereotypes of language forms and their users (Thomas, 2004: 205). Speakers in a particular community make their judgements on the basis of what qualities they have learnt to associate their varieties with. For instance, in the United States women who speak with a southern accent may be perceived as 'sweet, pretty and not very bright' because people have learnt to associate southern accent with lack of intelligence (Lippi-Green, 1997: 215).

The present study

The tendency to evaluate speakers of the local dialect negatively on competence-related traits and positively on solidarity/attractiveness-related traits is also very much apparent in the Greek-Cypriot (GC) society in Cyprus. It has been observed that GCs have stigmatised the dialect and its users are perceived to lack some of the characteristics of SMG users (Papapavlou, 1998). Several factors including political and social factors have influenced this stigmatisation, but this issue will not be discussed here as it is beyond the scope of this study.

A pattern that was observed to dominate in the results of previous unpublished studies I carried out is that GCD speakers received relatively lower evaluations in comparison to their SMG counterparts on most traits examined. This trend was consistent on all competence related traits, where GC speakers were perceived to be using 'incorrect' speech, and they were characterised as less *intelligent, educated*, and *ambitious* than their SMG counterparts. Interestingly, it was observed that the more GCD elements speakers used in their speech, the more negative evaluations they received on all competence related traits. On the contrary, the more SMG elements they used in their speech, and hence the closer their speech was to SMG, the more positive the evaluations they received. The findings from these studies suggest that GCD is not a single, fixed variety but has a number of 'subvarieties' which I have categorised following a preliminary survey. Hence, the purpose of this study is to examine which subvariety GCs consider more 'marked' than others and which one they use to express their GC identity.

It is probable that not all GCs evaluate negatively all components of the dialect (phonological, morphological, lexical, and syntactic). If that was the case they would not be using the dialect on an everyday basis and in their inter-actions. The current study does not explore the phonological, morphological, lexical and syntactic features of each subvariety to observe which elements of the dialect GCs tend to downgrade, but it deals with a more broad and informal categorisation of each subvariety which the preliminary work has proved to be one that is recognised by GC speakers.

Preliminary work

For the purpose of categorising these subvarieties, I spent seven hours observing and partly transcribing the language use of ordinary people, presenters, com-mentators and politicians on the radio and television, as well as interacting with strangers, acquaintances and friends, to uncover the linguistic differences there are in the speech of these different speakers. These differences were arranged in four different categories and placed on a dialectal continuum of the GCD. This preliminary work was carried out prior to the study for the purpose of selecting the different subvarieties.

1.SMG   2.POLISHED GCD   3.MODERN GCD   4.RURAL GCD

To confirm the categorisation of these four types or 'subvarieties' of the dialect, 15 GC – female (9) and male (6) – adult speakers from various backgrounds, ages (23–50) and levels of education were asked to read a collection of phrases and extracts I had transcribed earlier, relating to each subvariety and then com-ment on them. In order not to emphasise differences between 'correct' versus 'peasant' (as the GCs call it) speech, I used the term 'style' in an attempt to make them turn their attention to stylistic differences in these extracts, for the purpose of this activity was not to examine their views on the 'correctness' of these subvarieties but on whether they can distinguish between them and employ them in their daily interactions. The two questions asked to generate their comments were *Can you detect any stylistic differences in these speech samples*? and *In which situations would you use each one of these styles*? This was a one-to-one procedure, where all responses with their permission were recorded and then analysed. All GCs who took part in this preliminary survey agreed that these subvarieties are distinct and general types/styles under which the speech of GCs can be classified.

Based on the findings collected from the literature (see Papapavlou, 1998; Giles and Coupland, 1991; Garrett et al., 2003) and from previous studies I have carried out (unpublished), it is predicted that the stronger the accent is, the lower the evaluations will be on the measure of competence, but the closer the accent is to SMG, the lower evaluations will be on the measure of attractiveness.

Method
The Matched-Guise Technique

A form of the Matched-Guise Technique (MGT) (Lambert, 1967) was employed, where eight male speakers performed in the four different subvarieties. The classic model of the MGT attempts to examine how listeners evaluate numerous speech characteristics. This is achieved by asking listeners to evaluate paired speech samples of bilingual or bidialectal speakers who use one language in one guise and another language in the other guise. Listeners are not aware that they are listening to the same speaker in each paired speech sample, as the order of these speech samples is manipulated. Hence, the listeners' evaluations are believed to reflect their feelings towards the language or dialect they are asked to evaluate.

Speakers

Out of the 18 male students from Intercollege[3] in Lefkosia who volunteered to perform as speakers in the study, eight of them were selected to represent speakers of the four subvarieties of the dialect. To have a homogeneous group of speakers and to avoid speaker differences due to gender, only male speakers were recorded. The speakers' age ranged from 21 to 26, with an average age of 23.3. All speakers were born and raised in Cyprus and have been using the dialect from a very young age, even before attending kindergarten when systematic learning of SMG began.

Procedures

Speaker narratives

Speakers were asked to narrate a personal experience in about two minutes that had surprised them, pleased them or stayed in their mind. They were informed that their narrative would be recorded and then used as a linguistic exercise with other students. They were asked not to prepare anything in advance, apart from thinking what they would talk about. I arranged to meet with each speaker separately to avoid causing feelings of anxiety which might have arisen if other students, whom the speakers did not know, were also present during their recordings.

To maintain spontaneity and natural flow in the recordings of the narratives, speakers were asked to tell their story in a way they felt most comfortable with. Hence, no mention was made with regard to the use of the four subvarieties in the GCD, as I did not want to influence them on which subvariety to use in their speech. Consequently, to find two speakers who would consistently use the same subvariety meant that I had to record far more than eight speakers. The total number of speakers recorded was 18, from whom the final eight were selected. This part of the study was the most time-consuming as speakers' stories were either shorter than two minutes, not very interesting for evaluation purposes or not audible. Time was the only part of the recordings that was monitored. Speakers were told from the beginning to narrate their story in about two minutes. As there was no rehearsal prior to the recordings, the narrations displayed most of the characteristics of natural/unprepared speech such as repetition, pauses, self-correction, and articulating certain syllables at a slower pace than others when thinking what to say next. After the completion of all recordings, the order of the eight selected guises that fell under the four subvarieties of GCD was manipulated and then copied onto a CD, which informants later heard.

It is worth noting that six of the speakers had lived their entire life in the suburbs of the capital and the other two come from two villages Aredhiou and Psymolofou outside the capital city. Interestingly, these two were the only speakers who employed the last subvariety on the dialectal continuum, Rural GCD. They opted for this subvariety in the recordings as this is the one they felt most comfortable with, and used in their everyday interactions with their peers at Intercollege and in the village where they lived. Even more interesting is the fact that, in their stories they made reference to their villages, thus making a clear association of their identity with the use of Rural GCD and the villages they come from. This association was apparent in their narratives, in contrast to the other six narratives where speakers made no reference to geographical identity.

Participants in the Matched-Guise Technique

A total number of 106 students from four different classes at Intercollege participated in the MGT (42 male and 64 female). To maintain homogeneity in the groups of participants observed, it was vital that all participants were born and raised in Cyprus. They were full-time and part-time GC students, who have been studying towards achieving a BA/BSc Degree in several fields of study such as Marketing, Hotel and Tourism Management, Computer Science, English Language and Linguistics, Business Administration, Primary Education, and training in Culinary Arts. The informants' age ranged from 18 to 36 years old; the average age of males was 22^4 and of females 20 years old.

Hypotheses

On the basis of the results obtained from my previous experiments and other similar studies (Lippi-Green, 1997; Papapavlou, 1998; Abrams and Hogg, 1987) it is predicted that in the Matched-Guise Technique:

1. Speakers of Rural GCD, the last subvariety on the dialectal continuum, will receive the lowest evaluations on the measure of competence, but they will be attributed with qualities such as *honesty, warmth, likeability, friendliness* and *humour*;
2. Speakers of SMG are expected to receive very low evaluations on the measure of attractiveness, but it is predicted that they will be attributed with qualities such as *ambition, education, intelligence* and *using 'correct' speech*;
3. GC subjects will not associate themselves with the speakers of Rural GCD and thus, their evaluations for these speakers on the scale of *speaks like me* will receive the lowest evaluations out of all the four subvarieties observed, as this is the subvariety that is the most stigmatised and associated with the speech of less educated people living in villages. This stigmatisation is also expected to be apparent on the trait of *modernity*, where speakers of Rural GCD will again receive the lowest evaluations;
4. On the contrary, speakers of Modern GCD will receive the highest evaluations on the measure of *speaks like me*, as this is the subvariety most commonly used by young GCs in their everyday interactions with friends and family.

Procedures
The Matched-Guise Technique

The MGT was replicated four times in a period of two weeks, as students from four different classes participated in it. They were told that they would hear eight narratives from eight different speakers, and their task was to characterise them on the basis of their vocal characteristics. All evaluations had to be marked on the evaluation paper (see Appendix A) by circling a number of one to five, which they thought corresponded to the specific trait for the specific speaker.

Each student was provided with an evaluation paper consisting of eight similar evaluation sheets, one for each speaker s/he had to rate. Each sheet contained the 13 traits they had to employ in order to characterise each speaker on the CD. All traits were presented on a 5-point Likert scale. Eleven of these traits related to three different dimensions:

1. *competence* (intelligent/unintelligent, ambitious/not ambitious, educated/uneducated, speaks correctly/does not speak correctly);
2. *attractiveness* (honest/dishonest, warm/cold, I like him/I dislike him, friendly/unfriendly, humorous/lacking humour, modern/old-fashioned);
3. *solidarity* (speaks like me/does not speak like me).

The reason for selecting these 11 traits is for the possibility of comparing the results to those obtained from earlier studies carried out in the GC community (Papapavlou, 1998) but also to other similar empirical studies carried out in various other linguistic communities (Garrett et al., 2003; Lippi-Green, 1997). Two additional scales were used to examine judges' opinions about the four different degrees of the dialect, which did not relate to the characteristics of the speakers, but to their actual language use. Here the judges had to rate speakers on whether they sound 'very Greek-Cypriot' and if their story sounds interesting in the particular subvariety. These two dimensions were also observed by Garrett et al. (2003) in their systematic study on Welsh teenagers' attitudes towards regional speakers. Hence, it was thought that the findings that will emerge from these two dimensions could provide a point of comparison with their work.

Following instructions on procedures, students were given sufficient time to familiarise themselves with the 13 semantic-differential scales, and they were then given the opportunity to listen once to each speaker. Listening to each speaker a second time would deviate from the naturalistic approach that was sought since the beginning of the experiment. Thus, judges heard each speaker only once, as is the case in actual interactions, and were asked to evaluate each one by providing their spontaneous reactions towards the speaker's speech. On average, judges required about a minute to fill in all their evaluations on the 13 semantic-differential scales. A brief and informal discussion followed each MGT session, where students were asked to provide their views on the language use of each speaker.

Moreover, four rather large focus-group sessions were carried out with 55 students (28 male and 27 female) from various fields of study. The majority of these students were studying Hotel and Tourism Management, Computer Science, Business Administration and Accounting. The discussions in Focus Groups were semi-structured where a few parts of each discussion were directed by salient questions that had the purpose of steering the discussion in a way that would allow me later to link and compare the information provided from focus groups with the data collected from the MGT. The work carried out in these focus groups and the interesting findings which emerged from them will be discussed in a future paper. In all sessions, after subjects finished rating all 8 speakers and commenting on their language use, they were informed about the real purpose of the study.

Results and discussion

Analysis of variance was used to examine students' evaluations in relation to the four subvarieties. With regard to the first hypothesis (see 'Hypotheses' above), it was observed that on all four competence related traits, namely on *ambition, education, intelligence* and *speaking correctly*, the same pattern of evaluations arose, where speakers of Rural GCD scored the lowest ratings out of all speakers.[5] However, it should be emphasised that on the trait of *ambition* statistical significance was not observed.

Despite the fact that Rural GCD was expected to receive the lowest evaluations on these traits, it was not predicted that Modern GCD would receive higher evaluations than Polished GCD on these traits, as Modern GCD is closer to Rural GCD, and differs significantly from SMG in terms of syntax, phonology and lexis. What are the reasons that influenced subjects to rate speakers of Polished GCD less positively than speakers of Modern GCD on these four scales, if Polished GCD is closer to the official language? This issue should be examined further; nonetheless it could also be linked to the comments that participants made in the short and informal discussion following the MGT. They characterised the speakers of Polished GCD less positively than the speakers of Modern GCD, saying that they do not sound very natural as they employ SMG, but occasionally add the GC element [ĵé] ('and'), an element that is not normally found in the official language instead of systematically using [ké] which is what they *should* be using.

Even so, they have agreed that Polished GCD is sometimes used, but the speakers who use it have a high status and have already gained the respect of others, like politicians making short announcements on the news, or their lecturers in class after the lecture (which is normally in English), who explain a few things in Greek. They added that their lecturers many times use the GC element [ĵé] with other GC elements like the augment [e] in front of verbs signifying past tense and final [–n] in nouns, both features of Ancient Greek which are still used in GCD, to reveal their GC identity and probably lessen the distance there is between them and their students.

The participants added however that, the speakers on the CD do not fall under the same category as their lecturers. Their own words were 'they are only students; we do not know who they are'. Thus based on the views of these informants, we can assume that if a speaker serves the community, becomes popular and accepted by showing that s/he is a knowledgeable, educated, and hence respectable person in the society, s/he is not negatively criticised by others when using GC elements in a rather formal speech. Yet again, this is another hypothesis that needs to be confirmed with further investigation.

As predicted, speakers of Rural GCD who scored the lowest ratings on all competence related traits received more favourable evaluations than their SMG counterparts on four out of the six attractiveness related traits observed, i.e. subjects characterised Rural GCD speakers as being *warmer*, more *likeable*, *friendlier* and more *humorous*[6] than SMG speakers. The results obtained from all attractiveness-related traits revealed statistical significance at the level of 0.1. Interestingly, two attractiveness-related traits, namely the traits of *honesty* and *modernity*, received the highest evaluations in Modern GCD, and not in Rural GCD.[7] Further investigation is needed to determine if speakers of Modern GCD are regarded as more *honest* than speakers of Rural GCD. However, it is possible that in the present study the two speakers who used Modern GCD in the MGT were perceived to be more *honest* than the two speakers of Rural GCD.

Despite the low evaluations SMG speakers received on the majority of attractiveness traits observed, they nonetheless received the highest evaluations of all speakers on all competence-related traits (no statistical significance was observed on the trait of *ambition*). The second hypothesis was also confirmed, as the results of the MGT suggest that speaking 'correctly' is directly related to SMG, the standard and prestigious language of the Greek-speaking part of Cyprus. This result did not seem at all surprising, since the Constitution concerning language use in Cyprus, which was formed in 1960 when Cyprus gained its independence from the English, states that the official languages of Cyprus are SMG and Turkish[7]. SMG is the exclusive medium of instruction in GC state schools, and it was observed that when pupils employ GCD lexis instead of their SMG equivalents, educators consider it their duty to correct them. Consequently, children learn from an early age that SMG is the 'appropriate' variety to use in the classroom and begin to associate GCD with the elderly who live in villages and rural areas (Papapavlou, 2004).

The third hypothesis was also verified, as the Rural GCD speakers received the lowest evaluations on the traits of *modernity*[8] and *speaks like me*[9]. A plausible reason why speakers of Modern GCD scored higher than their Rural GCD counterparts on these traits is because Rural GCD is a subvariety which students in the informal discussions expressed to associate with people living a quiet life in villages, with farmers and with the elderly who are not regarded as modern as those living and working in the city, who dress fashionably, and attend various social events. A plausible reason why the majority of young GCs make no association between the dialect and the trait of *modernity*, could be due to the fact that from a young age at school they are taught to believe that SMG is not only the prestigious and appropriate form that relates to intelligence and education, but also to progress and modernisation of ideas and style. For many centuries, Cyprus was under the occupation of various invaders, which led to the island's isolation from mainland Greece, to its socio-economic deprivation, and to the low educational level of its people. Consequently, GCs admired mainland Greeks for their good education and considered them intelligent and well-read. Although nowadays the educational level of GCs and mainland Greeks is very much similar, young GCs still form negative associations about the dialect and its users and thus do not consider themselves as members of the same group of speakers as those using Rural GCD. This rationalisation can account for the low evaluations Rural GCD received on the trait of *speaks like me*.

The fourth hypothesis was the only hypothesis that was not confirmed from MGT results, since speakers of Modern GCD did not receive the highest evaluations on the measure of *speaks like me* as it was expected. Surprisingly, participants did not express solidarity with the speakers of the variety they most often use, but with the speakers who used SMG[10]. As mentioned above, it is possible that the less favourable evaluations towards Modern GCD might be linked to the negative attitudes GCs form from an early age towards all the dialectal elements, including phonology, morphology, lexis, and syntax.

Conclusion

The interesting findings of the present study demonstrate that GCs receive the highest evaluations on a number of attractiveness related traits when they speak in Rural GCD. Speakers of this subvariety are perceived as the *warmest*, most *likeable, friendliest*, and the most *humorous* out of all other speakers observed. A finding which was consistent in the MGT is that GCs receive the highest evaluations on competence-related traits when they speak in SMG. On the contrary, when they use Rural GCD, they are perceived as the least *educated*, *ambitious* and *intelligent*.

In the discussions following the MGT, students expressed that they know they undervalue their own dialect. They all agreed that the dialect will gradually cease to exist, as they admitted they tend to replace more and more GCD lexis with their SMG equivalents. In their response to 'what can we do about it?' they addressed the state as being responsible for the less positive associations GCs have learnt to make about the dialect and its users, but also for having the power to do something about this issue and teach GCs not to consider the dialect less worthy than SMG.

This great undertaking can be achieved by including in the school curriculum subjects which focus on the value and importance of the dialect to GCs, to their life and to their identity such as folk literature, poems and songs based on GCs' experiences before and after the 1974 Turkish occupation. Although the school curriculum does incorporate GC literature, it depends entirely on the teacher how often this subject will be taught in class. According to students, many educators prefer to do Greek literature in class on a regular basis as opposed to teaching GC literature only once or twice in the whole academic year.

Students also added that apart from the government, parents can also contribute to teaching their children to value the dialect parallel to the standard variety. This can be achieved by letting their children express themselves at home in the dialect and refraining from correcting them by replacing some of their GCD words with their SMG equivalents. Evidently, conscious and systematic work is needed from the government which as an authority has the power to change the current language attitudes. Such work is also needed from the adults, whom young learners look up to, imitate, and with whom they employ their language use in their daily interactions.

Limitations of the study

It is plausible that a number of limitations might have influenced the results obtained from the study. To begin with, the number of speakers who used each subvariety on the CD was limited. Second, the content in speakers' stories might have brought about differences in evaluations. It is very likely that subjects might have judged some narratives more negatively than others if they did not like the content, or the way the speaker handled the situation he was in. A good example is Rural GCD-5 who was characterised as someone who was not 'very *intelligent*' because of his reckless actions. In this case there is no direct connection between language use and competence, as the latter in this case does not relate to his competence in the language used to narrate his story, but to his actual behaviour and irresponsibility in driving under the effect of alcohol.

An additional example showing content effect was evident on the traits of *education, intelligence, ambition* and *speaks correctly*. Although, it was clear in the statistical part that the two speakers who used SMG scored the highest evaluations, it was observed that one of these two speakers scored the highest evaluations out of all other speakers on these four competence-related traits. The favourable evaluations are most probably connected to the content of his narrative where he mentioned that he owns a business and after briefly talking about it he explained the process of cleaning sea sponges. This speaker sounded very familiar with the process he was explaining, for the steps he described were explained with clarity and examples; thus giving the informants the impression that he was an experienced and a well-informed person on his subject.

Third, the educational and formal environment where the study was carried out might have led the participants of this study to react somewhat negatively towards the speakers who used dialectal items in their narratives despite the fact that the medium of instruction at Intercollege is English. Fourth, since the focus of the present study was to observe the attitudes of a particular group of informants toward four subvarieties used in Lefkosia, there is a possibility that dissimilar evaluations would have arisen if the study was carried out in a different city. Fifth, it is possible that different results from the MGT might have been produced if the number of male and female participants (64 and 42 respectively) was somewhat equal. Finally, the use of Polished GCD is not as systematically used as the other three subvarieties. Thus, its restricted use could account for the negative evaluations it received in the majority of the traits examined. Normally, GC speakers switch from the dialect to SMG when issues such as the degree of formality, differences in status, age and gender between interlocutors become salient during interaction. However, quite a few instances have been observed informally where speakers use Polished GCD, including politicians in short and impromptu speeches when addressing a small audience, being interviewed, or participating in discussions on the television.

Future work

Although the present study proved to be very fruitful and brought to the surface many interesting findings, more light will be shed on the issue of GCs' language attitudes towards their dialect with systematic observation of educators' language use in class. It would be very interesting to see how educators in primary and secondary education handle students' use of GCD and how they influence their students'/pupils' language use in class. Clearly, the school environment and the teachers' attitudes towards the dialect have the potential to influence to a certain extent – if not to a significant extent – learners' attitudes towards the dialect in relation to the official language.

Acknowledgement

I am grateful to my supervisor Clarissa Wilks for her constructive criticism and encouraging comments on an earlier draft of this paper.

Notes

1   A measure associated with humour and authenticity.
2   A measure associate with high competence and achievement of very good grades at school.
3   The study was carried out at Intercollege, a HE institution in Lefkosia where English is used as the medium of instruction.
4   GC males normally attend tertiary education rather later than females, as they prefer to complete their obligatory two-year service in the Army before they begin their tertiary education.

5

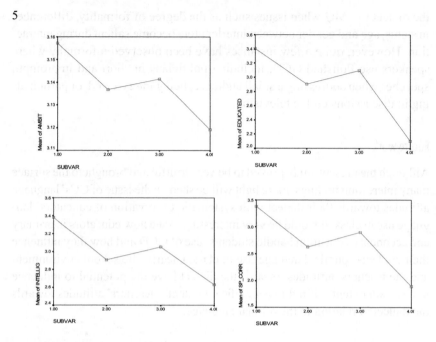

Figure 4.2: Means plot for the traits of 'ambition', 'education', 'intelligence' and 'speaks correctly'

6

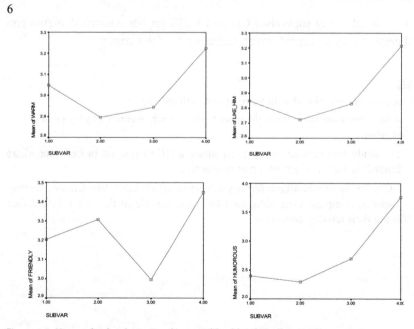

Figure 4.3: Means plot for the traits of 'warm', 'likeable', 'friendly', and 'humorous'

7　　Turkish is used in various formal documents bearing the emblem of the Greek-Cypriot Republic such as passports, stamps and banknotes. The Turkish language is used as a medium of communication only amongst Turkish-Cypriot speakers who live in southern Cyprus and those who live in the north (Karyolemou) [my translation].

8

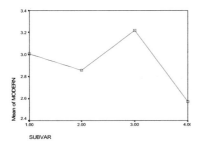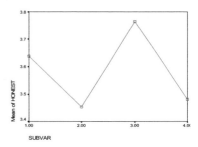

Figure 4.4: Means plot for the traits of 'modern' and 'honest'

9

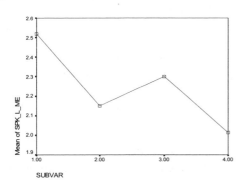

Figure 4.5: Means plot for the scale of 'speaks like me'

10

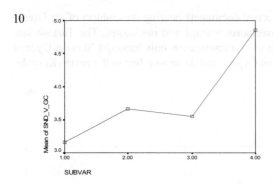

Figure 4.6: Means plot for the scale of 'sounds very GC'

References

Abrams, D. and Hogg, M. A. (1987) language attitudes, frames of reference, and social identity: a Scottish dimension. *Journal of Language and Social Psychology* 6: 201–13.

Garrett, P., Coupland, N. and Williams, A. (2003) *Investigating Language Attitudes*. Cardiff: University of Wales Press.

Giles, H. and Coupland, N. (1991) *Language: contexts and consequence*. Milton Keynes: Open University Press.

Καρυολαίμου, Μ. *Η ελληνική γλώσσα στην Κύπρο*. [Karyolemou, M. *The Greek Language in Cyprus*]. Retrieved on 12 November 2005 from http://abnet. agrino.org/htmls/D/D005.html#top

Lambert, W. E. (1967) A social psychology of bilingualism. *Journal of Social Issues* 23: 91–109.

Lippi-Green, R. (1997) *English with an Accent: language, ideology and discrimination in the United States*. London: Routledge.

Papapavlou, A. (1998) Attitudes toward the Greek Cypriot dialect: sociocultural implications. *International Journal of the Sociology of Language* 134: 15–28.

Papapavlou, A. (2004) Verbal fluency of bidialectal speakers of SMG and the role of language-in-education practices in Cyprus. *International Journal of the Sociology of Language* 168: 91–100.

Pavlou, P. (2004) Greek dialect use in the mass media in Cyprus. *International Journal of the Sociology of Language* 168: 101–18.

Thomas, L. (2004) Attitudes to language. In I. Singh and J. S. Peccei (eds) *Language, Society and Power* 193–209. (Second edition) London: Routledge.

Appendix A: Students' evaluation paper in English (translated from Greek)

Circle the number that best describes the speaker you have just heard
(5 highest, 1 lowest rating).

Speaker						
warm	5	4	3	2	1	cold
honest	5	4	3	2	1	dishonest
ambitious	5	4	3	2	1	not ambitious
I like him	5	4	3	2	1	I dislike him
he speaks like me	5	4	3	2	1	he does not speak like me
friendly	5	4	3	2	1	unfriendly
educated	5	4	3	2	1	uneducated
humorous	5	4	3	2	1	lacking humour
modern	5	4	3	2	1	old-fashioned
intelligent	5	4	3	2	1	unintelligent
speaks 'correctly'	5	4	3	2	1	does not speak 'correctly'
interesting story	5	4	3	2	1	boring story
he sounds very Cypriot	5	4	3	2	1	he does not sound Cypriot

5   Perceptions of varieties of spoken English: implications for EIL

Sue Fraser

Introduction

Assuming that English is to be taught worldwide to speakers of other languages, discussion centres upon what the purpose of learning English is, and hence what variety/ies should be taught. As the argument for English as an International Language (EIL) gains ground, the central question is which model of English is most appropriate for international communication with global intelligibility. Although there is much debate over whether native-speaker models (see Davies, 2003, 1991) or a Standard English model (Strevens, 1983: 88) should be adopted, or whether regional varieties are also acceptable, it is advocated here that a standard form of grammar and vocabulary (Strevens, 1992: 40) is most suitable for English language teaching, especially at lower levels. However, as the central concern of this research is pronunciation, consideration of whether there should be a standard model such as Received Pronunciation (RP) or General American (GA) for EIL or whether localised varieties are equally appropriate is required.

'Periphery-English countries' (Phillipson, 1992: 17), with little contact with 'inner circle' countries such as America or Britain (Kachru, 1992: 356), may have few practical reasons for learning traditional EFL native-speaker models. Hence, it could be argued that a model containing features of all varieties of EIL, and as such recognisable to all users, should be taught. However, if native-speaker models are to be abandoned, the problem of intelligibility arises if variations become too diverse. While Jenkins (1998: 121) identifies phonological elements of core segmentals, nuclear stress and appropriate articulatory setting, as crucial to maintaining mutual understanding, no restrictions on choice of regional varieties are suggested. As this research focuses on the appropriacy and desirability of varieties of spoken English for Japanese learners, the relevance of whether EFL or EIL is more appropriate for the specific situation of language teaching in Japan will now be addressed.

EFL/EIL in the Japanese context

Since 1873 it has been recognised that learning English is essential for the future commercial development of Japan (Mori, 1873, cited in Kachru, 1992: 5). The most recent Ministry of Education, Culture, Sports, Science and Technology (MEXT) reforms for English education are still stressing this importance: 'For children living in the 21st century, it is essential for them to acquire communication abilities in English as a common international language' (MEXT 2003a: i). Despite resistance from supporters of *nihonjinron* (uniqueness of the Japanese) such as Suzuki (1971) and Tsuda (1990, 1993) (summarised by Tanaka and Tanaka, 1995: 127–8), who feel threatened by Western hegemony and potential linguistic imperialism, there is much enthusiasm for *kokusaika* (internationalisation) from the media, politicians and the population at large, who see it in their interest to become functional in English. This in turn translates into the pressure felt within schools to succeed in English. With Japan being an 'expanding circle' country (Kachru, 1992: 356), English has been taught as a FL, but recent emphasis on international usage has fuelled the argument for teaching EIL in Japan.

As this paper concentrates on pronunciation, it is necessary to ascertain which models of spoken English are currently used for pedagogical purposes, and whether they are still appropriate for the present aims. While advocating that 'The Language elements should be contemporary standard English in principle [...], consideration should also be given to the fact that different varieties of English are used throughout the world as means of communication' (MEXT, 2003b: 8), MEXT does not propose any specific model of pronunciation. But, on closer examination of the documents, EIL intentions revert to EFL targets, with reference to models of spoken English stating or implying native-speaker (NS) pronunciation.

Based on my own involvement with Japanese senior high schools, my impression is that almost all English teaching relies on native-speaker models and EFL goals. All Assistant Language Teachers (ALTs) in schools are native speakers, predominantly North American (61 per cent: MEXT, 2002). Published audio materials all use General American (GA) pronunciation recordings and authorised textbooks mainly provide inner circle cultural content (Fraser, 2005) with a plethora of pronunciation exercises forcing Japanese English teachers to aim for near-NS articulation and stress patterns. Public proficiency examinations all exclusively use GA speakers, as will the new listening component (piloted March 2005) of the state-run universities entrance examination.

From the above evidence, it seems indisputable that EFL with GA pronunciation is the model for ELT in Japanese schools, regardless of theoretical arguments for EIL and public claims of the internationalisation of Japan.

Preferred models of pronunciation

From personal observation and discussion in Japan, it is clear that the ability to speak English is a matter of prestige, and achieving native-like pronunciation is especially valued. It is noted that in expanding circle countries 'the ideal goal is to imitate the native speaker of the standard language as closely as possible. Speaking English is simply not related to cultural identity. It is rather an exponent of one's academic and language-learning abilities' (Andreasson, 1994: 402).

It is similarly suggested that Japanese 'learners may feel that it is unnecessary for them to study different varieties of English that they do not intend to use and regard as inferior' (Morrow, 2004: 94), which also include Japanese English. Japanese linguists also report that English as EFL with British or American 'Standard' English is desired, and there is a problem of not acquiring NS-like ability if people do not start learning English when young (Tanaka and Tanaka, 1995: 127). As parents inaccurately consider that attainment of native-speaker pronunciation is the most evident indicator of language proficiency, they are prepared to pay for private tuition, from exclusively inner circle teachers, for their children from a very early age. Moreover, media reports on *ikita eigo* (living, real English) and an ever greater demand for *eikai wa gakko* (English conversation classes with native-speaker instructors) increase business opportunities for language schools and publishers. Such opinions may be influenced by the purpose to which they will use English, such as in business and economics with the West, as Kubota (1998) rather resignedly concludes: 'As long as Japan continues to negotiate and struggle for power within the hegemony of the West, it will probably continue to regard the Inner Circle variety of English as a model to acquire' (Kubota, 1998: 302). Indeed, the apparent Japanese desire to be associated with the West, rather than with Asia, may influence, consciously or otherwise, reactions to non-native speakers of English.

To examine the opinions of those at the receiving end of English education in Japan, an investigation was conducted to elicit perceptions and impressions of different examples of spoken English, having discovered little previous research into whether Japanese learners can actually identify native speakers,[1] and what their attitudes to varieties of English and the cultural backgrounds of different speakers are.

Related studies

Several studies have examined second language learner reactions to different accents, but very few pertaining solely to Japanese learners have been traced. In earlier studies, students from Asian countries listened to readers from Asia and America 'to compare the degree of intelligibility between native and non-native varieties of educated English' (Smith and Rafiqzad, 1983: 49), and Indian, Thai and Singaporean students' opinions on ELT and target varieties were surveyed (Shaw, 1983). Others examined the effect of using speakers of different varieties on listening comprehension scores in published proficiency tests (Smith and Bisazza, 1983; Major et al., 2005).

Particularly relevant is the work of Hiroko Matsuura, who, as part of research teams, has conducted attitudinal studies on Japanese university students. Matsuura, Chiba and Yamamoto's (1994) exploration of students' attitudes to Asian and American pronunciation found a strong preference for American speakers, which formed the basis of hypotheses for their 1995 study into how familiarity, motivation and respect for indigenous languages affect acceptance of different accents. Similar preferences were expressed to taped readings of an English text by native and Asian, including Japanese, speakers (Chiba et al., 1995). Further relevant studies focusing on intelligibility and perceived comprehensibility of spoken English noted differences in perceived and actual comprehension of both NS varieties (Matsuura et al., 1999) and Japanese English (Matsuura et al., 2004). Also of interest is the work of Aya Matsuda (2003), whose qualitative case study on final-year Japanese high school students ascertained that NS, especially American, pronunciation was highly esteemed and desired as a model, whereas Japanese English was not respected.

Differences in foci

The present research is not a replication of previous studies, and represents four distinct differences in focus and design. This study aims to:

- examine attitudes of younger students without specialist knowledge or other advantage. In studies led by Matsuura (1994, 1999, 2004) all subjects were university students, and in Chiba et al. (1995) all were English or International Business undergraduates. I would suggest that Matsuda's (2003) subjects are not typical of Japanese high school students, being at a private school, and with 85 per cent having travelled or lived abroad. My target group contained no returnees, and considerably fewer had been outside Japan;

- examine if students can recognise and name different varieties, rather than give options to choose from, as do Chiba et al. (1995: 79), which can lead to a process of elimination. Matsuda (2003) has no listening/recognition component;
- examine intelligibility as well as attitudes, since what students think is easy to understand needs to be substantiated by testing comprehension. Only Matsuura et al. (1999) addresses this to some degree;
- examine if attitudes are changing over time, especially for identifying speakers. The effects of changes in MEXT guidelines and ELT practice, increase in foreign media and foreign residents and visitors to Japan, may produce significantly different responses from earlier studies of Matsuura et al.

The research

In order to explore whether attitudes of younger, non-specialist learners are changing due to increased exposure to non-Japanese speakers, and how closely inter-related recognition, perception and comprehension of varieties are, three research questions were elaborated:

i)   Are Japanese high school students aware of different varieties of spoken English?
ii) Do they have preferences for certain varieties?
iii) Do they find certain varieties easier to understand?

More specifically, the first question investigates whether students can identify native speakers or not, and can perceive and recognise phonological distinctions related to different countries. The second investigates whether personal experiences, familiarity, cultural preconceptions or prestige of certain nationalities cause any preferences. The third question tries to determine reasons why students find some varieties easier to understand.

Subjects

The research was conducted in April/May 2005 at two academic high schools in Japan, hereafter referred to as schools F and Y. Seventy-six final-year (17/18 year-olds) male and female students took part in the experiment and survey. All had studied English for at least five years, since commencing at the age of 12 at junior high school. The 38 students at school Y, academically one of the highest in the county, were following the 'maths and science course', where although more emphasis is placed on those subjects, English is still considered as very important. In general, students on this course are of above average ability for their year group. School F, although ranked a little lower academically, offers an 'International Understanding' course, which schedules more English classes per week than for students following a general course for high schools. The 38 students from school F constituted the third-year class of this special course.

Method and instruments for the research

A tape-recording of six speakers in conjunction with attitudinal statements on a 5-point Likert scale, a listening comprehension task and a short question-naire (see Appendix A), all piloted previously with multilingual L2 learners, were used for data collection. The recording consisted of different speakers describing their favourite place to visit, with the content being unplanned and monologic. The six adult speakers were from Inner Circle (England, America, Scotland), Outer Circle (Zimbabwe) and Expanding Circle (Taiwan, Japan) countries (Kachru, 1992), and were likely to represent familiar and unfamiliar varieties. While or after listening, students were to record their impressions of each speaker in relation to the ten statements on the response sheet, ticking agreement boxes as appropriate to their immediate reaction. Each recording was played only once.

In the second task, students listened to and took notes on recordings of the same six speakers giving brief self-introductions. Students could write in English, Japanese or phonetically, as L2 linguistic accuracy was not being assessed here. The purpose of this part was to explore the actual comprehension aspects of the listening experience, and how this related to the evaluation task. Again students could listen once only to each speaker. In addition, students completed a questionnaire on their opinions on accents, countries and cultures, and ELT, to elicit any preconceived judgements which may have influenced their responses in the attitudinal listening experiment (see Appendix B).

Data analysis and discussion

The data were analysed in relation to the three research questions of (i) aware-ness of different varieties of spoken English (ii) preference for particular varie-ties and (iii) ease of comprehension. Results from the response sheet, listening comprehension task and attitudinal questionnaire are cross-referenced and explained, and similarities with findings of other researchers are discussed. For ease of comparison with previous studies, the raw data from both schools are collated and presented as percentages. Complete data are tabulated in Appendix C.

Awareness of different varieties

The first research question investigates whether learners are aware of differences in the way English is spoken, especially between native and non-native speakers. When examining if the students could distinguish who were the native speakers (Question 4), there was only an overall 28.5 per cent accuracy rate for identification of the three NSs in the recording. However, this rose significantly when considering Speaker 3 alone – there was 63.1 per cent accuracy in identifying her as a NS, with 50 per cent correctly placing her as American. With Speakers 2 and 6, only one student in each case was able to correctly identify them as English and Scottish respectively. In contrast, it was found that identification of Speaker 5 as Japanese proved considerably easier, with 81.5 per cent answering correctly. Some common features of East Asian pronunciation may have been recognised, as 41.2 per cent placed Speaker 1 as Asian. 3.9 per cent suggested she was Chinese, and a further 11.8 per cent thought perhaps Japanese, although none actually identified her as Taiwanese.

The above results indicate some awareness of typical phonological features of certain native and local speakers' English, which may be due to familiarity. To substantiate this proposition, cross-referencing with Question 8 data shows that 90.7 per cent said they were familiar with the pronunciation of Speaker 5, whereas only 34.2 per cent were with Speaker 1, and a negligible 6.5 per cent with Speaker 4. Suggested home countries of Speaker 4 produced no distinct pattern, as this was probably the first time any student had heard a speaker from Africa. It is worth noting that as these learners have had very little exposure to Europeans speaking English, 'Europe' was a frequent suggestion when a voice was very unfamiliar. In this case, 13.1 per cent said Speaker 4 was European, with a further 22.3 per cent (the highest percentage) specifying French, although there seems little grounding for this, as to my knowledge, neither school has had contact with French speakers of English, and no student had visited France. It is interesting, however, that although Speaker 4 is an Outer Circle bilingual, only 7.8 per cent suggested she was a native speaker.

Matsuda (2003: 488) reported that students interviewed were unaware of other varieties of English except American and British. In the present study, several NS and L2 varieties were raised (Canadian/Australian/Scottish/Indian), and awareness that English is spoken by many nations with different pronunciation was apparent. Whereas Chiba et al. (1995: 80) found identification of NSs, but with no distinction between American and British, my results indicate fairly high (50 per cent) recognition of American speakers. This may be due to exclusive exposure to GA in published ELT materials and tests (Fraser, 2005), and also because recent ALTs at both schools have been Canadian and American.

Preference for particular varieties

The second research question aims to identify any preference or prestige attached to specific varieties or accents, and to examine reasons for this. Preference may depend on variables such as personal experiences, familiarity, gender, cultural conceptions or status, or could simply result from aesthetic appreciation of someone's voice. All these factors are closely related in the case of Speaker 3. Second only to Japanese Speaker 5, American Speaker 3 was well liked (Question 5: 56.5 per cent) and sounded quite familiar (Question 8: 44.7 per cent), and was the first choice as a model of English, with 71 per cent wanting to speak like her (Question 7). In the questionnaire, American pronunciation was most appreciated (51.3 per cent), and, except for Britain, was considered the most desirable overseas destination (86.8 per cent). The popularity of this variety may also be influenced by recent ALTs in school, availability of American media, movies and music, and 10.5 per cent having visited the USA. Matsuda (2003: 488) reported that 84 per cent of her interviewees wanted to pronounce English as the Americans or British, and likewise Matsuura et al. (1994) found students preferred American English as a model. The present data support these findings in that 89.4 per cent think having NS pronunciation is important.

An ambivalence can be seen in relation to the home variety, despite being the most familiar (90.7 per cent) and most liked (65.7 per cent). Indeed, 34.2 per cent said they wanted to speak like her (Question 7), perhaps because being a fluent Japanese English speaker is a realistic goal, but only 26.3 per cent wanted her as their English teacher (Question 9). Matsuura et al. (2004) found that only 23.8 per cent considered Japanese English an acceptable variety, and Matsuda's (2003: 492) data revealed that Japanese English pronunciation is 'not cool', 'less fashionable than American English', and concluded that 'the Japanese accent is still positioned negatively and as an 'incorrect' form of English' (ibid). While the present results did not display such low prestige, attaining NS pronunciation was shown to be overwhelmingly important (89.4 per cent).

Preference for speakers in the experiment may also involve factors of tone and quality of voice, being male or female, and apparent age and personality. Responses to Question 1 ('sounds friendly') and Question 6 ('is well educated') not analysed here, may add to perceptions of personality, and may thus influence choice. Moreover, responses to the actual language samples and expressions of pre-conceived ideas may differ, with students stating they prefer accent *x* in the questionnaire, yet in reality not knowing which speaker is *x* or how *x* speakers actually sound. Hence, contradictory answers, as regarding the speaker from England, whom only 18.4 per cent thought was a NS, may arise. Only 9.2 per cent both liked how Speaker 2 spoke and wanted to speak like him, despite 23.6 per cent preferring British pronunciation in the questionnaire, and a very high 93.4 per cent wanting to visit the UK.

Ease of comprehension

Data relating to which speaker(s) were perceived as being easy to understand (Question 3) are discussed next, and possible reasons for these impressions examined, in order to address the third research question. There was almost unanimous agreement (94.7 per cent) that Speaker 5 was easy to understand, and similarly the majority agreed that Speaker 4 was not. Only 11.8 per cent considered her easy to understand. These results parallel the findings for Question 8 where familiarity with a variety of pronunciation was focused upon. 90.7 per cent reported being used to Speaker 5's accent, while only 6.5 per cent felt the accent of Speaker 4 was familiar.

Previous studies conclude similarly that familiarity influences comprehension. Smith's (1992: 83–4) test and perception study found that 90 per cent of Japanese on a subjective questionnaire thought they could understand a Japanese speaker of English, and could identify him very easily, yet in a multiple-choice comprehensibility test only 60 per cent did understand the Japanese speaker well. He concluded that 'being familiar with the topic and speech variety did affect the subjects' perceptions of how well they had understood' (ibid: 88). Smith and Bisazza (1983: 66) likewise surmise that Japanese subjects' ability to understand a Japanese speaker better than American or Indian is due to familiarity and 'limited active exposure to English outside the classroom' (ibid). However, 45 per cent of students interviewed in Matsuda (2003: 492) believed that Japanese English was not intelligible to non-Japanese, but perhaps this resulted from aforementioned fashionable attitudes (ibid: 492) and their strong desire (84 per cent) to acquire a NS accent (ibid: 489).

A further factor thought to affect comprehension is speed, as comparison of data for Question 3 and Question 2 demonstrates. Speaker 5, deemed easiest to understand, was also considered to speak at a reasonable pace, with only 5.2 per cent saying she was too fast. Similarly, Speaker 1, who was considered fairly easy to understand (52.6 per cent), perhaps for reasons speculated upon above, was only thought to speak too quickly by 17.1 per cent. Reactions to Speaker 2 imply that speed and comprehensibility are closely linked, in that he was regarded as speaking rather quickly (50 per cent), with only 18.4 per cent ease of understanding. Interestingly, although Speaker 4 was considered the most difficult to understand, with just 11.8 per cent perceiving her easy to comprehend, her speed was not problematic, as only 26.3 per cent thought she spoke too quickly. In contrast, Speaker 3 was considered the fastest speaker, with 67.1 per cent saying she spoke too quickly, but was still intelligible to 38.1 per cent of the respondents. As other researchers did not comment upon perceptions of speaking speed, no comparisons can be made. As texts in other experiments were read aloud, rather than spoken spontaneously as here, speed of delivery may have been indicated or controlled, and would therefore not have been an issue.

To support perceptions of comprehensibility, evidence from the listening comprehension task needs to be taken into account. Smith (1982: 83–4) and Matsuura et al. (1999: 57) both noted that even if students perceived that they had understood, test results did not reflect that opinion. To explore these conclusions, further analysis of scores of the listening task for individual students compared with their perceptions of understanding and attitudes toward different speakers needs to be undertaken to see if there are generalisable patterns for different types of learners. However, samples so far show that those learners of English, who scored highly on the comprehension task, had made fairly accurate estimations of their understanding.

Summary of findings

To summarise, it seems that students are aware that there are many varieties of English, but have little idea when identifying where speakers are from exactly. Nonetheless, they have preconceived ideas of high-status or fashionable accents (usually American), which may be due to exposure in ELT and the media. Despite finding Japanese English easy to understand, they do not value it highly as a variety, neither particularly wanting it as a model for teaching nor production. This tends to underline the general Japanese attitude, noted above, that NS pronunciation is still highly valued and desired. The majority of students in the sample expressed a desire to travel, and stated that learning about other cultures is very important, implying that they are open-minded about other nations. In addition, many students appear motivated to learn (89.4 per cent) and speak (76.3 per cent) English, therefore indicating that learners should be taught about and exposed to different varieties.

The present study concludes that both specialist 'International Understanding' and 'maths and science' course students agree that language and culture should be taught simultaneously (96 per cent). This represents a significant increase in interest in the importance of teaching culture in ELT, contrasting with Matsuura et al.'s (2004) study, where only 41.8 per cent advocated the teaching of language + culture. Although too small a sample to prove conclusive, this present study does indicate that attitudes to learning English, and tolerance and interest in other countries and cultures, are changing, perhaps due to more possibilities of travel, study and work abroad. Thus, this interest should be exploited in the language classroom.

While there are limitations in this small-scale study, the results set out patterns which may be of value to other language learning contexts where replication is possible. Such attitudinal studies identify reasons for rejection of NNS varieties, be they due to prestige, prejudice, unintelligibility or unfamiliarity, and indicate ways of broadening opinions and experiences through development of ELT materials.

Implications for ELT

The results discussed above present implications for materials designers, teachers and students. There seems to be a consensus, both in general and specific to ELT in Japan, that more exposure to different varieties of English would be beneficial to learners. The Japanese Ministry of Education *Course of Study for English* states that: 'consideration should […] be given to the fact that different varieties of English are used throughout the world as a means of communication' (MEXT, 2003b: 8). Crystal (1999: 17) mentions the importance of varieties students are likely to hear 'in their own locale' (ibid), which should provide the majority of linguistic input, a point of great relevance for Japan. To fulfil MEXT's objective 'to acquire communication abilities in English as a common international language' (MEXT, 2003a: i), students need to develop familiarity with varieties of English spoken by those they are likely to interact with in their future careers. Thus, becoming accustomed to East Asian varieties such as Chinese, Malaysian and Thai English, as well as Australasian NS pronunciation, would be beneficial, as 'exclusive native speaker use should be kept to a minimum, as it is chiefly irrelevant for many learners in terms of potential use in authentic settings' (Widdowson, 1998, cited in Alptekin, 2002: 63). Tolerance of different speakers is to be encouraged (Smith, 1983: 4) for English to be successfully used internationally. As concluded from the present research, students are not intolerant of varieties, and hence of their speakers and cultures, but are on the whole ignorant of the differences in English spoken around the world, having not encountered varied input in class.

As most exposure to English is through textbooks and accompanying recordings, it is this deficiency that ELT material writers must address. As currently a sanitised, American-biased impression and model of English, with staged GA pronunciation is provided in Japanese English textbooks (Fraser, 2005), learners are not receiving input to increase exposure and appreciation of other varieties. As well as providing accurate information about other countries, materials, both printed and recorded, need to include authentic input to demonstrate a range of Englishes. Moreover, it is imperative to raise teachers' awareness of distinctive features of different varieties, so they can identify and explain them in class. Increasing the amount of team-teaching, and extending the range of ALTs to include fluent non-native speakers, would also increase exposure to different varieties.

As the focus is shifting from EFL to EIL, there is more acceptance of flexibility of form. Students, therefore, should be encouraged to participate in interactions in English without embarrassment about their own Japanese pronunciation, and to recognise that effective communication can occur regardless of the variety. Explicit phonological work should not be overlooked in class, but a change from the present focus on stress patterns and choral repetition toward 'contrastive work, to make the differences salient for learners, and thus to enhance their receptive competence for EIL' (Jenkins, 1998: 125) is more appropriate. Nonetheless, students should not be denied access to NS models and techniques for approximating to NS speech should they desire it. Through such varied exposure, learners, and teachers, will develop familiarity with different Englishes, and no longer make judgements on the desirability of a particular variety without any knowledge or understanding of it.

Conclusion

To conclude, it is suggested that for the Japanese context a situation halfway along the continuum from EFL to EIL may be most appropriate. EIL where language and culture are separated is too extreme, especially as MEXT (2003a: 4) advocates 'deepening the understanding of language and cultures' through ELT, and this research indicates much interest in other cultures. Thus, examples of how people use English in a variety of NS, bilingual and FL situations should be integrated into teaching materials and classes, so that learners become prepared to exchange information about their own culture with anyone in the world, and appreciate the global purpose of English.

Therefore, a move away from *only* NS (i.e. American) culture, models and pronunciation, to a situation of Standard English (Strevens, 1983: 88) form, intelligible universally, with input from worldwide sources for interest, general educational development, and to teach pragmatic appropriacy for future intercultural interaction is suggested. Hence, not EFL with one GA model and monocultural context, but EIL with varied cultural and phonological input, seems appropriate for the Japanese, and perhaps many ELT situations.

Encouragement in appreciating all forms of communication is important. Broadening knowledge and tolerance by increased exposure to different people, ways of thinking, speaking and living should help students attain the goals of MEXT and empower them for life in a globalised world.

Notes

1   For the purposes of this study, the more generally held meaning of 'native speaker' is assumed, rather than referring to any specific academic definition and debate over the existence thereof (see Davies, 2003, 1991). More pertinently, as the aspiration of many Japanese learners is to speak like those whose mother tongue is English, the author does not enter into discussion on the concept of native speaker, nor offer a definition of her own. Since the aim of this research is to investigate Japanese attitudes towards speakers of different varieties, the image of 'native speaker' of those learners has been adopted. Perhaps on account of their almost exclusively monolingual context, the assumption is that those born and raised within a society are native speakers of that language; hence Americans, British and so on are native speakers of English.

References

Alptekin, C. (2002) Towards intercultural communicative competence in ELT. *ELT Journal* 56(1): 57–64.

Andreasson, A-M. (1994) Norm as a pedagogical paradigm. *World Englishes* 13(3): 395–409.

Chiba, R., Matsuura, H. and Yamamoto, A. (1995) Japanese attitudes toward English accents. *World Englishes* 14(1): 77–86.

Crystal, D. (1999) The future of Englishes. *English Today.* 15(2): 10–20.

Davies, A. (1991) *The Native Speaker in Applied Linguistics.* Edinburgh: Edinburgh University Press.

Davies, A. (2003) *The Native Speaker: myth and reality.* Clevedon: Multilingual Matters.

Fraser, S. (2005) Insight or stereotype: cultural content of ELT materials for Japanese high schools. Unpublished Ed.D. paper. University of Durham.

Jenkins, J. (1998) Which pronunciation norms and models for English as an International Language? *ELT Journal* 52(2): 119–26.

Kachru, B. B. (ed.) (1992) *The Other Tongue. Englishes across Cultures.* (Second edition) Urbana and Chicago: University of Illinois Press.

Kubota, R. (1998) Ideologies of English in Japan. *World Englishes* 17(3): 295–306.

Major, R. C., Fitzmaurice, S. M., Bunta, F. and Balasubramanian, C. (2005) Testing the effects of regional, ethnic, and international dialects of English on listening comprehension. *Language Learning* 55(1): 37–69.

Matsuda, A. (2003) The ownership of English in Japanese secondary schools. *World Englishes* 22(4): 483–96.

Matsuura, H., Chiba, R. and Yamamoto, A. (1994) Japanese college students' attitudes towards non-native varieties of English. In D. Graddol and J. Swann (eds) *Evaluating Language* 52–61. Clevedon: BAAL/Multilingual Matters.

Matsuura, H., Chiba, R. and Fujieda, M. (1999) Intelligibility and comprehensibility of American and Irish Englishes in Japan. *World Englishes* 18(1): 49–62.

Matsuura, H., Fujieda, M. and Mahoney, S. (2004) Research report: the officialization of English and ELT in Japan: 2000. *World Englishes* 23(3): 471–87.

MEXT (The Ministry of Education, Culture, Sports, Science and Technology) (2002) 平成１４年度「語学指導を行う外国青年招致事業（JETプログラム）新規招致者の決定について」Retrieved on 25 August 2005 from http://www.mext.go.jp/b-menu/_shingi/_chousa/_shotou/020/sesaku/020701d.htm

MEXT (The Ministry of Education, Culture, Sports, Science and Technology) (2003a) Action plan to cultivate 'Japanese with English Abilities'. Retrieved on 12 October 2004 from http://www.mext.go.jp/english/topics/03072801.htm

MEXT (The Ministry of Education, Culture, Sports, Science and Technology) (2003b) Elementary and secondary education: the course of study for foreign languages. Retrieved on 12 October 2004 from http://www.mext.go.jp/english/shotou/030301.htm

Morrow, P. R. (2004) English in Japan: the World Englishes perspective. *JALT Journal* 26(1): 79–100.

Phillipson, R. (1992) *Linguistic Imperialism*. Oxford: Oxford University Press.

Shaw, W. D. (1983) Asian student attitudes towards English. In L. E. Smith (ed.) *Readings in English as an International Language* 21–33. Oxford: Pergamon Press.

Smith, L. E. (1983) English as an international auxiliary language. In L. E. Smith (ed.) *Readings in English as an International Language* 1–5. Oxford: Pergamon Press.

Smith, L. E. (1992) Spread of English and issues of intelligibility. In B. B. Kachru (ed.) *The Other Tongue. Englishes across Cultures* 76–90. (Second edition) Urbana and Chicago: University of Illinois Press.

Smith, L. E. and Bisazza, J. A. (1983) The comprehensibility of three varieties of English for college students in seven countries. In L. E. Smith (ed.) *Readings in English as an International Language* 59–68. Oxford: Pergamon Press.

Smith, L. E. and Rafiqzad, K. (1983) English for cross-cultural communication: the question of intelligibility. In L. E. Smith (ed.) *Readings in English as an International Language* 49–58. Oxford: Pergamon Press.

Strevens, P. (1983) What is 'Standard English'? In L. E. Smith (ed.) *Readings in English as an International Language* 87–93. Oxford: Pergamon Press.

Strevens, P. (1992) English as an International Language: directions in the 1990s. In B. B. Kachru (ed.) *The Other Tongue. Englishes across Cultures* 38–53. (Second edition) Urbana and Chicago: University of Illinois Press.

Tanaka, S. O. and Tanaka, H. (1995) A survey of Japanese sources on the use of English in Japan. *World Englishes* 14(1): 117–35.

Appendix A: Attitudinal statements

(1) This person sounds **friendly.**
(2) This person speaks **too quickly**.
(3) It is **easy to understand** this speaker.
(4) This person is a **Native Speaker** of English.
(5) I **like** the way this person speaks.
(6) This speaker is **well-educated**.
(7) I want to speak English like this speaker.
(8) I am **used to** this type of pronunciation.
(9) I'd like this person as my English teacher.
(10) I want to **learn** about this speaker's **country and culture**.

1

	strongly agree	agree	don't know	disagree	strongly disagree
1.	☐	☐	☐	☐	☐.
2.	☐	☐	☐	☐	☐.
3.	☐	☐	☐	☐	☐.
4.	☐	☐	☐	☐	☐.
5.	☐	☐	☐	☐	☐.
6.	☐	☐	☐	☐	☐.
7.	☐	☐	☐	☐	☐.
8.	☐	☐	☐	☐	☐.
9.	☐	☐	☐	☐	☐.
10.	☐	☐	☐	☐	☐.

1

Listening Comprehension

1. Name _____.

2. Country _____.

3. Job _____.

4. Hobbies or interests _____.

5. Write anything else

Appendix B: Questionnaire

1. male / female age.

2. I prefer (American / British / Australian / Asian / Japanese) English pronunciation.

3. I prefer (male / female) teachers.

4. I (have / have not) visited foreign countries.
   If yes, which countries?

5. I prefer a (Japanese / native-speaker / both) as my English teacher.

6. I think having native-speaker-like pronunciation is important.
   (2 = very much 1 = yes 0 = No)

7. I think learning about culture is important when learning a foreign language.
   (2 = very much 1 = yes 0 = No)

8. I like learning English.
   (2 = very much 1 = yes 0 = No)

9. I like speaking in English.
   (2 = very much 1 = yes 0 = No)

10. Which countries would you like to visit?
    (2 = very much 1 = yes 0 = No)
    India   Australia   Africa   South Korea
    Britain (England)   Malaysia   USA

Appendix C: Tabulated results

Agreement with statements

(2) 'This person speaks too quickly.'

	Speaker 1	Speaker 2	Speaker 3	Speaker 4	Speaker 5	Speaker 6
agree	17.1%	50%	67.1%	26.3%	5.2%	5.2%

(3) 'It is easy to understand this speaker.'

	Speaker 1	Speaker 2	Speaker 3	Speaker 4	Speaker 5	Speaker 6
agree	52.6%	18.4%	38.1%	11.8%	94.7%	31.5%

(4) 'This person is a native speaker of English.'

	Speaker 1	Speaker 2	Speaker 3	Speaker 4	Speaker 5	Speaker 6
agree	25%	18.4%	73.6%	7.8%	9.2%	17.1%

(5) 'I like the way this person speaks.'

	Speaker 1	Speaker 2	Speaker 3	Speaker 4	Speaker 5	Speaker 6
agree	36.8%	9.2%	56.5%	6.5%	65.7%	32.8%

(7) 'I want to speak English like this person.'

	Speaker 1	Speaker 2	Speaker 3	Speaker 4	Speaker 5	Speaker 6
agree	18.4%	9.2%	71%	2.6%	34.2%	17.1%

(8) 'I am used to this type of pronunciation.'

	Speaker 1	Speaker 2	Speaker 3	Speaker 4	Speaker 5	Speaker 6
agree	34.2%	17.1%	44.7%	6.5%	90.7%	21%

(9) 'I'd like this person as my English teacher.'

	Speaker 1	Speaker 2	Speaker 3	Speaker 4	Speaker 5	Speaker 6
agree	10.5%	2.6%	43.4%	1.3%	26.3%	15.7%

(10)   'I want to learn about this speaker's country and culture.'

	Speaker 1	Speaker 2	Speaker 3	Speaker 4	Speaker 5	Speaker 6
agree	39.4%	28.9%	51.3%	35.5%	28.9%	36.8%

(totals of 'Strongly agree' + 'Agree' with statement)

Correct identification of speakers:

	Speaker 2	Speaker 3	Speaker 6
Country	1.3%	50%	1.3%
N – S	10.5%	13.1%	9.2%

Speaker 5 = Japanese = 81.5%

Speaker 1 = Asian = 41.2%

2. I prefer (<u>American British Australian Asian Japanese</u>) English pronunciation.
       51.3% 23.6% 1.3% 3.9% 18.4%

4. Have been abroad: 50%

Countries visited

Australia	USA	Canada	China	Others
36.8%	10.5%	3.9%	3.9%	1.3%

5. I prefer a (<u>J N-S both</u>) as my English Ts:
       18.4% 18.4% 63.1%

6. I think having N-S -like pronunciation is important:
       Total: 89.4% <u>very important</u> <u>important</u>
             32.8% 56.5%

7. I think learning culture in FLT is important:
   Total: 96% <u>very important</u> <u>important</u>
   52.6% 43.4%

8. I like learning English:
   Total: 89.4% V<u>ery</u> Y<u>es</u>
   23.6% 65.7%

9. I like speaking in English.
   Total: 76.3% <u>Very</u> <u>Yes</u>
   23.6% 52.6%

10. I'd like to visit:

USA		UK		Africa		S. Korea		Malaysia	
Very	Yes	Very	Yes	Very	Yes	Very	Yes	Very	Yes
61.8%	25%	81.5%	11.8%	14.4%	44.7%	32.8%	28.9%	26.3%	46%
86.8%		93.4%		59.2%		61.8%		72.3%	

6   Variation in disciplinary culture: university tutors' views on assessed writing tasks

Hilary Nesi and Sheena Gardner

Introduction

Most empirical research supports the view that there are important cultural differences between disciplinary groupings. These differences are apparent to many of those involved in higher education research and staff development (e.g. Lattuca and Stark, 1994; Braxton, 1995; Neumann, 2001; Neumann et al., 2002), and also to faculty members involved in the teaching of the various disciplines. QAA (n.d.) benchmarking statements reveal important contrasts in disciplinary identity and practice, and Healey (2000: 173) claims that 'there is a strong perception among [academic] staff that there are significant differences among disciplines in what academics do and how these activities are described and valued'.

Variation across disciplines is frequently described in terms of the broad groupings derived by Becher (1989) from the earlier work of Biglan (1973) and Kolb (1981). Becher's typology classifies disciplines according to whether they are hard or soft (on the basis of their level of paradigm development), and whether they are pure or applied (on the basis of the extent to which they are concerned with practical application). Braxton (1995) represents the hard disciplines as being characterised by greater concern for career development and cognitive goals (such as the learning of facts and concepts), and the soft disciplines as being characterised by greater concern for general education development, character development, critical thinking and 'scholarly' activities (such as the reading of research articles). Squires (2005) draws a distinction between the pure disciplines and the applied 'professional' disciplines such as Education and Medicine, concluding that whereas the primary concern in the pure disciplines is to interpret or understand the world, 'the professions differ from other disciplines in being concerned primarily with *acting* rather than knowing' (2005: 130). According to Squires, professional practice needs to be fine-tuned to meet the requirements of each new situation; its unpredictable and irreversible nature (you can't 'repeat' a patient or a student) also leads to a greater need for reflection.

The same sort of variation across the hard/soft and pure/applied categories was observed by Smart and Ethington (1995), who gathered opinions on the goals of undergraduate education from over 4000 university faculty members who regularly taught undergraduate students. Responses were reduced to three factors: 'knowledge acquisition' (the acquisition of multidisciplinary general knowledge), 'knowledge application' (the in-depth knowledge of a specific subject that prepares the student for a career), and 'knowledge integration' (the use of knowledge to think creatively). These factors were found to vary in importance according to discipline, with soft and applied disciplines placing greater emphasis on knowledge acquisition, and hard disciplines having more concern for knowledge application. Knowledge integration and application were both perceived to be more important in the applied disciplines than in the pure.

These differences of approach and emphasis have also been observed in published academic writing. Bazerman (1981) and Becher (1987), for example, found that whereas expert science writers, working within a well-developed paradigm, assumed that their readers shared the same body of knowledge as themselves, writers in the social sciences needed to persuade readers to accept findings based on methodologies or theoretical frameworks not universally accepted in the discipline, whilst writers in the humanities tried to convince their readers of interpretations they had arrived at through personal insight. Purves (1986: 39) comments on the clear distinctions between scholarly journals in different disciplines, and describes each discipline as 'a rhetorical community, which is to say a field with certain norms, expectations and conventions with respect to writing'.

Disciplinary variation in the writing of doctoral students has been examined by Parry (1998), who looked at focus, language, structure, and citation practices in 24 theses (eight from science, social science and the humanities). By and large, her findings support the established distinctions between disciplinary groupings. She found that theses in the sciences were mainly placed within an established paradigm, whilst social scientists worked with 'co-existing but competing paradigms' and in the humanities paradigms were found to be 'individualistic' or were replaced by 'intellectual fashions'. Parry's findings are complex, however, and there was some overlapping of features across the groupings. For example she classed the text structure of the science theses as 'report and explanation', that of the social science theses as 'explanation and argument', and that of the humanities theses as 'argument with recounting and narrative' (Parry, 1998: 297)

Purves (1986: 39) points out that 'instruction in any discipline is accultura-tion, or the bringing of the student into the 'interpretative community' of the discipline'. This may be a long process, especially as undergraduate students are often required to write in a much wider range of knowledge areas than the experts do. Variation in epistemology and discourse occurs not only across disciplines, but also within disciplines, and students may be required to apply different sets of rhetorical conventions to meet the demands of different course modules. Neumann et al. (2002: 407) note that some disciplines straddle catego-ries (for example Biology, which has both hard/pure and soft/pure elements), and some disciplines contain 'deviant' specialisms (for example Sociometrics, as a hard/pure subfield within Sociology which is predominantly soft/pure). Further evidence of the crossover between hard/soft and pure/applied divides can be found in the titles of the following undergraduate course modules (all within single-subject degree programmes at Warwick University):

- Human Computer Interaction (Computer Science)
- Mathematical Economics (Economics)
- Introduction to Mathematical Biology (Mathematics)
- Psychology and the Law (Psychology)
- Physics in Medicine (Physics)

As such titles suggest, boundaries between scholarly domains are permeable; Klein (1996: 42) writes of the 'continued fissioning of knowledge into greater numbers of specialities', and the 'ontological gerrymandering' that takes place to create new domains for subjects which do not share classical disciplinary characteristics.

Undergraduate modules for students from different disciplines could be regarded as further hindrance to the process of disciplinary acculturation. North (2005a, 2005b) examined an undergraduate course in the history of science, attended by students from both arts and science backgrounds. She found considerable linguistic and rhetorical variation in the writing produced by the two groups, and also noted that the arts students received higher marks for the course than their counterparts from the sciences, presumably because the academic conventions they had already mastered matched more closely to those of the course tutors.

Nevertheless there is also evidence that academics in different disciplines value many of the same qualities in the written assignments their students produce. Elander et al. (2006: 72) analysed published assessment criteria in psychology, business studies and geography and found that 'critical thinking, use of language, structuring and argument' were 'core criteria that have a central role in the shared perception of what is important in good student writing'. In interviews with academics in the humanities, sciences and social sciences, Lea and Street (2000) found that 'structure,' 'argument' and 'clarity' were commonly identified as crucial to student writing success (although their informants had difficulty in explaining what a well-developed argument actually looks like in a written assignment).

Surveys of student writing tasks have noted these variations within and connections across disciplines. Horowitz (1986), for example, found many of the same broad types of undergraduate task recurring in different fields. Horowitz's 'synthesis of multiple sources', which he describes as a sort of 'essay', was set in hard, soft, pure and applied disciplines, although some disciplines, such as Psychology, also set tasks of many other different types. Similarly Currie (1993) found a wide range of conceptual activity and genre in assignments for an introductory course in Organisational Behaviour, although in this case all papers were referred to simply as 'assignments', a label which did not 'accurately reflect the characteristics of the skills required to carry out the writing tasks' (1993: 12). Stierer (2000) found that for an Open University MA programme in Education a single student could be required to produce up to 12 different genres, including, for example, essays, reports, research proposals, critical literature reviews, personal position papers, and case studies.

It would appear that the variety of written tasks is on the increase, particularly within emergent disciplines (Baynham, 2000). Lea and Stierer (2000) link this escalation to recent rapid changes in British higher education, arguing that applied disciplines are under pressure to prove both their academic status and their practical relevance, resulting in tensions between 'real world' and 'academic' learning, and between 'traditional essayist genres of academic writing and new styles of writing developed to support the acquisition and consolidation of professional knowledge' (2000: 9). Evans and Abbott (1998: 115) ascribe the change to 'the increasing pressure for experimentation in relation to course design, delivery and assessment', but point out that innovation has often been promoted without any clear justification – much of the published material on alternative approaches to teaching and learning is not, they claim, based on findings from empirical research (1998: 17).

Undergraduate student writing is clearly complex, with many variations in practice dependent not only on discipline, level of study and educational approach, but also on the nature of the higher education institution, the particular focus of the department within that institution, and the idiosyncrasies of the lecturers who assign written work. In this paper we are able to provide a more comprehensive inventory of genres of student writing than has previously been documented in a British university context, and identify, from the perspective of the academic, a number of important trends in the assignment of student writing tasks.

The study

As part of an ESRC funded project entitled 'An investigation of genres of assessed writing in British Higher Education'[1] we have been conducting semi-structured interviews with academic staff responsible for course planning and assessment at undergraduate level, to discover views on the types of assignments students are required to write, perceptions of the differences between assignment types, and the qualities valued in student writing at various levels. In the process of interviewing we have been particularly attentive to responses that reflect fundamental differences of approach between the soft and hard disciplines, or the pure and applied, or alternatively any indication of commonality and shared values. Our interviews also offer academics the opportunity to reflect on changes and developments in student writing tasks, including the introduction of new genres. (See Appendix A for interview protocol.)

This paper reports on 55 interviews conducted in 20 departments at the Universities of Warwick, Reading and Oxford Brookes. To assist in relating our findings to the literature on student writing practices and disciplinary variation, we assigned subject areas to disciplinary groupings as indicated in Table 1.

Disciplinary grouping	Subject area	Number of interviews
Arts and Humanities	Archaeology English Studies History Philosophy Publishing Theatre Studies	16
Life Sciences	Biological Sciences Food Sciences Health Medicine Psychology	10
Physical Sciences	Computing Engineering Mathematics Physics	14
Social Sciences	Anthropology Economics Hospitality and Tourism Law Sociology	15

Table 1: Subject areas and disciplinary groupings

Findings

In what follows, we first review the types of assignment we found and their distribution across subject areas. We then discuss the three main groups of assignments: 'pedagogic' genres such as the traditional student essay, 'research-academic', and 'professional' genres. This is followed by observations on four innovative trends identified, and two common values expressed.

Assignment types and spread

Although in some modules students are assessed partially on oral presentations, or entirely by examination, for the majority of staff we talked to 'assignment writing is the core of how we examine and assess students' (Sociology). As Table 2 shows, in some disciplines such as Philosophy the essay is the principal assignment type undergraduates write, whereas in other areas undergraduates are expected to produce assignments of many different kinds.

The labels used for the assignments are those from the departmental discourse communities. Such labels are known to be unreliable indicators of genre across disciplines (Currie, 1993: 102), as many tutors recognised. Some tutors explicitly differentiated 'research projects' from 'project reports', although these terms were not always used consistently and others realised that what they called 'essays' others might call 'projects', or (in the case of longer essays) 'dissertations'. The examples in Table 2 have been selected to illustrate not only the range of labels, but also the spread of assignment types across the disciplines.

Essay	Anthropology, Archaeology, Biology, Computing, Economics, Engineering, English Studies, Food Sciences, Health, History, Hospitality and Tourism, Law, Mathematics, Medicine, Philosophy, Psychology, Publishing, Theatre Studies
Report	Computing, Food Sciences, Hospitality and Tourism, Law, Psychology
Laboratory Report	Archaeology, Biology, Physics
Project Report	Biology, Economics, Engineering, Mathematics, Sociology
Research Project	Biology, Mathematics, Theatre Studies
Dissertation	Anthropology, Archaeology, Biology, Computing, Law, Medicine, Publishing, Sociology, Theatre Studies

Group Project	Archaeology, Engineering, Health, Physics, Publishing
Poster	Anthropology, Biology, Engineering, Mathematics, Physics, Psychology
Book Review	History, Psychology, Sociology, Theatre Studies
Website Evaluation	Medicine, Theatre Studies
Problem Sheets	Biosciences, Economics, Food Sciences, Hospitality and Tourism, Mathematics
Case Studies	Health, Publishing
Case Notes, Draft Appeal to House of Lords, Advice Notes to a client, Submissions in preparation for a case, Moots, Problem Question (judgment),	Law
Field Study/ Ethnography	Sociology
Patient Case Report	Medicine
Letter from publisher to author	Publishing
Reflective writing / journal / blog	Engineering, English Studies, Hospitality and Tourism, Philosophy, Medicine, Theatre Studies
Critical evaluation (of own production or practical task)	Anthropology, English Studies, Computing, Theatre Studies
Marketing Proposal / Plan	Engineering, Publishing
Fiction	Sociology, Law
Press Release, Fact Sheet, Technical Abstract, persuasive writing	Biology, Physics
Letter of advice to friend written from 1830s perspective; Maths in Action project (lay audience)	Mathematics

Table 2: Assignment types and spread

These diverse assignment types differ not only in rhetorical structure, but also in audience and purpose. In Engineering, for instance, scientific papers are written to report findings to an academic audience, funding proposals are written to persuade a professional readership, posters are designed to inform a lay audience (e.g. visitors to a transport museum), and reflective journals are written for personal and professional development. The writing process also differs. Some assignments are written individually whereas others involve group work.

Variation is particularly typical of the applied disciplines where, as Lea and Stierer (2000: 9) point out, there is inherent tension between the discourse requirements of the professional and the academic communities (although the trend to develop 'transferable skills' is evident in most disciplines). Some tutors were proud to draw attention to writing tasks that indicate the practical relevance of their degree programmes. Publishing tutors, for example, argued that there was 'little point' in writing academic essays in some modules, as Publishing is a vocational degree and assignments 'try to replicate what goes on'. In contrast, tutors of Hospitality and Tourism, an 'emergent' discipline (Baynham, 2000), seemed more concerned to emphasise the academic respectability of their programme, commenting on the need for students to grasp the link between practice and theory.

Our interviews with tutors suggest that university writing can be grouped into 'pedagogic' genres such as the traditional student essay; 'research-academic' genres such as the research project and book review; and 'professional' genres such as moots in law, patient case reports, and critical evaluation of computer code design. In addition to these three groups, we identified trends towards the use of tasks involving fiction, self-reflection, writing for a general audience, and / or writing relating to the use of new technologies. These groups and trends are now presented.

Pedagogic genres

The prototypical pedagogic genre is the traditional student essay. It is used by all departments in our sample with the exception of Physics, which has only recently abandoned it. When defined by tutors, it is taken to be discursive prose. Length and frequency varies: some tutors expect short essays every two weeks, others require a 3000-word essay per module per term, and possibly one longer 'essay' of 8,000–10,000 words in the final year. 'Law as a discipline is very focused on adherence to the brief.' Biology is equally in favour of concision in that 'there has never been a penalty for an essay being too short'.

Essays have a basic, generally three-part structure:

- Introduction, body, conclusion (Biological Sciences)
- Introduction, logical sequence of argument, conclusion (Medicine)
- Argument, counter-argument, conclusion (Hospitality and Tourism)

This general structure allows for more variation in approach than in other assessed genres:

- Greater scope than other assignment types in terms of what they're writing about (Engineering)
- Generally more 'rangy', with a freer structure (Law)
- Less prescribed structure (Theatre Studies)
- More flexible than practical reports; possibly addressing only a subset of the classic RA (Psychology)
- More open-ended, with less structured investigation (Hospitality and Tourism)

An Engineering tutor suggested that students find essays frightening for this very reason: 'Having become accustomed to writing structured reports, the prospect of an essay on professional ethics is daunting'. In recognition of this open-endedness, problem sheets may be assigned instead of essays because they are 'shorter, more specific and more direct' (Health).

Essays were also thought to involve critical thinking:

- 'A chance to show ... that you can think deeply about a subject' (Anthropology)
- Evidence of independent thought, assessing a particular debate, critical analysis (Archaeology)
- 'The traditional Law essay would probably take the form of a critical discussion of a proposition' (Law)
- 'It has an argument, a critical argument, critique is crucial' (Sociology).
- 'An essay has got to be an argument of some sort ... not simply reportage or narrative' (Theatre Studies)

Particularly in essays, progression is marked by an increasingly critical and original response:

- 'We'd expect much more of a critique of their work from a third year ... [student] than we would from a first year' (Computing)
- Students become 'more critical in the final stages' (Hospitality and Tourism)

- First year writing should be accurate, concise, explicit, but by the third year 'originality should be added to the mixture' (Psychology)
- Good students 'develop a genuine personal voice' (Theatre Studies)

Within and across departments, however, there are different views on originality. For instance, student opinions may or may not be valued:

> I am not overly concerned about students' own opinions – it's more about structure, argumentation and engagement with the text, but some colleagues are more interested in what students think about something. (Sociology)

In Theatre Studies, essay writing is used to develop an appropriate balance of critical rigour, open-mindedness, and creative imaginative responses ('the ability to think outside the box'). Similarly in English Studies a balance is sought between students' own viewpoints and substantiation from and engagement with the field.

The value of the essay would appear to lie in its relatively loosely structured ability to display critical thinking and development of an argument within the context of the curriculum.

Research-academic genres

In contrast to the pedagogic genres of student essay and problem sheet, a project report in Psychology is 'structured like an academic article' and must adhere to the conventions of a publishable scientific paper. This view is one that resonates across a number of departments: 'Over time, student writing should approximate ever more closely to the writing that academics submit for publication in learned/scientific journals' (Economics). In Psychology, practical reports, project reports and essays are all meant to be written in the style of the classic research article, and in Food Sciences student writing is expected to conform to 'the style you'd expect in a research paper' – 'publishable in style, but not in content'. Biology students are advised to 'write in the style of current opinion journals'. Physics tutors reported 'trying to get [students] to write a scientific paper – as might be published in a scientific journal, for an audience of their peers'. However, although publication constitutes recognition of success in academia, opinions varied as to the likelihood of this occurring at undergraduate level. According to Psychology tutors only a minority of undergraduate students reach publication standard, whereas in Biochemistry, a 'flagship' within Biology, it was reported that 'many year three essays are of publishable quality'. Clearly although the research article is used as a model in these disciplines, the purpose of writing is educational, and publication is not a primary aim.

The typical research-academic genres identified in our interviews are scientific reports (which mirror research articles), and book reviews. In certain disciplines, case studies may also prove to belong in this category. Reports and case studies, however, may also be labels for assignments which emulate professional rather than academic genres.

Professional genres

Professional genres position student writers as professionals. In the Medical School assignments such as the case report, involving patient description and a management plan, are used to assess competence to progress as a medical practitioner. Engineering students are required to consider their legal liability for the recommendations they make in their site investigation reports. Publishing students write publishing project proposals and letters to authors, in the persona of a publisher. Law students write case notes and appeals, which are 'common forms of legal writing', as well as 'problem questions' which apply the law 'rather as barristers and solicitors have to do'.

These professional genres tend to have clear schema, often made explicit by section headings. For instance, in Law the three sections of an appeal are 'precedent, principle and policy', while in case notes they are 'facts, decisions and implications'. Highly structured genres present very different demands to the essay, and are assessed by different criteria. Practice in the applied disciplines can be contrasted with the 'purer' approach taken in Theatre Studies, where an informant spoke of his dislike of 'writing to a formula' which he can 'tell a mile off'. Several members of Theatre Studies explicitly valued writing that takes risks, and encouraged students to 'write dangerously' (a positive example of this being one student's analysis of 'King Kong as a Wagnerian Opera').

Some informants spoke of progression towards employment. In Engineering, for example, formative writing tasks in the first year progressed through structured academic laboratory reports to assignments written for professional audiences in the final year.

Innovative trends

Evans and Abbot (1998) discuss the rise of the staff development industry and the increasing value placed on innovative practice in British higher education, particularly since the reforms of 1992. Our interviews also reflected this; some tutors were almost apologetic about their use of the 'essay', perceived as being 'standard' and 'traditional', and by implication unimaginative and old-fashioned:

- 'The fact that essays are still used as the only mode by the majority of English literature assessors seems to me very limiting'. (English Studies)
- 'It has been the convention to use essays. I would like to break away from that'. (Psychology)
- 'We are a traditional department and we still use mainly essays and we're very conscious that we would like to, and perhaps need to, do something about that. More and more colleagues are doing different things'. (Sociology)

Creative writing

Students in English Studies and Theatre Studies produce creative work and then critique their own output. More unexpected and rather experimental examples of innovation come from Sociology and Law, however. For instance in one Sociology module students may produce a piece of crime fiction (intended to demonstrate understanding of the sociological theories taught, and assessed on these terms rather than literary merit), and in another students are set a creative writing task which the tutor calls a 'story'. In a recently approved Law module students are encouraged to produce a dramatic dissertation that takes the form of a playscript of the facts or trial of a legal case, together with a reflective commentary.

Empathy writing

In addition to the professional writing where students write assignments specific to their intended work situation, growing numbers of tutors offer assignments written for a general, non-professional, or non-academic audience. In Philosophy students are encouraged to write for educated peers: 'if they can explain the essence of a debate to a fellow student in the hall of residence who is not studying Philosophy, they have understood what they have read', whereas in Physics, Biology, Mathematics and Engineering we see students writing, informed by their disciplines, for school children, friends, museums, or newspapers. Here they have to consider not only scientific content, but also the audience and purpose. Lea and Street (2000: 39) have coined the term 'empathy writing' for such new ways of communicating disciplines outside the academic community.

Reflective writing

A third type of innovation could be called reflective writing. This encompasses a range of assignment types, each of which relates to different strands within national initiatives in Personal (and Professional) Development Planning (PDP), defined by the Higher Education Academy (2005) as:

> a structured and supported process undertaken by an individual to reflect upon their own learning, performance and / or achievement and to plan for their personal, educational and career development.

Reflection on learning appears in different guises in our interviews. Students may be asked to evaluate their own work (Computing, English Studies, Theatre Studies), to reflect on their experiences during group work (Engineering, Hospitality and Tourism), on the educational value of a practical task (Anthropology), or on past personal experiences (Medicine). Such writing may take the form of a learning journal, as Creme (2000) found in Social Anthropology courses at Sussex University. She points out how journals 'foreground ... the idea of writing as a process and a tool for learning rather than as a product and occasional demonstration of knowledge' (Creme, 2000: 99).

Squires (2005) comments on the particular need for reflective practice in the professional disciplines, and the six Health and Social Welfare academics interviewed by Hoadley-Maidment (2000) ranked the ability to draw on personal experience very highly. According to our informants, however, medical students find this kind of writing particularly hard, because it differs so greatly from the factual reports they are used to writing in the pure sciences.

New technologies

New technologies can influence emergent assessment trends. For instance, with the introduction of weblogs or blogs for student writing as part of PDP at Warwick, some reflective writing has been submitted online, and there are indications this might become increasingly the norm (reflective journals in Engineering might move to blog format, for example). Website evaluations have been introduced in Medicine and Theatre Studies. This assignment type is similar to the book review, but with at least partially different evaluation criteria. Web-page design in Publishing certainly involves different skills, and reportedly appeals to students who feel less comfortable with academic essay writing. Powerpoint presentations are also increasingly assessed. These have not been included in our study – our current scope is solely written text – but the trend towards multimodal assignments is clear. While the innovations described above are indicative of trends, a stronger consensus emerged in terms of common values.

Common values

Two themes emerged across the disciplines: Firstly, subject tutors take responsibility for introducing students to the expectations of writing in their subject area. Secondly there was a consensus on what constitutes 'good' writing.

Learning discipline specifics

Tutors across disciplines commented on the difference between university writing and A-level writing. In Theatre Studies, first-year essays were used to 'make the break from A-level style of thinking', and Physics tutors changed the laboratory report section heading 'Materials and Methods' to 'Experimental Details' – 'that may well be the title they have used in school, and one that we try to beat out of them'. Requirements at A-Level relating to the use of secondary sources may also be very different, as tutors in Hospitality and Tourism and English Studies pointed out.

Tutors introduce students to the writing practices of their subject area in many ways. In English Studies and Philosophy there is explicit attention to pieces of writing that move students towards the essay as the final goal, such as reflective diaries, and responses to texts. In Sociology all students follow a Professional Skills Programme in their first year to learn what is expected in essays. Similarly in Philosophy students follow a first-year module entitled Doing Philosophy, where they work through a series of preparatory tasks building up to an essay every three weeks. Assignments called 'critical review' are set in Archaeology with the explicit goal of teaching students how to engage in critical reading and thinking.

Students also learn how written products are organised. In Law and Physics, among others, clear guidelines are given not only on the expected sections and subsections of specific genres such as Moots and Laboratory Reports, but also on the content and language expected in each section. Where tutors assume students are familiar with a text type, there may be less instruction, although Psychology tutors reported surprise that some students did not know the expected structure for a book review (summary plus evaluation). In History norms are not clear-cut and different tutors may give different advice. For instance one academic claimed to value 'signposting of the argument' and 'flagging up of significant points', but realised that some of his colleagues disliked scaffolding and did not feel the need to underline the structure of the argument.

Good writing

When we asked tutors about desirable characteristics of student writing, there was remarkable consistency within the group, and indeed with the literature. Economics tutors mentioned critical analysis and logical development, History tutors clarity of argument, taking the reader on 'a journey through conflicting ideas'. Tutors in Sociology and Medicine valued 'a clearly stated argument'. Engineering tutors liked succinct and well-structured writing, while Philosophy tutors liked clarity and clear signalling. These comments support Lea and Street's (2000) findings regarding argument, structure and clarity. Next to coherent structure, the most frequently stated desirable quality was originality or creativity, and we have seen how this interacts with logical thinking. Other desirable qualities included 'understanding', 'insight', and 'application', as well as 'succinct expression' and 'adherence to academic conventions'. Given the differences that have emerged surrounding writing purpose, audience and rhetorical structure, it is perhaps surprising that there are nevertheless shared qualities valued across the university. This is not at all to suggest that what counts as 'good' writing is similar across the disciplines, as tutors are well aware: 'An excellent English student would still have to learn how to write in Law'.

Conclusion

This study acknowledges widespread use of a set of core assignment types that sit easily within the traditions of university education (essay, dissertation, book review, laboratory report). Writing of this type may simply serve as evidence of educational achievement, or it may reflect the output of the professional academic (we distinguish between 'pedagogic' genres and 'research-academic' genres). In addition the study identifies a substantial number of different 'professional' genres, reflecting the conventions and purposes of workplace texts, and also the assignment of 'empathy' writing tasks for general readerships. While pedagogic and research-academic genres tend to occur in the pure disciplines, and professional genres tend to occur within the applied disciplines, it is also the case that modules in some pure disciplines require writing for non-academic audiences, such as school children or museum visitors. Concern with the requirements of the world of work, together with trends towards increased reflective writing, seem to serve essentially formative, developmental and personal or professional development goals, as captured by recent PDP initiatives. We also note the use of creative writing tasks, even for students outside the humanities (Law, Medicine, Sociology), and an increasing emphasis on the creation and evaluation of multimodal and web-based texts.

The differences highlighted by Braxton (1995), Bazerman (1981) and Becher (1987) persist between those disciplines that engage in reporting facts within one paradigm, in comparison with those that require interpretation and reflection on ideas and texts within the context of competing paradigms. The danger for universities currently attempting to harmonise assessment criteria is the temptation to agree on the 'common' values and not interpret them sufficiently for students. Indeed one striking feature in our interviews was the sense in which tutors felt it was the subject area's responsibility to introduce students to norms specific to their area, irrespective of norms in other areas. Some tutors did refer to faculty wide assessment criteria, but in their interpretation, they were always subject- (or module-) specific. In this way our study underscores the findings of others (e.g. Neumann et al., 2002) concerning the need for students to be alert to differences not only across subject areas, but also across assignments.

Notes

1   The ESRC funded project (RES-000-23-0800) aims to compile and analyse a corpus of 'good' student assignments, at all levels from first-year undergraduate to masters degree, across the disciplines. It aims to characterise proficient student writing produced for degree programmes in British universities in terms of genres and subgenres through interviews with members of the discourse communities (here university tutors), multidimensional analysis of registers, and systemic functional genre analysis. Further details can be found at www.warwick.ac.uk/go/BAWE.

References

Baynham, M. (2000) Academic writing in new and emergent discipline areas. In M. Lea and B. Stierer (eds) *Student Writing in Higher Education: new contexts* 17–31. Buckingham: The Society for Research into Higher Education and Open University Press.

Bazerman, C. (1981) What written knowledge does. *Philosophy of the Social Sciences* 2: 361–87.

Becher, T. (1987) Disciplinary discourse. *Studies in Higher Education* 12: 261–74.

Becher, T. (1989) *Academic Tribes and Territories*. Buckingham: The Society for Research into Higher Education and Open University Press.

Biglan, A. (1973) The characteristics of subject matter in different academic areas. *Journal of Applied Psychology* 57: 195–203.

Braxton, J. (1995) Disciplines with an affinity for the improvement of undergraduate education. In N. Hativa and M. Marincovich (eds) *Disciplinary Differences in Teaching and Learning* 59–64. San Francisco: Jossey-Bass Publishers.

Creme, P. (2000) The 'personal' in university writing: uses of reflective learning journals. In M. Lea and B. Stierer (eds) *Student Writing in Higher Education: new contexts* 97–111. Buckingham: The Society for Research into Higher Education and Open University Press.

Currie, P. (1993) Entering a disciplinary community: conceptual activities required to write for one introductory university course. *Journal of Second Language Writing* 2: 101–17.

Elander, J., Harrington, K., Norton, L., Robinson, R. and Reddy, P. (2006) Complex skills and academic writing: a review of evidence about the types of learning required to meet core assessment criteria. *Assessment and Evaluation in Higher Education* 31: 71–90.

Evans, L. and Abbott, I. (1998) *Teaching and Learning in Higher Education.* London: Cassell.

Healey, M. (2000) Developing the scholarship of teaching in higher education: a discipline-based approach. *Higher Education Research and Development* 19: 169–89.

Higher Education Academy (2005) Professional Development Planning. Retrieved on 12 January 2006 from http://www.heacademy.ac.uk/PDP.htm

Hoadley-Maidment, E. (2000) From personal experience to reflective practitioner: academic literacies and professional education. In M. Lea and B. Stierer (eds) *Student Writing in Higher Education: new contexts* 165–78. Buckingham: The Society for Research into Higher Education and Open University Press.

Horowitz, D. (1986) What professors actually require: academic tasks for the EFL classroom. *TESOL Quarterly* 20: 445–62.

Klein, J. T. (1996) *Crossing boundaries: knowledge, disciplinarities, and interdisciplinarities.* Charlottesville: University Press of Virginia.

Kolb, D. A. (1981) Learning styles and disciplinary differences 232–55. In L. A. Chickering (ed.) *The Modern American College.* San Francisco, CA: Jossey-Bass.

Lattuca, L. and Stark, J. (1994) Will disciplinary perspectives impede curricular reform? *Journal of Higher Education* 65: 401–26.

Lea, M. and Street, B. (2000) Student writing and staff feedback in higher education: an academic literacies approach. In M. Lea and B. Stierer (eds) *Student Writing in Higher Education: new contexts* 1–14. Buckingham: The Society for Research into Higher Education and Open University Press.

Lea, M. and Stierer, B. (2000) Editors' introduction. In M. Lea and B. Stierer (eds) *Student Writing in Higher Education: new contexts* 1–14. Buckingham: The Society for Research into Higher Education and Open University Press.

Neumann, R. (2001) Disciplinary differences and university teaching. *Studies in Higher Education* 26: 135–46.

Neumann, R., Parry, S. and Becher, T. (2002) Teaching and learning in their disciplinary contexts: a conceptual analysis. *Studies in Higher Education* 27: 405–417.

North, S. (2005a) Disciplinary variation in the use of theme in undergraduate essays. *Applied Linguistics* 26: 431–52.

North, S. (2005b) Different values, different skills? A comparison of essay writing by students from arts and science backgrounds. *Studies in Higher Education* 30: 517–33.

Parry, S. (1998) Disciplinary discourse in doctoral theses. *Higher Education* 36: 273–99.

Purves, A. C. (1986) Rhetorical communities: the international student and basic writing. *Journal of Basic Writing* 5: 38–51.

Quality Assurance Agency (QAA) (n.d.) *Subject Benchmark Statements.* Retrieved on 10 January 2006 from http://www.qaa.ac.uk/academicinfra-structure/benchmark/default.asp

Smart, J. and Ethington, C. (1995) Disciplinary and institutional differences in undergraduate education goals. In N. Hativa and M. Marincovich (eds) *Disciplinary Differences in Teaching and Learning* 49–58. San Francisco: Jossey-Bass Publishers.

Squires, G. (2005) Art, science and the professions. *Studies in Higher Education* 30: 127–36.

Stierer, B. (2000) Schoolteachers as students: academic literacy and the construction of professional knowledge writing Master's courses in Education. In M. Lea and B. Stierer (eds) S*tudent Writing in Higher Education: new contexts* 179–95. Buckingham: The Society for Research into Higher Education and Open University Press.

Appendix A: Academic interview guidance notes

- What role does assignment-writing play in your department?

- What different types of written assignment do you set your students?
    - o Could you tell us more about ZZ?
    - o Are there other types of assignment task?
    - o Do you set assignments of type [pre-existing genre] as well?
    - o Do you use other formats, e.g. videos?

- How do the assignment types you set differ?
    - o How could we tell a YY from an XX?
    - o e.g. an experimental report from a case-study?
    - o e.g. a critical review from an essay?

- What sort of differences do you expect to find between the written work of first or second year students and final-year undergraduates or masters-level students?

- What do you value most in student written work?

- What sorts of things do you most dislike in student's written work?

- In your opinion, how much does presentation matter?

- How do the various assignment tasks reveal evidence of the qualities you value?

- Do you find that overseas students have particular problems with written assignments?
    o Do you have ways and means of helping them?

- Who should we talk to about collecting assignments?

- Is there a good time to collect assignments on module MM999?

- Are there any modules we should definitely include in our sample?
    o If so, which? and why?

7 Interdisciplinarity and writer identity: students' views and experiences

Bojana Petrić

Introduction

There is a clear relationship between disciplinarity and writer identity. As research shows, scholars in the same discipline share not only disciplinary worldviews but also genres and discourses (Swales, 1990; Hyland, 2000). To become a member of a disciplinary community, one must take on the identity of a member and appropriate its discourses (Ivanič, 1998). Regardless of whether this process is seen as disciplinary enculturation (Prior, 1998) or as a gradual move from the periphery to the core of a disciplinary community of practice (Lave and Wenger, 1991), it is clear that gaining expertise in a discipline has implications for the individual's identity, which is reflected in her ways of writing.

It is much less clear, however, to what extent these concepts apply to inter-disciplinarity. It is still debatable what constitutes interdisciplinarity and what fields qualify to be called interdisciplinary (see, for example, discussions within the 'Interdisciplines' project at www.interdisciplines.org). Research focusing on particular interdisciplinary fields from an applied linguistics perspective (e.g. Baynham, 2000, on nursing studies; Samraj, 1995, on environmental studies) has shown that writing in interdisciplinary fields is characterised by the existence of more than one discourse coming from the disciplines that contribute to it and that these discourses are often contradictory. In other words, interdisciplinary discourse communities (if we accept that such a concept has relevance) are by definition more heterogeneous than disciplinary discourse communities. This places special demands on students studying in interdisci-plinary programmes. Baynham (2000), for example, describes how students in a nursing studies programme have to learn to write like a biologist in one class and a practising nurse in another. This raises important questions: How does the existence of competing discourses in interdisciplinary fields affect students' enculturation into them? How does the existence of more than one discipline in their field of study affect students' sense of their academic identity and, in turn, their writing? Such questions motivated this study.

Studying writer identity is a complex endeavour since identity is composed of a multitude of layers that are difficult to untangle. In an effort to approach writer identity in a more analytical way, Ivanič (1998) and Clark and Ivanič (1997) distinguish between its three aspects, i.e. autobiographical self, discursive self, and self as author, at the same time acknowledging the inevitable overlaps among them. This study focuses on the area largely covered by the latter two aspects, focusing primarily on the writers' sense of their academic affiliation. In interdisciplinary fields, where many possible patterns of disciplinary affiliation exist, this aspect of writer identity is particularly complex. At the same time, it is important to understand the effect of disciplinary affiliation on students' academic achievement in the interdiscipline as some patterns of disciplinary affiliation may facilitate this while others may hinder it.

In this study I explore disciplinary affiliation as part of writer identity in an interdisciplinary field by focusing on student writers' own views and experiences of writing a master's thesis in an interdisciplinary master's programme. In contrast to previous work using text analysis and discourse-based interviews with writers, here writer identity is approached from the students' perspective only. As a consequence, some of the reported aspects of writer identity may not have a visible presence in students' texts. They are nevertheless important since they help shape the (inter) disciplinary boundaries of students' writing and position them in relation to their chosen interdisciplinary field.

The method and the context of the study

To understand how students conceptualise their identity as authors of their master's theses, I conducted semi-structured interviews with 30 students in the master's programme on gender studies at an English-medium university in Central Europe[1]. The participants come from 18 different countries, of which 17 are in the Central and Eastern European region and one in Latin America. The interviews were conducted immediately after the students submitted and defended their master's theses. I was particularly interested in how these students viewed themselves as authors in relation to their primary disciplines and the interdiscipline of gender studies. Further, I aimed to discover the patterns of affiliations that constitute their sense of writer identity. To gather information on students' affiliation, I asked the participants to discuss their work in relation to the disciplines they drew on and to describe what image of themselves they wanted to create in their texts.

The interviews were then transcribed and analysed following Coffey and Atkinson (1996) and Holliday (2002). First, the transcripts were coded for reference to the themes related to the research questions, such as 'affiliation with gender studies' or 'affiliation with the primary discipline', and 'projected image'. Other themes emerged from the data themselves, such as 'language as a marker of affiliation'. Data segments from different interview transcripts were then compiled into thematic files so that all data related to one theme were included in a single file. In the next step, each thematic file was further analysed for common patterns and points of divergence. This process started with establishing large categories, such as 'affiliation with the primary discipline' or 'affiliation with the interdiscipline'. In the next step, the analysis focused on the patterns of affiliations. Subcategories were introduced where data supported further division. For example, the initial category of 'affiliation with the primary discipline' was shown to occur in combination with either acceptance or rejection of the interdiscipline; therefore, these two subcategories were established. In contrast, 'affiliation with the interdiscipline' remained an undivided category since data did not support its further classification.

The decision to locate this investigation within the interdisciplinary field of gender studies was motivated by two main reasons. First, unlike many other interdisciplinary fields, which basically combine two fields into one, gender studies is characterised by a specific philosophical perspective applicable to research on topics belonging to a variety of social science disciplines. This field, therefore, attracts students and scholars from a wide range of primary disciplinary backgrounds, which makes it suitable for the study of students' affiliations with the primary discipline and the interdiscipline. Secondly, gender studies is a relatively novel scholarly field in the academic tradition of Central and Eastern Europe: while there is a history of activist work, in some of the countries in the region, gender studies is still struggling for academic recognition, and degree programmes in this field are only slowly becoming accepted. This implies that none of the participants in this study had a previous degree in gender studies; they all held bachelor's degrees in other disciplines, in most cases in the humanities and social sciences.

The choice of gender studies is significant for yet another reason: the specific nature of writing in this field. According to Delamont (2003), a feminist sociologist, writing in gender studies is characterised by 'a multiplicity of voices' within a single text. This is in line with the findings about discourses in interdisciplinary fields in general, as explained above. The difference, however, may lie in the fact that in gender studies this multiplicity of voices, i.e. heterogeneity of discourses, is acknowledged since one of the premises of scholarship in the field is that knowledge is socially constructed. This has led to the acceptance of openly personal elements in writing (e.g. the use of

'I', the incorporation of personal experience) and a mixing of 'objective' and 'subjective' modes of writing. It has to be borne in mind, however, that the participants in this study are writers of master's theses, a genre relatively standardised and generally not very open to experimentation.

In what follows, I explore the issue of disciplinary affiliation in an interdisciplinary field based on analysis of students' accounts of their writer identities in their master's theses.

Disciplinary affiliation in an interdisciplinary field

The issue of disciplinary affiliation of student writers in interdisciplinary fields is an interesting one since there are at least three disciplines involved: 1) the students' primary discipline, i.e. the one they studied for their first degree; 2) the interdiscipline into which they are being enculturated, and 3) the secondary discipline, in case of students who become interested in an area different from their primary discipline via the interdiscipline. For example, in this study, a student whose first degree was in English studies wrote a thesis based on historical analysis of Hungarian early feminist writings. The interest in history grew out of the student's interest in gender studies.

The analysis of the interview data shows five patterns of disciplinary affiliation among students writing in the interdisciplinary field of gender studies:

1. Affiliation with the primary discipline and acceptance of the interdiscipline
2. Affiliation with the primary discipline and rejection of the interdiscipline
3. Affiliation with the interdiscipline
4. Integrative affiliation
5. Ambivalent relationship to the interdiscipline

Each will be discussed separately, with excerpts from the interviews to illustrate students' views. The names of students have been replaced by pseudonyms.

Affiliation with the primary discipline and acceptance of the interdiscipline

This type of affiliation was found in cases when students continued to work within their primary discipline but from a gender studies perspective, as in the case of, for example, a student whose first degree is in history, and who is writing a master's thesis about a historical issue from a gender studies standpoint. Hector, a student who identifies himself with his primary discipline, explains this:

> Well, I don't know if this would be a nice position to say in a gender department, but I see gender more as an approach than as a discipline, an approach that could be used in different disciplines. I would classify my work as mainly a political science work. I tried to use that language, and it's the language I was usually reading, so that language related more to political science and international relations, political philosophy. Of course I discuss and bring in the gender issues. (…) I think it's a feminist approach in political science or something like that.

For Hector, whose first degree was in political science and international relations, the gender studies interdiscipline provides a specific approach to a political science problem. He clearly feels that his work belongs to the discipline of political science. It is significant that he refers to language as an indicator of the discipline a text belongs to. Using language as a criterion of disciplinary affiliation, he chose to follow the discourse of his primary discipline as the most suitable for his work. In this way, he also signalled his own belonging to, or desire to join that discourse community.

In cases when students affiliate with the primary discipline, the question arises as to the role of the interdiscipline within which they are framing their research project. For many students, as the interviews suggest, the interdiscipline represents a point of identification in terms of underlying philosophical perspectives. The interdiscipline provides a distinct paradigm, which informs the work in ways that would not be possible if the work were conceptualised solely within the epistemological boundaries of the primary discipline. This, from the students' perspective, enriches their work in the primary discipline by making them more alert historians or sociologists. The example of Lavinia, a student whose first degree was in psychology, is a case in point. Lavinia's BA thesis, written within the framework of social psychology, focused on the attitudes of hospital staff towards domestic violence. For her MA thesis in gender studies, she continued research in the same general area but from a feminist perspective[2]. This perspective allowed her to see the research problem in a new light:

> I learnt about the constructivist approach to domestic violence and I also wrote my paper on feminist epistemologies based on that. So in a way this changed my work; this allowed me to formulate my questions and hypotheses in other way than I would have done it last year.

As can be seen, becoming familiarised with the perspective of the interdiscipline changed Lavinia's conceptual framework. It allowed her, as she says, to formulate different questions. In this case, the interdiscipline enabled the student to step out of the epistemological boundary of the primary discipline.

Although these students affiliate primarily with their primary discipline, it is clear that the interdiscipline constitutes an important ingredient of that affiliation.

Affiliation with the primary discipline and rejection of the interdiscipline

In the course of their studies, some students perceive an insurmountable gap between their primary discipline and the interdiscipline, which leads them to reject the interdiscipline. Natalia, whose previous degree was in psychology, and whose thesis in gender studies received a low grade, felt that her research would have been evaluated more positively in a psychology department:

> My thesis is, for me it was interesting, and I think it's a good work, but my supervisors don't think so. They were not very much happy with my thesis, but, I don't know, it's because if I wrote it in psychology and my supervisors were psychologists, it would be completely different. And gender studies, it's something different, and different disciplines, and it's called interdisciplinary, but I don't think so.

Natalia relates her supervisors' criticism not to the features of her thesis but to the fact that they evaluated it from the perspective of gender studies. She acknowledges that she did not apply a gender studies perspective in her research; furthermore, she questions its basic premise of interdisciplinarity. She perceives an incompatibility between ways of doing research in her primary discipline and the interdiscipline, which, in her view, led to her underachievement. In this case, then, writing a master's thesis in an interdisciplinary field is not perceived as enrichment and enlargement of one's perspective but rather as a source of additional burden since it involves, in the student's view, the requirement to meet conflicting demands.

For Natalia, the rejection of the interdiscipline went hand in hand with resistance to the ways of writing associated with the interdiscipline:

> In Russia we have a completely different academic style. We never use expressions like 'I argue'. It was difficult to add my voice in my thesis. My supervisor said 'You have to add your voice'. I studied phrases to use but I felt indifferent. I don't think it's very important.

Natalia resists the values and the discourse of the interdiscipline by referring to the values and discourses of her primary discipline and the academic tradition of her country, in which she clearly feels firmly rooted.

Affiliation with the interdiscipline

Students who strongly associate with the values of the interdiscipline typically express affiliation with the interdisciplinary field rather than the primary discipline. Many also abandon their primary discipline and start researching an issue within the boundaries of another discipline. To these students, the interdiscipline offers entrance to other disciplines and allows movement between fields as long as the research problem falls within the scope of the interdiscipline. Dragana, whose first degree was in literature and cultural studies, explains this when talking about her thesis:

> I see it very much as a work of a feminist. I positioned myself very much as a feminist and a gender scholar as well, because I was analyzing masculinity, and I did social science. Now, I've never done that before but [the supervisor] said I've done a good work of it so ... I think it's like feminist sociology of sport maybe.

This excerpt shows that basing her work on a feminist perspective is of primary importance to Dragana, and that the image of herself she wants to project to the reader is that of a feminist. She is less certain about how to characterise the other elements of her work, as is shown in her use of tentative expressions in the last sentence. It seems that to her, and other students sharing this position, the choice of discipline is secondary to the values of the interdiscipline she subscribes to and strongly identifies with.

Students are aware that expressing their strong affiliation with the interdiscipline can be achieved through their choices of language and rhetorical devices. Olga explains her use of language features identified with gender studies:

> Yes, I think I had a voice, and this is one of the premises of the feminist literature; I don't know much about other types of research. This is, like, there is no pretence to objectivity; I clearly acknowledge that knowledge is subjective, and I use the 'I' pronoun consciously, because I know that, if somebody else would write this work having the same data, they would write a different work. So I think it's also ... It's not only that my respondents answer, but it's also my personal experience that shaped this work, so yes, I do think I had a voice. So it was like this ... the feminist approach 'the personal is political'.

In some cases, students' desire to write like a feminist clashed with the requirements of thesis writing. Csilla, for example, wanted to signal her identity of a feminist scholar by using her personal voice. When her supervisors advised her against it, she resisted, referring to published feminist scholars' writing as a model, thus revealing her desire to identify herself with feminist writers rather than MA thesis writers:

> When my supervisors told me that it [one of the chapters] was a bit too personal, I was thinking like, 'Yes, so what? It is personal, but then why shouldn't it be?' I mean, I don't agree with this strong separation between these spheres and I think in feminist scholars' works it's quite usual that they really put them together.

Integrative affiliation

Integrative affiliation is noted in cases where students express affiliation with multiple disciplines, including the interdiscipline. The following excerpt illustrates this position:

> I think it's three different things in one, and they are equally important to me. I think about it [her thesis] as an anthropological work, cultural anthropology, with the gender perspective, which is very important, I insist on that, and the Bulgarian context, that is also very important to me. So the work tried to put all three: anthropology plus gender plus Bulgaria. (Dimitrina)

By emphasising that all three elements are equally important ingredients of her work, Dimitrina also gives an indication of her sense of her multiple academic identities. It is significant that she places her national background together with her disciplinary affiliation, a point revealing that ways of doing gender studies in the context of a particular country may place the researcher in a specific position and therefore become an important element of her positioning.

Ambivalent relationship with the interdiscipline

Students are attracted to interdisciplinary fields for a variety of reasons. In the course of their studies, however, some may discover that they do not subscribe to its values. In this study, a small number of students expressly stated that they felt uncomfortable identifying with some of the premises of gender studies, which they felt was required of them. Here is a telling example:

> I was beginning to feel a little ill after finishing the second chapter because I've written the word 'patriarchy' and 'patriarch' so many times that I was beginning to feel guilty. I was like: 'I'm not that much of a feminist! Am I that sure of what I am saying?' I was feeling like I was really pushing myself into this 'gender thing', you know, like I was maybe overdoing it a little bit. I just kept writing: 'patriarch, patriarch, patriarch, horrible, evil'. Because, you know, your condition is to be this academic animal, and you sort of know

> what expectations you have to fulfill and what sort of arguments you have to make and half of time you don't even know if you really believe the argument. (Valeria)

Valeria questions what she is writing, yet at the same time feels the pressure of expectations in terms of the 'sort of arguments' she has to make. Although, in her view, she fulfils these expectations by appropriating key terminology (e.g. 'patriarchy') and perspectives of the interdiscipline, it is clear that she herself is not convinced by these arguments. Her affiliation with the interdiscipline seems only superficial.

This issue was addressed by one of the interviewed thesis supervisors in the department as well:

> You can perfectly produce an essay, a paper, where gender is used in every other paragraph, but it doesn't mean that it's going to be a critical thinking piece or project. In a way you can have the relationship to it as a subject matter which you have learnt, you have done it, like in any other degree, you can produce degrees without ever being committed to what you are doing, except it is more visible here, because feminism in itself has this self-definition which is being critical, being political, with an explicit agenda of empowerment, etc. So it's much more visible and painful if the work doesn't live up to the self-defined objectives. You can learn the tricks. So you can be an insider to the discourse and remain untouched.

The supervisor points to the possibility that some students may complete the master's thesis seemingly in accordance with the requirements of the interdiscipline but without being committed to its underlying values. The first and last sentence in this excerpt are particularly illuminating: as this supervisor states, appropriating the language of the interdiscipline does not necessarily imply that the student has embraced its main values nor that she has taken on the identity of a member of its community. This shows that although taking on the identity of a member of a disciplinary discourse community implies appropriating its discourses (Ivanič, 1998), the reverse may not always be true: taking on the language may not lead to nor be an indication that the writer is becoming a member of the discourse community. The person can, as this supervisor explained, 'remain untouched'.

It is useful to refer here to Bakhtin's division of discourses into authoritative and internally persuasive (Bakhtin, 1981). Authoritative discourses, such as the discourses of the state, the church, and, in this case, experts in the discipline, are distant to students trying to enter the discipline. In contrast, internally persuasive discourses are those students can use with ease and which they feel are 'theirs'. By appropriating elements of the authoritative discourses of the discipline, they slowly enlarge their repertoire of internally persuasive discourses. But this process is not an easy one; as Bakhtin states:

> [N]ot all words for just anyone submit equally easily to this appropriation, to this seizure and transformation into private property: many words stubbornly resist, others remain alien, sound foreign in the mouth of the one who appropriated them and who now speaks them; they cannot be assimilated into his context and fall out of it; it is as if they put themselves in quotation marks against the will of the speaker. (Bakhtin, 1981: 294)

This seems an apt description of Valeria's use of words like 'patriarchy', which make her feel uncomfortable as they still belong to an authoritative discourse rather than her. It seems that Valeria is unsure about whether she wants such words to become part of her internally persuasive discourses; she uses them only to the extent that she feels is required of her.

Another type of ambivalent relationship to the interdiscipline is expressed by students who framed their research within gender studies primarily in order to fulfil the department's requirements. These accounts do not reflect the kind of passionate commitment as, for example, Dragana's, who considers it crucial that her work be seen as the work of a feminist. The relationship to the interdiscipline in these cases is reduced to affiliation to the department rather than the interdiscipline itself. The following excerpt provides a clear example. Here Oana describes how she gave her thesis a 'department taste':

> I use so much feminist theory, I mean, in a different department I would have probably approached the issue of teenage girls in a different way, using more psychology sources or social research but here I knew that this is the kind of vocabulary and the kind of conceptual framework that people expect so I think in this way it's got a department taste.

Her reference to 'the kind of vocabulary ... that people expect' points to her awareness of the importance of language and ways of writing for a work to be considered as belonging to a certain field. Her decision to use the language signaling affiliation with the interdiscipline seems to have been motivated most of all by her awareness of departmental expectations. Another student, Beata, expresses a similar motivation for her use of the framework of the interdiscipline:

> I didn't know how much material I would find on feminism and chaos theory, because in the library I couldn't find any at first. And I thought: 'Well, I might focus more on literature on chaos theory, but of course, I'm a gender student, so I should somehow put the whole thing in this framework'.

Both Oana and Beata show awareness that a master's thesis needs to reflect the approaches and discourses characteristic of the field within which it is written in order to be successful. It is not clear, however, to what extent their use of gender studies 'vocabulary' and 'framework' is a result and indication of their affiliation with the interdiscipline itself. The above excerpts can be interpreted as their desire to, above all, be successful students and write good theses.

Conclusions

This study shows that in interdisciplinary fields disciplinary affiliation is an important part of writer identity. It affects many decisions relevant to writing, such as how writers position themselves, what sources they use and what rhetorical choices they make. The five patterns of affiliation described in this paper show the various possible positions students may take when writing in an interdisciplinary field. While it is possible that some of these patterns may reflect the specific nature of the interdisciplinary field of gender studies, it is plausible to expect that similar patterns can be observed with student writers in other interdisciplinary fields as well.

Patterns of disciplinary affiliation are particularly important in higher education as they may be related to students' academic achievement. For example, in Natalia's case, the rejection of the interdiscipline correlates with the low mark for her thesis. However, the relationship between disciplinary affiliation and thesis grade is not so clear-cut. In this study, students showing an ambivalent relationship to the interdiscipline, i.e. affiliation with the department but no particular commitment to the discipline, wrote excellent theses, which received top grades. Clearly, this is an area worth further exploration.

Another issue deserving attention is how patterns of disciplinary affiliation evolve and change over time. In this study there are cases of students showing an ambivalent relationship to the interdiscipline or open rejection of it. Presumably, these students were initially attracted to the interdiscipline, but in the course of their one-year study their attitudes changed. In contrast, some students developed a strong sense of affiliation with the interdiscipline. It is of interest to study how these attitudes form and develop and what factors impact on this process.

Related to this is the theoretical issue of the changing relationship between discourse and identity in the process of disciplinary enculturation: while it is widely recognised that becoming a member of a disciplinary community is accompanied by appropriating its discourse(s), the opposite, as this study suggests, may not necessarily be the case. In other words, the fact that a student writer uses the discourse of a discipline does not necessarily imply that she identifies with it nor that she regards, or would like to regard herself as a member of it.

Finally, studying writer identity in interdisciplinary fields may also provide important insights into the nature of interdisciplinarity itself. In particular, such studies may reveal whether the concept of interdisciplinary discourse communities is relevant in fields characterised by hybridity of discourses and in what ways this concept differs from that of disciplinary discourse communities.

Notes

1   This paper is based on the data collected for a larger research project, reported in Petrić, B. (2005) *Citation Practices in Student Academic Writing.* Unpublished doctoral dissertation. Budapest: Eötvös Loránd University.
2   Throughout this paper, I use the terms 'gender studies' and 'feminist studies/ feminism' interchangeably, following the practice in the department where this study was conducted.

Acknowledgements

I would like to thank the editors for useful comments on the earlier draft of the paper. I am also indebted to BAAL for the grant which enabled me to present this paper at the 2005 BAAL conference in Bristol.

References

Bakhtin, M. M. (1981) Discourse in the novel. In M. Holquist (ed.) *The Dialogic Imagination. Four Essays by M. M. Bakhtin* 259–422. Austin: University of Texas Press.
Baynham, M. (2000) Academic writing in new and emergent disciplines. In M. R. Lea and B. Stierer (eds) *Student Writing in Higher Education. New Contexts* 17–31. Buckingham: The Society for Research into Higher Education and Open University Press.
Clark, R. and Ivanič, R. (1997) *The Politics of Writing.* London: Routledge.
Coffey, A. and Atkinson, P. (1996) *Making Sense of Qualitative Data.* Thousand Oaks: Sage.
Delamont, S. (2003) *Feminist Sociology.* London: Sage.
Holliday, A. (2002) *Doing and Writing Qualitative Research.* London: Sage.
Hyland, K. (2000) *Disciplinary Discourses. Social Interactions in Academic Writing.* Harlow: Longman.
Interdisciplines (n.d.) Discussions. Retrieved on 11 January 2006 from http://www.interdisciplines.org
Ivanič, R. (1998) *Writing and Identity. The Discursive Construction of Identity in Academic Writing.* Amsterdam: John Benjamins.

Lave, J. and Wenger, E. (1991) *Situated Learning: legitimate peripheral partici-pation*. Cambridge: Cambridge University Press.

Prior, P. A. (1998) *Writing/Disciplinarity. A Sociohistoric Account of Literate Activity in the Academy*. Mahwah, NJ: Lawrence Erlbaum.

Samraj, B. (1995) *The Nature of Academic Writing in an Interdisciplinary Field*. Unpublished doctoral dissertation. Ann Arbor: University of Michigan.

Swales, J. M. (1990) *Genre Analysis. English in Academic and Research Settings*. Cambridge: Cambridge University Press.

8   Who or what is the students' audience? The discoursal construction of audience identity in undergraduate assignments

Lynda Griffin

Introduction

Student academic writers not only demonstrate what they know about a topic when they produce written assignments for their tutors: they also represent themselves in their writing and convey an academic voice and identity (Ivanič, 1998). This identity is constrained and shaped by the context and culture within which they write, including disciplinary cultures (Hyland, 2000). Student writers at the same time anticipate a response from their readers, drawing on their own understanding of and sensitivity to the social context, and these assumptions about the reader also influence the ways in which they represent themselves in their writing. Although students may be aware of the existence of the 'real' audience for their texts, the one who will assess their work, they also construct and embed within their texts a more abstract concept, an 'identity' with whom their own academic voice can engage in dialogue: but who, or what is this students' audience? As a tutor with the Open University, I was in a position to research student writing in the context of its production. This was a Level 3 undergraduate distance-learning course, English language and Literacy (E300) offered by the Faculty of Education and Language Studies. As a result of my research, I argue that notions of 'the student's audience' can be inferred from close analysis of real texts in the context of the practices surrounding them. Furthermore, by starting from the perspective of practice, and engaging with the issues arising from students' own experiences, the theoretical notions surrounding what student writers 'ought to do' and are encouraged to do when they write for an academic audience can be evaluated in the light of actual student practices. I argue that 'the students' audience' as evidenced in their written texts ought to be considered alongside existing notions of audience as derived from academic theory, popular study skills texts and tutors' and students' own views of audience. A sense of audience is central to the development of successful academic writing, and for this reason deserves to be the focus of research. I would further suggest that a strong motivation for exploring 'the students' audience' is because students themselves deserve a response to their question: 'what do *they* want?'

My research reveals that students' texts contain interesting and often unexpected linguistic strategies, which reveal varied, complex but nevertheless successful encounters between writer and audiences. Pardoe (2000) raises the issue of how the language used to discuss student writing can reveal a 'deficit view' which equates unsuccessful writing with failure, and warns of the folly of focusing upon 'what is not there, rather than what is there' (2000: 150). By focusing upon what *is* there, I support the notion that a future direction in this field ought to be a reflexive one, in which students' own writing practices inform current theorising about audience in academic writing, and vice versa, as well as offering a basis for any future writing development.

I decided to focus upon more experienced student writers who had studied at least one previous undergraduate course at Level 2 or 3. They seem to be a rather under-represented and overlooked group in writing research, yet such students are at an interesting stage of development as academic writers, seeking their academic voices and identities in new contexts within the institutional constraints of a distance learning university, and the personal constraints of managing part-time study alongside other commitments. However, Open University students are used to 'switching' (Jones et al., 1999) between disciplinary contexts and cultures as they construct a flexible programme of study from the course choices available, and this also means that they are used to shaping their writing to suit changing circumstances, and therefore audiences.

Academic and popular notions of audience

Hyland refers to audience as 'notoriously elusive' (2001: 550) and 'very much a contentious area of debate' (2002: 35). Students find it difficult to articulate what they understand by audience, and what they *think* they do when they write may be rather different from the sense of audience embedded within their written texts. For example, when asked to try and explain in writing 'who/what you see as the reader(s)', student writers on E300 expressed a notion of an abstract but nevertheless humanised entity, reflected in the use of the indefinite pronoun 'someone':

> Most of the time, I think of the reader as someone that has more knowledge

and experience than myself ...

The reader will be someone who requires a reasoned answer ...

(Questionnaire response, Griffin, 2004)

The use of 'someone' grammatically is a personal reference, commonly used in conversation and fiction (Biber et al., 2002: 100), and is used to refer to human entities: in some style and study skills guides, audience is similarly 'human-ised' for example as 'the intelligent person in the in the street' (Chambers and Northedge, 1997: 178), a fictional character who has to be 'imagined'. Yet as Hoey states, 'no writer, however skilled, can ever get inside someone else's mind so completely as to know exactly what they want ...' (2001: 187), though some study guides do nevertheless encourage an investigative approach: 'find out as much as you can about your readers and try to match your vocabulary and style of writing to their needs' (Barrass, 1995: 89). But is audience a 'who' or a 'what'? Some style guides seem unsure: 'you need to be careful to write to your audience and provide it with all the help it needs to make sense of your work', but later, 'think of your reader as a student like yourself – as someone who is acquiring a general understanding of the field ...' (Wallace et al., 1999). Ivanič (1998) also questions what students mean by 'their', concluding that the students in her study are referring to the individual tutor and a more abstract 'them' such as the institution, who the tutor represents, a view reflected in the definitions provided by some OU students:

I also regard the 'academic world' of which the tutor is a part, as the potential audience for the essay.

Tutor and I suppose the OU as an institution.

(Questionnaire response, Griffin, 2004)

However, in the following example, taken from an email sent to the real tutor, 'they' can take on an identity which seems to separate 'them' from the tutor:

I am also having difficulty in understanding what they mean by 'the ideas underpinning my study'. Here are they looking for where I got my ideas from and why or are they looking for the ideas from the course that underpin my study?

(Email to tutor, E300, 2005 presentation.)

In the literature on audience, two models, the audience 'external' to and 'internal' to the text, have emerged. A variety of terms have been used for the embedded, internal audience: a 'fiction' (Ong, 1975) implied (Park, 1982), invoked (Ede and Lunsford, 1984), reader-in-the-text (Thompson and Thetela,

1995). Recent research into academic writing as social practice has focused upon audience as embedded in the rhetorical choices of the writer (Hyland, 2001: 551):

> Essentially, it represents the writer's awareness of the circumstances that define a rhetorical context and the ways that the current text is multiply aligned with other texts. Writers construct an audience by drawing on their knowledge of earlier texts and relying on readers' abilities to recognise intertexuality between texts.

Hyland's definition is an extremely useful one to adapt when carrying out detailed textual analysis, and 'awareness', 'circumstances' and 'intertexuality' are key words of the analysis. I will address the significance and importance of these terms when I present examples from student writing.

The risky business of simulated meetings with strangers

The notion of writing as interactive is central to views of writing as a form of social practice and of meaning as jointly created (Fairclough, 1992, 2001). Bakhtin's (1986) notion of language as dialogic, i.e. a conversation between reader and writer with traces of other texts (1986), also embraces 'addressivity', i.e. the notion that all utterances are addressed to 'someone'.

> Both the composition and, particularly, the style of the utterance depend on those to whom the utterance is addressed, how the speaker (or writer) senses and imagines his addressees, and the force of their effect on the utterance. (Bakhtin, 1986: 95)

Students produce assignments in anticipation of a 'response' and the motivating factor for 'speaking out' in the first place is being asked a question (or set an essay) by the course team or tutor:

> From the very beginning, the speaker expects a response from them, an active responsive understanding. The entire utterance is constructed, as it were, in anticipation of this response. (Bakhtin, 1986: 94)

Bakhtin's role for the 'others' is an active one in the 'chain of speech communion', and I would suggest that this might be a much more helpful way of representing what it is that students do as they write, as opposed to asking them to 'imagine' a reader who does not reply. Novice writers are 'joining a conversation' (Murray, 2005: 59) and raising student awareness of their role in the academic dialogue might help them to see what they do as less about pleasing the reader and more about offering a response to a question that will generate further active responses. Notions of writing as a conversation have found their way into some study skills books, too, for example, Chambers and Northedge (1997: 128) point out that 'Writing is a very special form of conversation. As you write, you are talking to someone you cannot see and who does not reply'. Similarly, Wallace et al. (1999: 179) observe that 'It is useful to imagine writing to a listener, as in face-to-face communication'.

However, writing is also a 'performance', not only in the sense that it is a form of action (Fairclough, 1992: 63), but it also necessitates taking on a 'role', an identity which may feel uncomfortable, unfamiliar, or 'fake' (Ivanič, 1998) and the responsibility for bringing to life, animating or ventriloquating the voices in the text falls with the student writer, too (Ivanič, 1998; Angélil-Carter, 2000). There is a tradition of theatrical analogies and metaphors in the literature on audience, including the representation of everyday behaviour as a theatrical performance (Goffman, 1969). Thompson, for example, refers to the way in which writers assign and bring to life the roles of readers as a 'stage-managed form of exchange' (Thompson, 2001: 59) and it is difficult to talk about audience without reference to roles and parts.

Expecting students to enter into a simulated dialogue with a stranger ('someone') who they do not know, who does not 'reply', and will assess their work represents the process as one which sounds rather daunting and difficult to get right, yet many students do succeed. As I will go on to demonstrate, one of the ways in which they do engage their audience is by 'animating' the interlocutor, i.e. 'bringing in the reader' (Hyland, 2001), lessening the distance and increasing the presence of their audience. Although writers and audiences are separated in time and space, student writers attempt to define a space in which this virtual debate can take place (Hyland, 2001). Anticipating the reader's response, they invite them into this space to share some of their experiences and, in some cases, influence their responses, as illustrated below.

The study: its scope and methodology

I carried out a small scale, ethnographic study of a group of undergraduate students from one regional area of the Open University. The data was collected in a 'real world', naturally occurring context. In the full study (Griffin, 2004) this data was considered alongside other texts and practices, including the course materials, text books, emails and letters, telephone conversations and data from face-to-face encounters such as tutorials. I focused on the texts and practices of my own tutorial group, and as an Open University Associate Lecturer I was a part of the context that I was researching.

The students were registered on a part-time, distance-learning course, English Language and Literacy (E300). Each presentation of the course lasts from February to October of a year. As a Level 3 course, it assumes a certain level of academic ability in students. Twenty-six students initially registered on the course, but I focused upon the writing of a 'core' group of ten who produced all six coursework assignments, or 'TMAs' (Tutor Marked Assignments). Although they were experienced writers, students nevertheless shared with me as their tutor their concerns and anxieties about particular writing practices on the course. One of these concerns was having to design, carry out and write up a 5,000 word tutor-assessed project report. Writing up their own research demanded of students a new identity as a researcher and brought about encounters with a new genre, the research report, and so the texts potentially offered interesting sites at which the tensions surrounding encounters with new identities, audiences and genres might be encoded within the language.

Taking an 'academic literacies' perspective (Lea and Street, 1998) I developed a set of analytical components which drew upon aspects of systemic functional grammar, sociolinguistics and critical discourse analysis. Central to my approach has been Hyland's notion of metadiscourse (Hyland, 2000; Hyland and Tse, 2004), which offers 'a very powerful way of looking at how writers project themselves into their work' and their 'stance towards either its content or the reader' (Hyland, 2000: 109). Metadiscoursal analysis focuses upon the interpersonal aspects of textual relations and the use of particular features (Hyland, 2000, 188–93), which reflect audience and contextual awareness on the part of the writer. As such, it offers a way of accessing 'the students' audience' through close analysis of the linguistic strategies that they use as they engage their audiences and create a context for their writing.

'Doing' research: inviting the reader along, too

In the project reports, students have to write up an account of a research activity which they have carried out during the course. It is a very different sort of assignment from the others on the course, in that they are presenting their own practical work and research activities to the reader and are seeking to persuade them that they have done this successfully. I will illustrate the work of two students, whom I shall refer to as Clare and Amy, focusing particularly upon the ways in which these students chose to write about their research activity as if it were still in progress. It raises interesting notions of audience in which the students anticipate the presence of the 'real' reader, i.e. myself whom I shall refer to as the 'tutor/reader' and at the same time, embedded within the text, audience(s) whom they have constructed for this particular set of circumstances. I will also make reference to and illustrate similar linguistic behaviour in other students' work at the end of this section, in order to further support the key points raised by the fuller analysis of the two case studies presented below.

Clare's report

Clare investigated the linguistic repertoire of a child, and early on in her report she starts off by switching between tenses in a way that at first seems inappropriate. Although clearly by this stage the research has been done, and these actions completed, she still writes in the present tense (though expressing future intentions):

(1)   In my small scale project I aim firstly to identify the linguistic variation
         which occurs in a monolingual child's speech repertoire …

She switches to the past tense, though, when providing an account of her methods:

(2)   I also used a tape recorder … I then transcribed selected sections … I
         decided to use a standard layout.

Later in her report, Clare brings to life for the reader the voices she encountered in the classroom as she gathered her data, evoking a highly interpersonal 'storytelling' style (Tannen, 1989) as she does so:

(3)   As it proved impossible to keep up with the speed of dialogue with a paper
         and pen, I also used a tape recorder … I was pretty confident that I had
         sufficient data.

In (4), the reader is taken into the classroom experience of Clare as researcher, and it is populated with the voices of those she encountered at the time, animating the event for the audience:

(4)   On my arrival the teacher explained to the class that I was going to be a
         special guest for the day …

Clare creates an opportunity for her audience in (4) to almost see and hear the process for themselves. Her movement between tenses draws the audience into the process of actually doing the research, not just in a practical sense but also the decisions, thoughts and reflections that she has experienced: this is particularly well illustrated at a moment when Clare delays the information for the reader, evoking a sense of the way she set about organising her thoughts and actions:

(5)   For my project, the first thing I needed to do was gather a selection of
         examples of a child holding natural conversations in different contexts … .

This manipulation of tense also extends to representing the ethical considerations surrounding her practical work (6):

(6)   I was aware that the teacher might consider the presence of a parent a little

> too intrusive on her teaching and too distracting for the children. However, she was extremely accommodating and more than happy for me to come and spend a whole day observing and recording conversations. She is aware that I am a classroom assistant …
>
> (Clare, TMA06, OU course E300, 2001 presentation.)

In her report, Clare moves constantly between making decisions and practical work carried out, maintaining a strong level of interpersonal involvement via the frequent use of person markers (*I, me, my*). In the wider context of the whole assignment, Clare's practice of writing about an activity that has already been completed as if it were still in progress achieves several purposes. It is an interpersonal strategy, which serves to create a context within which an audience is constructed who she anticipates may want to share in a journey, i.e. the process of carrying out the research, in as immediate a way as possible. Clare invites the audience into the classroom in order to do this. She creates the illusion that she is still doing her research, which in a sense she is. She has engaged in the writing process in order to produce a written representation of all her work for assessment purposes, her linguistic choices and behaviour helping the reader to share in parts of the actual practical work external to the written report. However, she is aware that the tutor/reader still has to formally assess the project, too, so in this sense it is not yet complete. Her enthusiasm for her research is evidenced in her storytelling style and use of interpersonal metadiscoursal features such as boosters (*extremely accommodating*/*I was pretty confident*) and this is conveyed to the tutor/ reader by bringing them in to the circumstances surrounding the research as it progressed, animating the contexts and influencing the reading and, potentially, the assessment process.

Amy's report

Amy carried out research on two media texts in their social context, and like Clare, she used linguistic strategies to represent her work as if still in progress, bringing the audience in to this process. In (1), she writes as if she has not actually started the work (*will be analysed*) but knows what she plans to do, yet at the same time the use of the progressive/passive tense (*are being approached*) sustains the illusion that the work is ongoing:

(1)   The texts are being approached for analysis from the standpoint of someone who is interested in a media story, how that story was created through language, presented and communicated to a readership.

The texts will be analysed for the ideological messages that they convey.

She presents the reader with a simulation of 'work in progress'. Amy creates the context for this to happen, and she interestingly also refers to her identity as a researcher, i.e. *someone* who is interested, and the stance, or *standpoint* that she took, indicating her awareness of her new role and identity, and distancing herself from this role as she 'now' writes up her research. Further on in the text (2), Amy again shares with the audience a sense of how she also moved between identities when carrying out other research-related tasks:

(2)   Notes were made as I compared the photographs

She conveys to the audience, through the use of the passive voice in (2), a more formal notion of the 'researcher identity' passively writing up notes, but through the use of the person marker *I* and the active voice, she uses a more interpersonal style to raise the audience's awareness of the process of another research activity – the more active role of reading and interpreting. There might almost be two identities at work here. The relationship encoded within these linguistic choices suggests a willingness to address the audience directly with a clear statement of her own involvement in the project work.

Amy seemed to find it difficult to sustain this direct relationship with the audience, in fact it does not seem to have been in her interests to do so in other parts of the essay. In a section where she had to discuss the theory behind her study (3), she moves between caution and certainty:

(3)   … in this study, how texts were chosen and how they are interpreted will be a personal reflection – it will not be possible to be totally objective.

Amy's identity as researcher is firmly in the past and complete (*texts were chosen*). However, the intellectual process of interpretation is represented as ongoing. She also commits herself to a future certainty (*will be a personal reflection/will not be possible*) that she anticipates her reader will accept. She may not be able to predict the audience's responses to her work, but here she reminds the reader of a key aspect of the theory and methods she has chosen to use (critical discourse analysis), anticipating that the tutor/reader may indeed interpret the data in a different way. Later in her 'evaluation' section, through the use of metadiscoursal features, Amy invites her audience to share in the intellectual process that she experienced as she carried out the research (4):

(4)   The images presented with the stories captured my attention and made me want to know more

But she also anticipates the audience's responses and shows awareness of the 'real' audience, the tutor/reader and their role as assessor as they read her assignment. Her choice of the passive voice, hedging and avoidance of person markers in (5), indicate that she hopes, perhaps, to influence audience response by evoking a 'less present' audience whom she anticipates will ask questions and view her work critically in role as course tutor:

(5)   A more thorough investigation could have been carried out using a narrower focus, using only one text for analysis, perhaps focussing in greater detail on the ideas in one suitable approach from the course.

(Amy, TMA06, OU course E300, 2001 presentation.)

It seems that it may, therefore, be preferable at times to evoke a more abstract notion of audience, moving them away from the worlds and contexts evoked within the text. Other student writers in the corpus also manipulated tense and time in order to influence the reader, yet did so in a variety of ways, enabling them to sustain and develop their own voices in their writing. For example, Beth (not her real name) in her study of code-switching in different domains, refers explicitly to time (6):

(6)   At the beginning of September I collated all the data and compiled this report

Beth's use of what Halliday (1994) calls a demonstrative determiner draws the audience's attention to the immediate context, though at the same time reminding them that it is the product of a longer process. Like Amy, Beth moves between identities as she writes, using the passive voice when referring to writing up her work, but using interpersonal person markers when referring to interactions with her subjects, who are her husband and children (7):

(7)   The taking of field notes proved more successful when I observed the children at play or in the company of my husband. Any further comments or questions were usually added later that day.

(Beth, TMA06, OU course E300, 2001 presentation.)

Thompson's notions of pastness as 'distance from reality' and future as 'uncertain until it happens' (1996: 185–6) are particularly useful here. Student writers frequently distanced their project work in this pastness whilst in the present 'circumstances', or 'reality', i.e. the moment of interaction with the audience, chose to write about their research as if it were ongoing, giving the project work a sense of uncertainty or incompleteness. I would suggest that such linguistic behaviour seems to reflect student writers' awareness as they write of the presence of the audience as assessor. They seek to sustain the illusion that their work is still in progress for as long as possible. At the same time, they often choose to animate processes which took place outside of the text, bringing them into the 'space' or context of the text, in order to influence the audience. Anna's (not her real name) intertextual evocation of the reading she did for her research (8) is a further example:

(8)   Turner's words led me to speculate on the type of understanding which may be gained about a condition of which we may have no personal experience, but are able to identify it by the term migraine

(Anna, TMA05, OU course E300, 2001 presentation).

Again the audience is taken back in time to the reading and interpretative process and, most importantly for assessment purposes, its influence on her own project work on the way migraine sufferers are positioned in advertising. The audience is constructed as someone who is invited to make these connections and so distance is decreased via the use of person markers (*me/we*). The use of the *to* infinitive, which Thompson (1996: 191) suggests is the 'non–finite equivalent of the modal verbs' also animates for the audience the mental process that took place as Anna engaged with the course materials.

Conclusions

This study represents an initial exploration of the academic writing of one group of undergraduates. Project reports were looked at alongside other aspects of text including introductions, and the use of personal examples in assignments. However, in drawing attention to 'the students' audience' I hope to start questioning some assumptions, held by tutors, students themselves and present in theoretical accounts of audience, about what students do when they write for an audience in particular texts and contexts. Existing notions of audience present a complex picture, and it may seem that bringing students' notions of audience into the picture complicates the issue further. However, I would suggest that this complexity needs attention, as student writers who ask 'what do they want?' are seeking clarification and clarity; in my brief survey of the kinds of guidance available to students, this is something that seems to be lacking. Part of the answer to their question might in fact lie in students' own texts, as my research revealed some examples of successful encounters with audience(s), and future directions might include addressing how these might be articulated and shared with the student community.

In student texts, I found that audience is not a stable entity, and therefore I would argue that it should not be viewed as such, though clearly some of the literature on audience perceives it in this way. As they write, students negotiate and develop their identities, and those of their audiences, whilst at same time contributing to shaping, changing and developing wider institutional practices and contexts, including institutional perceptions of and expectations of genres, for example as to what constitutes a report. In this sense, they are engaging in social practice, and acting upon the world, as well as representing both themselves and their audiences (Fairclough, 1992: 63). I found this to be particularly interesting where more experienced writers, as opposed to novice or professional writers are concerned, since they represent a large part of the higher education student population and potentially contribute a great deal to the shaping of institutional practices. Furthermore, it is a context of changing practices, both in 'traditional' contexts and non-traditional such as the Open University (Lea and Stierer, 2000), a process which can be reflected in writing practices within institutional and disciplinary contexts.

The model of academic writing which views writing as a set of practical skills and that which views it as a culturally, socially and historically situated practice are sometimes positioned at opposing ends of a continuum. However, I would argue that this notion is unhelpful, and one way forward is through stronger links between theory and research and current higher education practices. By adopting a reflexive approach, research might start to provide some answers to the questions posed by student writers. We must continue seeking an answer to the question, 'who or what is the students' audience', but I would argue for less emphasis on the human referent 'who' and more upon the 'what': the discoursally constructed fictional identities which populate student writing.

References

Angélil-Carter, S. (2000) *Stolen Language? Plagiarism in Writing*. Essex: Pearson Educational Ltd.

Bakhtin, M. M. (1986) The Problem of Speech Genres. In C. Emerson and M. Holquist (eds) *Speech Genres and other Late Essays*. Austin: University of Texas Press.

Barrass, R. (1995) *Students Must Write: a guide to better writing in coursework and examinations*. London: Routledge.

Biber, D., Conrad, S. and Leech, G. (2002) *Longman Student Grammar of Spoken and Written English*. Essex: Longman.

Chambers, E. and Northedge, A. (1997) *The Arts Good Study Guide*. Milton Keynes: The Open University.

Ede, L. and Lunsford, A. (1984) Audience addressed/audience invoked: the role of audience in composition theory and pedagogy. *College Composition and Communication* 35(2): 155–71.

Fairclough, N. (1992) *Discourse and Social Change*. Cambridge: Polity Press.

Fairclough, N. (2001) *Language and Power*. (Second edition) London: Longman.

Goffman, E. (1969) *The Presentation of Self in Everyday Life*. London: Penguin.

Griffin, L. (2004) Students' notions of audience as revealed by the academic writing of a group of Open University undergraduate students. Ed.D thesis: The Open University.

Halliday, M. A. K. (1994) *Introduction to Functional Grammar*. London: Arnold.

Hoey, M. (2001) *Textual Interaction: an introduction to written discourse analysis*. London: Routledge.

Hyland, K. (2000) *Disciplinary Discourses: social interactions in academic writing*. London: Longman.

Hyland, K. (2001) Bringing in the reader: addressee features in academic articles. *Written Communication* 18(4) 549–74.

Hyland, K. (2002) *Teaching and Researching Writing*. London: Longman.

Hyland, K. and Tse, P. (2004) Metadiscourse in academic writing: a reappraisal. *Applied Linguistics* 25(2): 156–77.

Ivanič, R. (1998) *Writing and Identity*. Amsterdam: Benjamins.

Jones, C., Turner, J. and Street, B. (1999) *Students Writing in the University: cultural and epistemological issues*. Amsterdam: John Benjamins.

Lea, M. and Stierer, B. (2000) *Student Writing in Higher Education: new contexts*. Buckingham: The Society for Research into Higher Education and Open University Press.

Lea, M. and Street, B. (1998) Student writing in higher education: an academic literacies approach. *Studies in Higher Education* 23(2): 157–72.

Murray, R. (2005) *Writing for Academic Journals*. Open University Press.

Ong, W. J. (1975) The Writer's audience is always a fiction. *PMLA* 90: 9–21.

Pardoe, S. (2000) Respect and the pursuit of 'symmetry' in researching literacy and student writing. In D. Barton, M. Hamiliton and R. Ivanič (eds) *Situated Literacies: reading and writing in context*. London: Routledge.

Park, D. B. (1982) The Meanings of audience. *College English* 24(3): 247–55.

Tannen, D. (1989) *Talking Voices*. Cambridge: Cambridge University Press.

Thompson, G. (1996) *Introducing Functional Grammar*. London: Arnold.

Thompson, G. (2001) Interaction in academic writing: learning to argue with the reader. *Applied Linguistics* 22(1): 58–78.

Thompson, G. and Thetela, P. (1995) The sound of one hand clapping: the management of interaction in written discourse *Text* 15(1): 103–27.

Wallace, A., Schirato, T. and Bright, P. (1999) *Beginning University: thinking, researching and writing for success*. Australia: Allen Unwin.

9   Revealing and obscuring the writer's identity: evidence from a corpus of theses

Maggie Charles

Introduction

In recent years there has been considerable interest in issues concerned with the academic writer's construction of identity. One strand of this research has seen the discipline as a key factor in identity development. Thus research on graduate writers has focused attention on students' socialisation into their disciplinary community (Belcher, 1994; Casanave, 1995, 2002; Prior, 1995). Changes over time in students' writing and thinking have been traced and linked to their gradual adoption of disciplinary norms, values and practices (Berkenkotter et al., 1988; Dong, 1996; Dudley-Evans, 1991; Swales, 1990). In addition, differences in the construction of knowledge have been explored in a range of disciplines and have been shown to be crucial to the writer's achievement of an appropriate written identity (see e.g. Cadman, 1997; Charles, 2004, 2006; Harwood, 2005; Hyland, 1999, 2000). The present work builds on research linking disciplinarity and identity. It uses a corpus approach to examine theses from two contrasting disciplines and shows how differences in disciplinary characteristics are reflected in different ways of constructing identity.

The second aspect of identity relevant here concerns what Ivanič refers to as the 'discoursal self' and may be defined as the impression that the writer conveys of themselves through their discoursal choices in any given text (Ivanič, 1998: 25). Several researchers have investigated specific linguistic features and linked them to the construction of identity. It has been proposed, for example, that the choice of grammatical subject indicates a cline of writer visibility (Davies, 1988; Gosden, 1993). Thus the writer is most visible when using *I* and least visible when they employ an existential subject, for example, *there*. Other researchers have focused particularly on non-native speaker students and have compared their use of specific linguistic features with that of expert writers. Thus Hewings and Hewings (2002) have examined introductory *it* patterns, while Tang and John (1999), Hyland (2002) and Petch-Tyson (1998) have all investigated the use of personal pronouns. A general finding from these studies is that in comparison with expert writers, students tend to over-use impersonal forms, constructing thereby a less authoritative stance and preferring to obscure rather than reveal their identity.

In this study, although I deal with the use of personal pronouns in one pattern, my major focus is on the use of impersonal patterns. I argue that although non-native speakers may indeed construct less powerful and overt identities, this does not necessarily imply that the use of impersonal forms obscures a writer's identity completely or leads to a text that is lacking in authority. Indeed I would suggest that all academic writers, whether student or professional, need sometimes to obscure and sometimes to reveal their identity within their texts. I argue that writers choose their level of visibility according to the rhetorical function they wish to perform and with reference both to their status in the community and the norms and practices of their discipline. Thus they attempt to construct an identity that is likely to persuade other members of the field to accept the validity of their research.

Corpora and method

This study is based on data from two corpora of theses written by native-speakers in two contrasting disciplines: a social science, politics/international relations and a natural science, materials science. The politics corpus consists of eight MPhil theses, giving approximately 190,000 words, while the materials corpus contains eight doctoral theses totalling 300,000 words. The corpora were searched using WordSmith Tools (Scott, 1999) and concordances were compiled and examined.

Several writers have drawn attention to the fact that certain grammar patterns are involved in the construction of stance and/or evaluation. These include patterns followed by *that* complementation (Biber et al., 1999; Hyland and Tse, 2005) and patterns with introductory *it* and an adjective (Charles, 2000; Francis, 1993; Groom, 2005). Since these patterns enable the writer to offer their own viewpoint on a given proposition, they are particularly suitable for the investigation of identity.

The present study examines five patterns. Three are reporting clauses which have a finite verb followed by a *that*-clause and which are used to report the writer's own work. The three patterns are distinguished according to the grammatical subject: a noun group with human reference (*I argue that*); a noun group with non-human reference (*These results show that*); introductory *it* followed by the passive voice (*It is suggested that*). The two remaining patterns have introductory *it* with a link verb and an adjective. The adjective is followed either by a *that*-clause (*It seems likely that*), or by *to* and an infinitive (*It is possible to obtain*). Patterns and examples are summarised in Table 1.

Pattern	Example	Example numbers
human subject + reporting verb + *that*	*I argue that*	1, 7, 8, 9, 10, 30
non-human subject + reporting verb + *that*	*These results show that*	2, 11, 12, 21, 22
it + passive reporting verb + *that*	*It is suggested that*	3, 13, 16, 25, 26, 29
it + link verb + adjective + *that*	*It seems likely that*	4, 5, 15, 18
it + link verb + adjective + *to-*infinitive	*It is possible to obtain*	6, 14, 17, 19, 20, 23, 24, 27, 28

Table 1: Patterns and examples

The use of patterns to reveal or obscure the writer's identity

The patterns listed above provide the writer with various options for revealing or obscuring their identity and indeed we can distinguish a cline in the visibility of the writer. The use of a reporting clause enables the writer to comment on the proposition in the *that*-clause. When used with a human subject, this pattern reveals the writer's identity most fully:

(1)   **I also argue that** the nature of the decision making system had an influence on the decisions made ... (Politics 8)

With a non-human subject, the writer's identity is more obscured, although the use of a noun that refers to the writer's work allows some writer visibility to be achieved:

(2)   **This present study argues that** Alpha also reveals a great deal about western policy ... (Politics 3)

The remaining patterns all obscure the identity of the writer to an even greater extent. It has been pointed out that introductory *it* clauses not only introduce propositions, but simultaneously evaluate them (Biber et al., 1999; Francis, 1993; Hunston and Francis, 1999). In Example (3) below, the proposition in the *that*-clause is evaluated as an assumption, while in (4) it is deemed *important*:

(3)   **It is assumed that** at the peak of the field pulse the applied field is quasi-static ... (Materials 4)

(4)   ... **it is very important that** materials scientists, engineers, physicists and chemists collaborate and pool their skills ... (Materials 5)

However the use of an introductory *it* clause leaves indeterminate who exactly is responsible for the evaluation; we are not specifically told who makes the assumption or who finds the proposition important. Thus the reader may interpret the responsibility as that of the writer alone or as that of a wider group: the writer together with other members of the disciplinary community. I suggest that writers make use of this indeterminacy in order to imply that their own comments or evaluations are shared more widely by the discipline as a whole. Thus, although the writer's individual identity may be obscured, they are able to take on the identity of a member of their disciplinary community. This is a particularly important strategy for the thesis writer since he/she is a novice whose thesis can be regarded as an attempt to gain full disciplinary membership.

Corpus data

Table 2 provides frequency figures per 100,000 words for each of the five patterns.

Pattern	Frequency per 100,000 words	
	Politics	Materials
human subject + reporting verb + *that*	33.2	11.0
non-human subject + reporting verb + *that*	18.4	87.7
it + passive reporting verb + *that*	34.2	109.0
it + link verb + adjective + *that*	58.9	50.7
it + link verb + adjective + *to*-infinitive	85.3	106.3

Table 2: Patterns and frequencies

Comparing the frequencies of these patterns in the two corpora shows certain disciplinary differences. In the verb patterns, politics uses three times as many instances of verbs with human subjects, the form which reveals the writer's identity most clearly. By contrast materials uses over four times as many examples of verbs with non-human subjects and over three times as many instances of introductory *it* with the passive, both patterns which tend to obscure the writer's identity to a greater extent.

   We can explain these findings by drawing on Becher and Trowler's (2001) study of the cultures of the disciplines, in which they characterise natural sciences as predominately 'impersonal' and 'value-free', while social sciences tend to be 'personal' and 'value-laden'. Thus, the higher frequency of human subjects in politics reflects the more personal construction of knowledge in a social science, while the higher frequencies of non-human and *it* subjects in materials are due to the greater impersonality of research in the natural sciences. Differences in frequency between the two corpora for the adjective patterns are not so significant in terms of identity construction, although they may be explained by characteristics of the subject matter in the two disciplines. Politics tends to use the adjective *that*-clause pattern in order to comment on propositions, often concerning political figures:

(5)   ... **it is far from clear that** Nasser and Ben Gurion would have formalised a deal. (Politics 3)

Materials, however, tends to use the *to*-infinitive pattern in order to comment on experimental procedures:

(6)   Hence **it is better to** evaporate solvent rapidly at the ccc, so that solidification occurs ... (Materials 5)

Revealing and obscuring the writer's identity: making claims

Next I discuss some of the rhetorical functions that writers perform using a revealed or obscured identity and suggest reasons why they choose a given level of visibility. I begin by examining the construction of identity that occurs when writers make claims. Achieving the acceptance of knowledge claims is fundamental to successful academic writing and thus the ability to make claims that are valid and persuasive to other members of the discipline is of the utmost importance. We would expect writers to reveal their identity when making such claims since a higher level of visibility enables the writer to take individual credit for their achievement. At the same time, new knowledge claims are potentially face-threatening to others in the field (Myers, 1989), since their acceptance may require other members to adjust, or even relinquish, their own claims. Thus the performance of this rhetorical function calls not only for detailed knowledge of the field, but also for particular sensitivity towards disciplinary norms and practices. Indeed we can distinguish differences in the level of writer visibility, both according to discipline and in relation to the importance and strength of the claim.

In politics, writers often make major claims using a reporting verb with a human subject, primarily *I*:

(7)   **I argue that** the very same motivations that convinced the international community to adopt a safe area policy in the first place persuaded them to lumber along despite the ineffectiveness of the project. (Politics 7)

The use of this pattern is particularly suited to this function because the choice of verb enables the writer to indicate their advocacy of the proposition in the *that*-clause, while the use of *I* as subject reveals the writer's identity most clearly and emphasises their exclusive and individual responsibility for this claim. The choice of *I* is, however, a high-risk option in that it isolates the writer from the rest of the disciplinary community, thus rendering them vulnerable in case of attack. Some protection can nonetheless be gained by using a hedged verb (e.g. *suggest, propose*):

(8)   **I suggest that** the preferences of the Treasury ... were central in influencing the early decisions of the new Labour Government ... (Politics 8)

The use of hedging has a dual effect here. It protects the writer if the evidence for their claim is insufficiently robust, but it also diminishes the face-threatening potential of the claim for other members of the community, making it more likely that the claim will be accepted.

As the thesis is a single-authored text, the use of *we* indicates an obscuring of the writer's identity, since the plural form suggests that there are others who share the writer's view. In fact, in the politics corpus *we* often occurs in conjunction with *if* or a modal form. In such cases *we* is interpreted as including both reader and writer and is thus not used to construct a claim:

(9)   ... **if we accept that** Segal et al.'s exclusion of Douglas from the model was valid on the grounds of clear measurement error ... (Politics 5)

In the materials corpus there are a small number of examples where *we* is indeed used to state a claim:

(10)   **We have shown using a mean field approach that** secondary recrystallisation is possible ... (Materials 7)

However as its use is confined to just two writers, it cannot be regarded as the most characteristic way of carrying out this function in theses in this discipline. Instead, materials writers tend to put forward their claims by using a reporting verb with a non-human subject, often the noun *result*:

(11)   **These results clearly demonstrate that** the erosion behaviour of a ductile and a brittle material is as expected. (Materials 3)

Here, the use of deictic forms with nouns that refer to the writer's text or research (e.g. *this thesis; these micrographs*) enables the reader to understand that it is the writer who is responsible for the statement made. A further signal of the claim is the use of factive verbs such as *show, demonstrate* and *reveal*:

(12)   **The work presented in this thesis has shown that** much common ground exists between ion-irradiation studies, the nucleation of fullerenes, and the use of a CEHRTEM. (Materials 2)

Thus there is a contrast between the way in which politics and materials construct their claims, which reflects the characteristic ways in which the two disciplines construct knowledge, in politics by putting forward individual arguments and in materials by providing experimental evidence. This leads politics writers to reveal their identity fully through the use of *I*, while materials writers tend to obscure their identity by attributing responsibility for the claim to a non-human entity. Nevertheless, I would argue that in materials the use of deixis makes it quite clear that the claim is ultimately that of the writer and the choice of a factive verb constructs a strong and confident assertion. Thus I would suggest that such forms do not obscure the writer's identity completely; rather they reveal as much of the writer's identity as is appropriate and persuasive, given the impersonal way in which the discipline constructs knowledge. Disciplinary factors, then, clearly play a considerable role in decisions as to level of visibility.

However not all claims are either sufficiently important or sufficiently robust to warrant the use of high writer visibility. In such cases writers tend to obscure their identity in order to protect themselves from possible attack. In particular, the indeterminacy inherent in an impersonal pattern dilutes the writer's responsibility for the claim, while hedging can modify the writer's level of certainty. This is seen particularly in the materials corpus, where the passive verb with introductory *it* is used in order to put forward more limited or less reliable claims. In the example below the claim is hedged through the choice of the verb *propose* and its applicability is limited to a specific sample:

(13)   This is the likely size of grains within the material and is not in conflict with the microstructure of this sample which is shown in figure 5.2. **It is therefore proposed that** this sample is weak linked under these conditions … (Materials 4)

Thus the level of visibility chosen depends not only on disciplinary factors, but also on the writer's specific purposes in the study reported.

Obscuring the writer's identity: evaluating the writer's work negatively

In the remainder of this paper I concentrate on rhetorical functions that are carried out using low writer visibility. One aspect common to all these functions is that impersonal patterns are used by the writer to suggest that they are not alone in their work, but are writing as a member of the disciplinary community. I would argue that the construction of an identity as a member of the discipline is a powerful strategy for students to employ in order to gain acceptance for their work.

I begin by showing how evaluations of the writer's own work are often appropriately carried out using a low level of writer visibility. By not revealing their identity overtly in such cases, the writer can take on the perspective of the disciplinary community, criticising or praising their own work as an informed and objective member of the discipline. First I discuss instances where writers draw attention to aspects of their work that are problematic. Examples of this rhetorical function are found in both disciplines, although they are more frequent in the materials corpus. The reason for this may be that, as this discipline uses experimentation as the basis for its construction of knowledge, it requires the extensive description and evaluation of research procedures. In the examples below, the three introductory *it* patterns are used in the context of reporting shortcomings in the writer's work:

(14)   … **it is impossible to** distinguish between the liberalism of Black, Douglas, Marshall and Brennan in COOKSIGN=5 cases because the small number of cases each voted in creates a rounding effect … (Politics 5)

(15)   **It is regrettable that** this investigation could not be performed quantitatively … (Materials 8)

(16)   After initial investigation **it was discovered that** the samples were not very parallel sided. (Materials 3)

I would argue that writers gain several distinct advantages from obscuring their identity under adverse circumstances. First, the use of impersonal forms means that writers do not have to attribute responsibility for flaws in their work directly to themselves. This has the advantage that they are able to indicate difficulties and limitations without risking damage to their credibility as competent researchers and thus they are able to maintain an acceptable professional identity. At the same time, by mentioning such problems overtly in the text, writers show themselves to be honest and reliable scholars, both attributes that are highly valued in the academic community. In fact it is precisely because the researcher draws attention to the limitations of the study, that the reader is more inclined to accept its reliability and validity.

Second, the use of impersonal forms also obscures the source of the negative evaluation. This means that writers are able to imply that the evaluation is one which all members of the discipline would share. This provides writers with a way of showing that they are familiar with disciplinary norms and expectations and thus enables them to construct an identity as knowledgeable members of the disciplinary community. The examples below show the writer's awareness that it would be desirable to be able to quantify the success of the department and to obtain more information from the analysis:

(17)   The Department of External Affairs was 'actively trying to shape public opinion' in the period; **it would be hard to** quantify its success, but by 1945 many Canadians shared the department's views ... (Politics 2)

(18)   **It was frustrating that**, owing to oxidation of the samples, slip-line analysis provided less information than it could have done. (Materials 6)

Although in this case the writers are not able to fulfil disciplinary expectations satisfactorily, they nevertheless succeed in showing that they are aware of what is required and are capable of judging their work according to the standards of the disciplinary community.

Obscuring the writer's identity: evaluating the writer's work positively

Writers also tend to use low visibility when they evaluate their own research positively. Here, obscuring their identity allows writers to emphasise their professional competence without appearing to boast. In fact, using a more overt construction of identity under such circumstances might well provoke criticism from other members of the discipline. Although all academic writers have to show a certain politeness and sensitivity towards members of the discipline as a whole (Myers, 1989), it is likely that the construction of academic modesty is particularly important and necessary for thesis writers, who are novice members of the community. In the following examples using the adjective and infinitive pattern, the writers imply that they, like other professionals in the field, are competent researchers for whom the described research procedures pose few problems:

(19)   **It is easy to** find examples of formal discrimination against women that should meet the persecution standard. (Politics 4)

(20)   Using the Orowan model for dislocation looping, **it is straightforward to** calculate the size and distribution of particles needed ... (Materials 7)

As with the negative evaluations of the writer's work analysed above, the use of this impersonal pattern implies that the evaluation is one that would be shared by all members of the discipline. In this way the writers obscure the fact that they are the source of the positive assessment, which makes it appear objective and thus it is more likely to be accepted by the disciplinary community.

A second way in which writers evaluate their research positively is to emphasise the care taken to ensure a thorough understanding of the research evidence. In the two examples below, the reporting verb is used with a non-human noun subject which is a nominalisation of a research process (*analysis*, *inspection*):

(21)   A first reading of clause 9 of Resolution 836 seems to indicate that UNPROFOR could use all measures necessary, including the use of force, to protect the safe areas. **A more careful analysis reveals that** the qualification of 'acting in self-defence' limited the employment of force to protecting UNPROFOR personnel. (Politics 7)

(22)   In (a)/(b) when g=220, dislocation lines are generally observed as two parallel lines. Double images, owing to g·b=4 can be ruled out as **closer inspection, with a magnifying eyepiece, of (d) and (e) ... show that** dislocations are indeed observed as two separate lines. (Materials 6)

The choice of this pattern opens a space for adjectival modification which the writers use in order to evaluate their research actions as particularly painstaking. By employing the comparative forms *more careful* and *closer*, the writers imply that they were not satisfied with their initial research actions and went on to investigate further and more deeply. In this way they construct the identity of a scrupulous researcher who is not content to accept their first impressions of the research data. Thus the writer's evaluation of their own work, whether positive or negative, is achieved highly effectively through obscuring their identity.

Obscuring the writer's identity: addressing the discipline with authority and modesty

Writers also frequently use low visibility when they directly address the dis-cipline. When carrying out such rhetorical functions it would be inappropriate to reveal their identity since the right to the attention of the disciplinary community is not one that can be claimed individually; rather it has to be earned by members through the production of work which is valued by the discipline. Further, given that the writers in these corpora are novices at the outset of their academic careers, the thesis may constitute the first major work they have submitted for disciplinary scrutiny. I would suggest, therefore, that it is particularly important for thesis writers to construct an identity which shows professionalism, but also takes account of their student status. One of the ways in which this may be achieved is through the use of impersonal forms which allow the writer to speak with authority, but at the same time to maintain a stance of academic modesty.

As noted earlier, introductory *it* clauses evaluate and comment on subsequent propositions. However indeterminacy in these patterns obscures the identity of the writer, making it unclear where responsibility for the comment lies: it can be understood as belonging to the writer alone or to the disciplinary community in general. This in turn enables writers to gain authority, as their use of these patterns implies that their individual evaluation is one which any disciplinary member would share.

In the examples below, the writers use the adjective and infinitive pattern in order to tell the reader how the research material should be understood:

(23)   … **it is necessary to** conceptualize socialization and competition as two aspects of a single process. (Politics 1)

(24)   Once the coverage reaches 0.8 ML or above … **it becomes helpful to** think of the clean dimers as the minority species. (Materials 1)

The choice of adjective enables the writer to vary the degree of authority and modesty. Thus, for example, *necessary*, *essential* and *important* construct highly authoritative statements, while *helpful*, *useful* and *reasonable* offer more modest suggestions.

The passive verb with introductory *it* subject is also used in order to address the disciplinary reader directly, particularly when it occurs with the modal forms *should* and *must* in conjunction with the verbs *note*, *emphasise* and *stress*:

(25)   **It must now be emphasised that** the act of observing the particles in the gas with the electron-beam was the means of the treatment that was being investigated. (Materials 2)

(26)   **It should be noted that** the predictions offered by the interpenetrative account are diametrically opposed to those offered by the competitive account. (Politics 1)

The choice of modal form and verb again enable the writer to adjust the level of authority and modesty, with *should* and *note* being less authoritative than *must*, *emphasise* and *stress*.

Obscuring the writer's identity: taking a critical position towards other researchers

Writers may also obscure their identity when they make a critical assessment of another researcher's work. The use of the adjective *hard* in the adjective and infinitive pattern provides a good illustration of how this function can be performed:

(27)   If Knight and Epstein (1996) are correct to argue that the rarity of formal
         alteration reflects the respect with which the norm of stare decisis is treated,
         then **it is hard to** see why ... Justices vote with such ideological rigidity.
         (Politics 5)

(28)   Swartzentruber et al. (1990) found that eb/kT = 1.2pm0.1 ... As they give
         almost no details of the calculation, **it is hard to** know where the differences
         might occur. (Materials 1)

In these examples the writer comments on the work of other researchers, constructing the identity of one who, in good faith, has tried but failed to understand a colleague's arguments or to use their methods. Clearly the effect is critical of the other researcher's work. However, the criticism is made in a modest and non-face-threatening way, since the pattern implies that it is the writer who finds the action hard. Thus the problem is that of the writer rather than the cited researcher. At the same time, the writer does maintain credibility, since the pattern also leaves open the possibility that others in the field would find the criticised arguments or procedures difficult as well.

A passive verb with introductory *it* subject can also be used to construct appropriate criticisms of other researchers. In the following example, there is indeterminacy in *it can be argued*, which could refer not only to the writer, but also to members of the discipline in general. The modal form *can* further reduces the effect of the criticism, since it casts doubt on whether the counter-argument is being made at all. By choosing this pattern, then, the writer mitigates the potentially face-threatening effect of arguing against earlier researchers.

(29)   Ling and Anderson (1992) comment that non-random particle distributions
         are to be expected in view of the enhanced reduction in the interfacial
         energy of the system. However since non-random particle distributions lead
         to smaller pinned grain sizes **it can be argued that** they have precisely the
         opposite effect. (Materials 7)

Although it is possible to find criticisms of other researchers in which the writer reveals their identity more clearly, examples seem rather more limited. Even in the politics corpus, with its higher writer visibility, there is only one writer who expresses opposition to other researchers using the pattern that reveals identity most fully:

(30)   I think recent commentators have underplayed the amount of antagonism and aggression present in Hegel's view of international relations. **I also think that** they have underestimated the extent of inequality between different nations in Hegel's philosophy. (Politics 6)

It is interesting to note that even in this highly critical example, the writer neither names nor gives specific references for the scholars attacked and this again diminishes the face-threatening potential of the criticism. Thus, although the examples discussed in this section are clearly critical, the negative evaluation of others' research is carried out with caution and sensitivity to the views of other community members. Given the position of the thesis writer as a novice in the discipline, the use of this low level of visibility may be particularly appropriate.

Conclusion

In this paper I have argued that the use of low writer visibility may not simply reflect a student's unwillingness to construct an authoritative identity. Rather I hope to have shown that obscuring identity may be appropriate for the performance of certain rhetorical functions, for example evaluation of the writer's own or others' research. This does not mean, of course, that low writer visibility is always appropriate. Thus we have seen that where individual credit is to be claimed, the writer chooses a higher level of visibility and it is here that disciplinary characteristics come particularly into play, with the writer's identity more clearly revealed in the politics than the materials corpus.

Although this study draws on data from a limited number of writers and it is possible that individual differences may exert an effect, my central concern here has been to provide a qualitative account of aspects of identity construction. What this research clearly indicates is that the achievement of an appropriate academic identity, whether for expert or novice, is an extremely complex task, which involves taking account of factors such as disciplinary practices, research purposes and professional status. It requires the writer to find a balance between modesty and authority, between deference to the discipline and the assertion of individuality. One of the ways in which writers may achieve this is through the use of grammar patterns that reveal or obscure their identity.

References

Becher, T. and Trowler, P. (2001) *Academic Tribes and Territories*. (Second edition) Buckingham: The Society for Research into Higher Education and Open University Press.

Belcher, D. (1994) The apprenticeship approach to advanced academic literacy: graduate students and their mentors. *English for Specific Purposes* 13(1): 23–34.

Berkenkotter, C., Huckin, T. and Ackerman, J. (1988) Conventions, conversations, and the writer: case study of a student in a rhetoric PhD program. *Research in the Teaching of English* 22(1): 9–44.

Biber, D., Johansson, S., Leech, G., Conrad, S. and Finegan, E. (1999) *Longman Grammar of Spoken and Written English*. Harlow: Pearson Education.

Cadman, K. (1997) Thesis writing for international students: a question of identity? *English for Specific Purposes* 16(1): 3–14.

Casanave, C. P. (1995) Local interactions: constructing contexts for composing in a graduate sociology program. In D. Belcher and G. Braine (eds) *Academic Writing in a Second Language*: *essays on research and pedagogy* 84–109. Norwood, NJ: Ablex.

Casanave, C. P. (2002) *Writing Games*: *multicultural case studies of academic literacy practices in higher education*. Mahwah, NJ: Erlbaum.

Charles, M. (2000) The role of an introductory 'it' pattern in constructing an appropriate academic persona. In P. Thompson (ed.) *Patterns and Perspectives*: *insights into EAP writing practice* 45–59. Reading: University of Reading.

Charles, M. (2004) *The Construction of Stance*: *a corpus-based investigation of two contrasting disciplines*. Unpublished PhD thesis, University of Birmingham.

Charles, M. (2006) The construction of stance in reporting clauses: a cross-disciplinary study of theses. *Applied Linguistics* 27(3): 492–518.

Davies, F. (1988) Reading between the lines: thematic choice as a device for presenting writer viewpoint in academic discourse. *The ESPecialist*. 9(1/2): 173–200.

Dong, Y. R. (1996) Learning how to use citations for knowledge transformation: non-native doctoral students' dissertation writing in science. *Research in the Teaching of English* 30(4): 428–57.

Dudley-Evans, T. (1991) Socialisation into the academic community: linguistic and stylistic expectations of a PhD thesis as revealed by supervisor comments. In P. Adams, B. Heaton and P. Howarth (eds) *Socio-cultural Issues in EAP* 41–51. London: Macmillan.

Francis, G. (1993) A corpus-driven approach to grammar. In M. Baker, G. Francis and E. Tognini-Bognelli (eds) *Text and Technology*: *in honour of John Sinclair* 137–56. Amsterdam: Benjamins.

Gosden, H. (1993) Discourse functions of subject in scientific research articles. *Applied Linguistics* 14(1): 56–75.

Groom, N. (2005) Pattern and meaning across genres and disciplines: an exploratory study. *Journal of English for Academic Purposes* 4(3): 257–77.

Harwood, N. (2005) 'We do not seem to have a theory ... the theory I present here attempts to fill this gap': inclusive and exclusive pronouns in academic writing. *Applied Linguistics* 26(3): 343–75.

Hewings, M. and Hewings, A. (2002) 'It is interesting to note that ... ': a comparative study of anticipatory 'it' in student and published writing. *English for Specific Purposes* 21(4): 367–83.

Hunston, S. and Francis, G. (1999) *Pattern Grammar*. Amsterdam: Benjamins.

Hyland, K. (1999) Disciplinary discourses: writer stance in research articles. In C. N. Candlin and K. Hyland (eds) *Writing: texts, processes and practices* 99–121. London: Longman.

Hyland, K. (2000) *Disciplinary Discourses: social interactions in academic writing*. Harlow: Longman.

Hyland, K. (2002) Authority and invisibility: authorial identity in academic writing. *Journal of Pragmatics* 34: 1091–112.

Hyland, K. and Tse, P. (2005) Hooking the reader: a corpus study of evaluative 'that' in abstracts. *English for Specific Purposes* 24: 123–39.

Ivanič, R. (1998) *Writing and Identity*. Amsterdam: Benjamins.

Myers, G. (1989) The pragmatics of politeness in scientific articles. *Applied Linguistics* 10(1): 1–35.

Petch-Tyson, S. (1998) Writer/reader visibility in EFL written discourse. In S. Granger (ed.) *Learner English on Computer* 107–18. London: Addison Wesley Longman.

Prior, P. (1995) Tracing authoritative and internally persuasive discourses: a case study of response, revision, and disciplinary enculturation. *Research in the Teaching of English*. 29(3): 288–325.

Scott, M. (1999) WordSmith Tools. (Version 3.0) Oxford: Oxford University Press.

Swales, J. M. (1990) *Genre Analysis*. Cambridge: Cambridge University Press.

Tang, R. and John, S. (1999) The 'I' in identity: exploring writer identity in student academic writing through the first person pronoun. *English for Specific Purposes* 18: S23–S49.

10   Face in L2 argumentative discourse: psycholinguistic constraints on the construction of identity

Doris Dippold

Introduction

'Face' is a fascinating metaphor. Frequently invoked in research in pragmatics and all its subfields, made famous by Goffman (1967), reinterpreted by Brown and Levinson (1978, 1987) in their theory of politeness, and subject of much debate and criticism (Chen, 2001; Blum-Kulka, 1987; Meier, 1995; Bargiela-Chiappini, 2003; Mao, 1994; Spencer-Oatey and Jang, 2003; Spencer-Oatey, 2000) face stands, as I will argue, for a speaker's desire to construct and protect both their own and their interlocutor's identity. In this paper, I will first introduce my particular account of face, arguing that Goffman's writings can be read as a theory of identity. Using data from a current study of undergraduate students of German, I will then show how second-language (L2) learners of German do facework in argumentative discourse and explore the impact the psycholinguistic processing implicit in this facework has on their performance. Finally, I contextualise those findings in the wider current discussions in both interlanguage pragmatics and second language acquisition, centring on learner identities, norms and targets of linguistic development.

Identity

The number and variety of approaches to and definitions of identity is manifold and a comprehensive treatment would go beyond the scope of this paper. My aim here is to describe identity using Goffman's face theory. According to Goffman, face is:

> the positive social value a person effectively claims for himself by the line others assume he has taken during a particular contact. Face is an image of self delineated in terms of approved social attributes. (Goffman, 1967: 5).

In other words, face is the self-image a speaker is constructing; it is how he or she wants to be seen by others. According to Goffman, a line is:

a pattern of verbal and nonverbal acts by which he [the speaker] expresses his view of the situation and through this his evaluation of the participants, especially himself. (Goffman, 1967: 5)

He later explains that 'the line taken by each participant is usually allowed to prevail, and each participant is allowed to carry off the role he appears to have chosen for himself' (1967: 11). Hence, a line is the propositional content of what the speaker says, feeding into the strategic goals he or she pursues. It also reflects what the speaker thinks of the other participants and of himself or herself, going back to the concept of face as self-image.

Furthermore, Goffman suggests that lines are an expression of the role a speaker has chosen to project. Therefore, the term 'role' is a concept very close to the aforementioned self-image, and both terms basically stand for a speaker's desire to show who they are and where they stand as a social person in relation to certain issues, thus constituting speaker identity. This relationship is summarised in Figure 1:

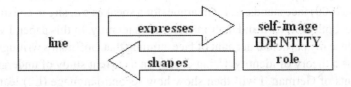

Figure 10.1: Line – role – identity

My interpretation of Goffman's approach to face is one rooted in the individual, in contrast to recent interactional approaches, which have interpreted face as a 'dyadic phenomenon' and the 'emergent outcome of communication' (Arundale, 2005: 9). Although face is interactional to the degree that protecting another person's face will at the same time also protect ones' own face, individual speakers retain agency for the kind of self-image they want to construct. Recent research on face also acknowledges the identity aspect of face. In her framework for 'rapport management', Spencer-Oatey (2000) suggests that face is made up of two components:

i)   *quality face* which is the 'fundamental desire for people to evaluate us positively in terms of our personal qualities, e.g. our competence, abilities, appearance';

ii) *identity face*, the 'fundamental desire for people to acknowledge and uphold our social identities as roles' (Spencer-Oatey, 2000: 215).

My data, and the discussion below, show that both quality face and identity face play a role in spoken learner discourse.

Research questions

The research reported here is work in progress and part of a larger research project, which focuses mainly on the identification of stages of pragmatic development and the factors which influence them. This article addresses the following research questions:

- What strategies do L2 learners of German at different proficiency levels use to do facework in spoken argumentative discourse?
- To what extent are learners' facework strategies in the L2 similar to or different from native-speakers' behaviours in the target language?
- What reasons can be suggested for the developmental patterns as well as those similarities and differences?

These questions will be answered by considering both qualitative and quantitative evidence, focusing on markers of epistemic modality and preference organisation.

Data

The data used for this project are from two major sources:

1. Elicitation tasks: transcriptions of argumentative conversation tasks in which subjects were asked to i) discuss different solutions to problems affecting students (e.g. binge-drinking); ii) prioritise different measures to deal with those problems, and iii) try to come up with a compromise.
2. Stimulated recall: transcriptions of retrospective interviews, conducted with some of the learner dyads after their conversations.

Subjects

The learner subjects were learners of German at a large UK university, most of whom studied German as part of their degree, and some of whom were enrolled in German classes as an optional unit. Most of the learner subjects were native speakers of English. Data were collected from learners at three levels of proficiency: lower-intermediate level (first-year university students), upper-intermediate level (second-year students) and advanced level (final-year students).[1] The native-speaker subjects were recruited from the student population at the same university. The German informants were either Socrates/Erasmus students or postgraduate students working for a Masters or PhD degree. The English informants were undergraduate and postgraduate students. Some of them were also enrolled in the German programme and took part in the data collection for learners as well as for native speakers.

Procedures

Six different tasks were designed for this study, the topics of which were related to student life (university admission criteria, binge-drinking, obesity, tips for first-year students of German, extra-curricular activities for students of German, tuition fees). Each dyad was allowed to choose their task for themselves. Each member of the dyad was then given a task instruction card with the discussion question (e.g. What should the University of X do to fight binge-drinking in the student population?), four different options to address the problem (e.g. close all campus bars), and a blank space to write down a fifth option of one's own choosing. Subjects first ranked the options individually and then discussed their ranking with their partner. After the conversations, retrospective interviews were conducted with some of the learner dyads.

	Conversation tasks	Retrospective interviews
German native-speakers	14	n/a
English native-speakers	12	n/a
Lower-intermediate L2 learners	10	6
Upper-intermediate L2 learners	9	6
Advanced L2 learners	9	4

Table 1: Summary of data collected in the different groups

Rationale for task choice

Argumentative discourse was initially chosen for data collection because it was felt that it would provide valuable insights into the workings of face in accordance with the lines speakers pursue during their argumentative discussions. By means of expressing their arguments (lines) speakers construct their identity, because they express what they think, who they are, where they stand as a social person in relation to the issue(s) discussed. In addition, the issue of face as positive social value also comes into play, as speakers cannot simply impose their views on their interlocutor in a blunt fashion. It is to this extent that face is actually interactional, as it would reflect badly on one's own face or identity if one tried to impose one's position too bluntly on an interlocutor. According to Goffman:

> the person will have two points of view – a defensive orientation toward saving his own face and a protective orientation toward saving the others' face. [...] In general one may expect these two perspectives to be taken at the same time. In trying to save the face of others, the person must choose a tack that will not lead to loss of his own; in trying to save his own face he must consider the loss of face that his action might entail for others. (1967: 14)

Hence, speakers are aware of how they could potentially impose on other speakers and their identities, while at the same time having the need to construct, project and protect their own face. They therefore need to use and develop mechanisms that allow them to balance both self-face and other-face, namely facework – 'actions taken by a person to make whatever he is doing consistent with face' (1967: 12).

Research findings

In this part of the paper, I will apply a psycholinguistic framework to explain how learners perform in the argumentative conversation tasks. In particular, I will draw on Bialystok's (1993) two-dimensional model of pragmatic development. According to this model, adults who embark on the task of learning a second language need to perform two different tasks. They have to form new symbolic representations, form-function matches which constitute a process of analysis. In addition they have to achieve processing control over those forms, i.e. they have to select and retrieve them as part of a process of control.

Markers of epistemic modality

Markers of epistemic modality signal a speaker's distance or lack of distance to the propositions expressed. In this analysis I shall only include downtoners, past conditionals and epistemic verbs used by the different speaker groups per 10000 characters of transcript.[2]

Those terms have been defined as follows:

- downtoner: sentence modifier used to moderate the impact an utterance is likely to have on the interlocutor by limiting speakers' commitment to the proposition, e.g. *vielleicht* (maybe);

- past conditional: use of the past conditional to distance the speaker from what is being said and decrease the face-threatening potential of the utterance, e.g. *das wäre* (you could);
- epistemic verb: verbs which describe the mental attitude of a speaker towards an issue, e.g. *ich denke* (I guess).

Table 1 shows the frequency of the above features per 10,000 characters in the transcripts for the different groups of speakers[3]:

	Epistemic verbs	Past conditional	Downtoner
German native-speakers	12.57	12.00	9.28
English native-speakers	25.53	29.45	13.58
Lower-intermediate L2 learners	29.71	8.68	4.34
Upper-intermediate L2 learners	22.86	17.33	16.12
Advanced L2 learners	21.56	13.50	16.14

Table 2: Modality markers per 10,000 characters

In terms of the question of how facework strategies develop in learner argumentative discourse it is interesting to see that their development is not necessarily linear from a very low frequency of use at lower-intermediate level to high frequency of use at advanced level. In fact, the frequency of use of epistemic verbs is at its highest at the lowest proficiency level (29.71/10,000), and remains far above native-speaker usage (12.57/10,000) at both upper-intermediate (22.86/10,000) and advanced level (21.56/10,000). In contrast, the number of downtoners is low at lower-intermediate level (4.34/10,000), but ahead of target level (9.28/10,000) at the upper-intermediate (16.12/10,000) and advanced levels (16.14/10,000). The frequency with which the past conditional is used is close to the target level (12/10,000) at the most advanced stage of development (13.5/10,000), falls short of it at lower-intermediate (8.69/10,000) but exceeds it at upper-intermediate level (17.33/10,000).

Given the fact that epistemic verbs, the past conditional and downtoners are the features that speakers most frequently used to limit their commitment to a proposition, the frequency count alone suggests that there are striking differences in the way with which speakers mitigate initiatives, agreement or disagreement in argumentative discourse. At lower-intermediate level, epistemic verbs are the dominant feature achieving a mitigating effect, as shown in Example (1). (Transcription conventions are given in Appendix A.)

Example (1) Stage 3.2 Binge

1 ASHLEY: =*ja (.) aber ich denke es nicht ein gute idee ist zum e: h*
=yeah (.) but I think it is not a good idea to eh: ban

alcohol aus allen allen campusbars verbannen!
alcohol from all campus bars!

2 BROOKE: *nein das ist em (.) ein bißchen streng ich denke*
no this is em (.) a bit strict I think

3 ASHLEY: *ja (.) ja ich denke dass alkohol ein grosses teil eh [des*
yes (.) yes I think that alcohol is a big part eh [of

studentleben ist
student life

4 BROOKE: [*ja (.) ja das*
[yes (.) yeah

stimmt (.) aber ich denke dass em (.) in eh campusbars em sie verkaufen
that's right (.) but I think that em (.) in eh campus bars em they sell

alkohol wenn jemand em schon zu viel getrunken hat=
alcohol when somebody em has already drunk too much=

5 ASHLEY: =[*ja*
=[yeah

6 BROOKE: [*ich glaube und dann ich denke dass das nicht gut ist*
[I believe and then I think that this is not good

Example (1) illustrates the quantitative trends mentioned above. Epistemic verbs are used by both speakers, both in initial actions – such as Ashley's initiative condemning a total ban of alcohol from all campus bars (Turn 1) – and in subsequent actions like Brooke's disagreement with this suggestion after initial agreement (Turn 4). There are no downtoners and no past conditional forms at all in this example.

At the higher levels, both initial and subsequent actions are mitigated more frequently by both past conditional forms and/or downtoners. Example (2) is from upper-intermediate level (underline is used to emphasise the features under discussion):

Example (2) Stage 5.6 Binge

1 EMILY: <u>*ich würde*</u> (.) *erschreckende posters machen* (.) *mit*
<u>I would</u> (.) produce scary posters (.) with

> *die em: auswirkungen em die passieren kann können wenn*
> the em: effects em that can can happen if

> *man zuviel trinkt em* (.) *und* <u>*ich glaube*</u> *auch dass* (.) *wie*
> one drinks too much em (.) and <u>I believe</u> also that (.) how

> *sie haben gesagt dass campusbars eh* <u>*sollten*</u> *die getränke*
> you said that campus bars eh <u>should</u> make drinks

> *teurer machen*?
> more expensive?

2 CATHERINE: *ja* (.) *weil wenn es sehr billig ist man kann*
yes (.) because if it is very cheap one can

> *zum beispiel fünf oder sechs [getränke trinken=*
> for example drink five or six [drinks=

3 EMILY: [*ja* (.) *ja*
                                     [yes (.) yes

4 CATHERINE: =*aber wenn wenn sie em teurer* <u>*würden*</u>
=but if if they em <u>became</u> more

> *em* <u>*würde*</u> *man nur* <u>*vielleicht*</u> *zwei oder drei*
> expensive em <u>would</u> one only <u>maybe</u> two or three

In Example (2), Emily mitigates her initiative – starting an advertising campaign featuring the dangers of alcohol and making alcoholic drinks more expensive in campus bars – with two past conditionals and one epistemic verb (Turn 1). In her reply, Catherine also uses the past conditional twice to present the proposition as purely hypothetical. Furthermore, the downtoner *vielleicht* also achieves a mitigating effect (Turn 4). These trends can be explained in a number of ways. First of all, House (1996) classifies epistemic verbs as minus committers which limit a speaker's commitment to a proposition.[4] Hence, the epistemic verbs fulfil a mitigating function just as downtoners do. Secondly and probably more importantly, epistemic verbs are frequently taught in textbooks as prototypical devices for the expression of opinion. They are, using Wray's (1999) term, formulaic sequences, i.e. sequences that are 'stored and retrieved whole from memory at the time of use, rather than being subject to generation or analysis by the language grammar' (1999: 214). The data show clearly that epistemic verbs are islands of reliability for learners, in that they structure discourse and serve as springboards into a turn or sentence. They serve the purpose of gaining time and easing processing, contributing to increased fluency and morphosyntactical accuracy. In contrast, the use of downtoners and the past conditional requires more advanced grammatical knowledge and processing control for their formation and use within a turn.

Preference organisation

In argumentative discourse, disagreement is usually a dispreferred turn, except for very heated discussions (Kotthoff, 1993). Dispreferred turns are more complex, i.e. they are often hedged, for example through markers of epistemic modality. Often, dispreferred turns featuring disagreement with another speaker's turn also contain elements of agreement. Three different ways of achieving agreement can be distinguished in my data:

- partial agreement: some aspects of the interlocutors' opinion are accepted, e.g. '*ja ja ich weiß aber wir müssen eh die fettsucht bekämpfen aber ich denke …*' ('yes yes I know but we have to fight obesity but I think …');
- agreement formula: a formula that is frequently used to express agreement, e.g. '*ja (.) ja das stimmt (.) aber ich denke …*' ('yes (.) yes that's right (.) but I think …');
- token agreement: agreement element using small discourse particles or adjectives (such as in '*na gut aber*'), followed by disagreement, e.g. '*ja aber*', 'yeah but'.

Table 3 shows the quantitative distribution of the three features.

	Token agreement	Partial agreement	Agreement formulas	Total
German native-speakers	36 = 62%	17 = 29.5%	5 = 8.5%	58 = 100%
English native-speakers	9 = 30%	16 = 53.5%	5 = 16.5%	30 = 100%
Lower-intermediate L2 learners	10 = 59.0%	4 = 23.5%	3 = 17.5%	17 = 100%
Upper-intermediate L2 learners	8 = 44.5%	8 = 44.5%	2 = 11%	18 = 100%
Advanced L2 learners	12 = 41.5%	9 = 31%	8 = 26.5%	29 = 100%

Table 3: Token agreement vs. Partial agreement vs. Agreement formulas

These figures show that the native speakers of German in the study have a preference for token agreement over partial agreement and agreement formulas. Those observations are confirmed and can be explained through the qualitative evidence. However, the same preference for token agreement also applies to learners at the lowest level of proficiency who therefore come closest to target level in terms of the agreement element preceding disagreement. Example (3) is from the lower-intermediate level.

Example (3) Stage 3.6 Activities

1 JIM: *die erste punkte wöchentliche deutsche filme wir haben eh jetzt*
         the first point weekly German films we have eh now

         em und das ist gut aber (.) eh man kann (.) nur ein bißchen deutsch
         em and his is good but (.) eh one can (.) only learn a little german

         eh von einem film lernen (.) man man muss nach deutschland oder
         eh from a film (.) one one has to go to Germany or

         östrich oder die schweiz em fahren um die eh lange lernen Austria or
         Switzerland to the eh learn the language

2 WENDY: *ja aber em es ist gut eh deutsch zu hören em und eh (.) man*
         yeah but em it is good eh to hear German and eh (.) one

         fühl eh fühlt gut man fühlt sich gut em wenn em wenn die anderen
         feels eh feels good one feels good when em one can

         verstehen kann?
         understand the others?

In this example, Wendy contradicts Jim's opinion that one cannot learn much from foreign-language films by saying that one feels good if one understands the language in the movie. Her disagreement features no marker of epistemic modality, but it is preceded by the token agreement '*ja aber*' ('yeah but', Turn 2). However, the fact that learners perform so close to L1 norms at the lowest proficiency level is not a case of conscious convergence to L1 norms of behaviour. Rather, psycholinguistic reasons may explain the quantitative and qualitative observations. Delaying disagreement further into a turn with partial agreement would require learners to construct this part of their turn from scratch, bringing with it many potential lexical and grammatical pitfalls. The foremost reason however is that '*ja aber*', the most frequently used token agreement, also has formulaic status. In the conversations recorded for this project, '*ja aber*' is not only used as a token agreement, but also as a turn starter, as in Example (4):

Example (4) Stage 3.1 Obese

1 ASHLEY: *ja aber em ich denke es ist fettsucht eine problem in der*
  yeah but em (.) I think it is obesity a problem at

2   *universität? ich weiß es nicht (.) aber ich denke dass kostenlose*
       university? I don't know (.) but I think that offering free

3   *sportkurse in allen teilen der universität em anbieten (.) ich denke=*
       sports classes in all parts of the university em (.) I think

4   *dass eine gute idee ist*
       that it is a good idea

This suggests that '*ja aber*' is easily accessible and easy to process, because there is less grammatical and lexical knowledge involved in its use compared to partial agreement and agreement formulas.

There are further trends that emerge from Table 2 supporting this interpretation. For example, agreement components within disagreement turns do become more complex at higher levels of proficiency, with more than 50 per cent constituting either partial agreement or agreement formula at the upper-intermediate and the advanced level. This suggests again that there is a broad relationship to overall proficiency, with students at higher levels of proficiency becoming more adept at using and retrieving more complex structures for performing facework in conversations.

Summary and discussion

Both the quantitative and the qualitative data suggest very strongly that both linguistic limitations and psycholinguistic processing constraints are at play in spoken argumentative L2 discourse, causing learners to opt for epistemic verbs as their preferred option of mitigation at the lowest level of proficiency and the use of increasingly complex structures at higher levels. In addition, learners use token agreement as their main form of agreement before disagreement at this level, while at the higher levels, disagreement is delayed further within the turn by more complex agreement components. Consequently, similarities and differences between the pragmatic behaviour of learners of German and native speakers of German cannot be attributed to pragmatic transfer or a conscious orientation towards or away from target norms; in fact, learners show little awareness of L2 pragmatic norms in the retrospective interviews. Rather, they must be explained by a combination of linguistic factors – not knowing certain structures, as might be the case with the past conditional – and limitations in processing control, resulting in lack of access to certain structures or inability to implement them in spoken discourse. Learners' comments in the retrospective interviews show that those problems and constraints have an impact on their perceived ability to construct identity and express how they feel about a problem. This applies in particular to learners from lower-intermediate and upper-intermediate levels. The following extract is from an interview at lower-intermediate level (5).

Example (5) Interview Stage 3.3

INTERVIEWER: Did you feel in any way uncomfortable with what you were asked to do – like arguing about a certain topic?

GOPAL: Not really.

JOHN: Not exactly uncomfortable with arguing. Only in as much as you are aware that you are a reasonably intelligent person but yet you are limited by your knowledge of stumbling halting incorrect German.

John perceives his performance to be severely restricted by his linguistic proficiency level. What is more, he also feels that he might not be able to come across as the person he would like to be seen as – namely 'reasonably intelligent', i.e. somebody who has an opinion, who has something to say. Only at a higher developmental level do learners seem to be able to liberate themselves from this identity and become able to construct themselves as competent speakers who can adequately represent and construct themselves despite some continuing limitations and problems, as the following extract from an interview at advanced level shows (6).

Example (6) Interview Stage 7.6

JENNY: Because we both say what we want to say even if it doesn't sound brilliant German. We can say everything that we – we have got a point obviously.

This change in perception is an effect of learners' generally higher linguistic proficiency as well as the fact that they have actually spent a year abroad in the target language community. What exact influence the year abroad has had is a question I cannot answer with the data available to me. Beyond those reasons, there is a further possible explanation for those patterns, and face does again play a role. In his definition of the term line – quoted earlier – Goffman suggests speakers have a choice of different roles which they can make relevant in discourse. Goffman also introduced the term 'footing', which 'implies a change in the alignment we take up to ourselves and the others present as expressed in the way we manage the production or reception of an utterance' (Goffman, 1981: 28). This means that a speaker can shift between different roles or self-images that he or she brings to the forefront in conversation, for example, a woman might speak in her private role as mother, but also her professional role as company executive. In the argumentative conversations recorded for this research, speakers not only acted within their conversational roles. Rather, they acted within their role as language learners or language students. Example (7) is an excerpt from a retrospective interview with learners from upper-intermediate level.

Example (7) Interview Stage 5.3

1 ((Interviewer stops recording after 'aber'))

2 INTERVIEWER: How did you decide to say what you said? What went
        through your mind?

3 ROBERTA: My stance (?) was that only the ones over the age of twenty
        one should ( ) but then I didn't know how to say it in German because I
        was thinking when do I have to put the verb and then the modal verb and
        then in the end I didn't know how to say it.

Roberta's comment illustrates a general trend observed in the interviews, again in particular at the two lowest levels. I replayed their conversations to my subjects in order to elicit comments about their thoughts and decision-making processes with regards to message content and form for the purpose of facework related to learners' conversational identities. However, learners' comments – like Roberta's – primarily relate to planning with regards to morphosyntactic aspects of language use. The comments suggest strongly that getting their grammar and their vocabulary right was an ongoing concern for a majority of the learners, and that they, in fact, were predominantly concerned with constructing a 'good L2 speaker' identity by aiming for morphosyntactical accuracy. They wanted to construct and present themselves as proficient speakers of the L2 who had successfully integrated what they had learned in class, and opting for structures that are easily accessible, such as token agreement and epistemic verbs, was a means to that end.

In terms of Spencer-Oatey's (2000) two interrelated aspects of face, this means that the L2 learners in this research oriented primarily to their quality face, aiming for positive evaluation in terms of their linguistic competence. At the same time, identity face is also attended to, as learners do try with whatever means they can to construct and protect their conversational roles, but linguistic problems and psycholinguistic processing constraints limit the amount and quality of attention identity face can be given.

Implications for research in interlanguage pragmatics

These observations have several implications for research in second-language acquisition (SLA) in general and interlanguage pragmatics in particular. In the past, interlanguage pragmatics has often evaluated non-convergence to the L2 'norm' or 'standard' as 'pragmatic failure' (Thomas, 1983). Looking back, House and Kasper (2000) criticise their own work of the early 1980s:

> We compared the interlanguage (IL) conversations of German non-native speakers of English to parallel conversations by native speakers (NS) of German, representing the learners' native language (L1), and to conversations by NS of British English, the learners' foreign language (L2). […] The observed IL-L2 differences were […] classified as 'over'- and 'under-use', and labeled 'pragmatic errors, 'deficiencies', and the like […].

> Looking back to our work after a passage of two decades of SLA research, we are amazed at the naivety of the projects' underlying assumptions. Clearly, the NNS did differ from the NS of both German and English in their politeness style and in their conversational organisation and management. But were we justified to regard these differences as deficits? (House and Kasper, 2000: 113)

My data show that labelling L2 pragmatic performance that is different to an L2 target as deficient is indeed not useful. Learners at low levels cannot be said to show no concern for face. Learners are indeed doing facework, but their performance is limited by linguistic limitations and psycholinguistic processing constraints, so that many of their cognitive resources are dedicated to constructing face associated with other identities, in particular their 'good L2 speaker identity' by way of emphasising fluency and morphosyntactical accuracy. These observations fit very well into the ongoing debate on concepts of non-native speaker (NNS), learner language and interlanguage (Firth and

Wagner, 1997). Firth and Wagner (1997) suggested that in SLA research, learners were often reduced to 'subjects', with only one of their social identities – that of learner – considered and inevitably sharply distinguished from native speakers. They also criticise the term interlanguage, through which, they claim, learners' performance is described as a predictable system in its own right, moving towards target performance. They suggest that instead:

> marked or deviant forms are not of necessity fossilisations of IL, nor can they on each and every occasion be accounted for by interference or a reduced L2 competence. Such forms may be deployed resourcefully and strategically to accomplish social and interactional ends – for example, to display empathy, or to accomplish mutual understanding. (Firth and Wagner, 1997: 293)

I cannot say for sure whether the deviations from native-speaker norms mentioned above – for example, the high frequency of epistemic verbs – are indeed conscious strategies. However, the retrospective interviews suggest that there is a rationale for them, as they are 'safe' strategies which can give learners time to plan their turns and therefore attend to morphosyntactical accuracy and the construction of the 'good L2 speaker' identity.

Conclusion

The research reported on in this paper found evidence that the degree to which L2 learners of German have developed processing control constrains their ability to do facework, to construct and protect their conversational identities in argumentative discourse. While this does certainly not have lasting implications in the context of those conversations recorded for research purposes, it might have more significance when more is at stake, as suggested by the frustration expressed in the retrospective reports by many learners. This research moves interlanguage pragmatics on from a focus on politeness, i.e. the use of language to ensure smooth social relations. Furthermore, it makes observations on an essentially social phenomenon – identity – within a cognitive framework. Consequently, it fills a gap in both the general SLA research and in interlanguage pragmatics research, asking how actual and perceived proficiency does actually affect learners' ability to construct their identity in spoken discourse.

Acknowledgements

I would like to thank Professor Ros Mitchell (University of Southampton) and the reviewers for their very helpful comments on earlier drafts of this paper.

178 *Language, Culture and Identity in Applied Linguistics*

Notes

1   The lower-intermediate level and the upper-intermediate level also include two conversations each by learners whose mother tongue was not English. Most of the final-year students had spent a year abroad in a German-speaking country.

2   Characters were chosen as a measure of reference because it was felt that they could provide the best measure of the length of the conversations.

3   In this paper, discuss group data only are discussed. Individual variation exists but it is beyond the scope of this paper to discuss it further.

4   According to Aijmer (1997) however, epistemic verbs can, in some cases, achieve the opposite of a mitigating or downtoning effect, being an expression of certainty and higher commitment.

References

Aijmer, K. (1997) I think – an English Modal Particle. In T. Swan and O. Westvik (eds) *Modality in Germanic languages: historical and comparative perspectives* 1– 47. Berlin: Mouton de Gruyter.

Arundale, R. (2005) Face as relational and interactional: alternative bases for research on face, facework and politeness. Ninth International Pragmatics Association Conference. Riva del Garda, Italy.

Bargiela-Chiappini, F. (2003) Face and politeness: new (insights) for old (concepts). *Journal of Pragmatics* 33(9): 1453–69.

Bialystok, E. (1993) Symbolic representation and attentional control. In G. Kasper and S. Blum-Kulka (eds) *Interlanguage Pragmatics* 43–58. New York: Oxford University Press.

Blum-Kulka, S. (1987) Indirectness and politeness in requests: same or different. *Journal of Pragmatics* 11(1): 131–46.

Brown, P. and Levinson, S. (1978) Politeness: some universals in language usage. In E. Goody (ed.) *Questions and Politeness*. Cambridge: Cambridge University Press.

Brown, P. and Levinson, S. (1987) *Politeness: some universals in language usage*. Cambridge: Cambridge University Press.

Chen, R. (2001) Self-politeness: a proposal. *Journal of Pragmatics* 33(1): 87–106.

Firth, A. and Wagner, J. (1997) On discourse, communication, and (some) fundamental concepts in SLA research. *Modern Language Journal* 81(3): 286–300.

Goffman, E. (1967) *Interaction Ritual: essays on face-to-face behaviour*. Garden City: Anchor Books.

Goffman, E. (1981) *Forms of Talk*. Philadelphia: University of Pennsylvania Press.

House, J. (1996) Contrastive discourse analysis and misunderstanding: the case of German and English. In M. Hellinger and U. Ammon (eds) *Contrastive Sociolinguistics* 345–84. Berlin: Mouton de Gruyter.

House, J. and Kasper, G. (2000) How to remain a non-native speaker. In C. Riemer (ed.) *Kognitive Aspekte des Lehrens und Lernens von Fremdsprachen* 101–18. Tübingen: Günther Narr Verlag.

Kotthoff, H. (1993) Disagreement and concession in disputes: on the context sensitivity of preference structures. *Language in Society* 22: 193–216.

Mao, L. (1994) Beyond politeness theory: 'face' revisited and renewed. *Journal of Pragmatics* 21(5): 451–86.

Meier, A. (1995) Passages of politeness. *Journal of Pragmatics* 24(4): 381–92.

Spencer-Oatey, H. (2000) Rapport management: a framework for analysis. In H. Spencer-Oatey (ed.) *Culturally Speaking*: *managing rapport through talk across cultures* 11–45. London: Continuum.

Spencer-Oatey, H. and Jang, W. (2003) Explaining cross-cultural pragmatic findings: moving from politeness maxims to Sociopragmatic Interactional Principles (SIPs). *Journal of Pragmatics* 35(10–11): 1633–50.

Thomas, J. (1983) Cross-cultural pragmatic failure. *Applied Linguistics* 4: 91–112.

Wray, A. (1999) Formulaic language in learners and native speakers. *Language Teaching* 32: 213–31.

Appendix A: Transcript conventions for conversation tasks

(.)	pause
em, eh	hesitation markers
?	rising intonation
!	very animated tone
(word)	utterance not clearly intelligible; transcriber's best guess
:	elongation of an utterance
((comment))	some sound or feature of the talk that cannot be very easily transcribed, e.g. laughing, coughing
[	simultaneous/overlapping utterances
( )	utterance unintelligible
=	latching or continuation of turn in new line after =

11 The effects of processing instruction and meaning output-based instruction on the acquisition of the Italian subjunctive of doubt and opinion

Alessandro Benati

Introduction
Input processing and processing instruction

Processing instruction (henceforth PI) is an instructional intervention used, as VanPatten (2002) argues, to ensure that a learner's focal attention during input processing is directed toward the relevant grammatical feature and not elsewhere in the sentence. Learners typically process only a portion of the input and this is due to processing limitations as not all the input to which learners are exposed is attended to during their exposure to it. Learners filter input through their internal processors. The question is: how do learners initially perceive and process linguistic data in the language they hear? Input processing is concerned with interpretation strategies by which learners derive intake from input. The input processing capacity of L2 learners is limited as only certain features will receive attention at any given time during the processing of a sentence. VanPatten has specifically proposed a set of principles concerning what learners attend to in the input:

P1. learners process input for meaning before they process for form (The Primacy of Meaning Principle);

P2. learners tend to process the first noun or pronoun they encounter in a sentence as the subject or agent (The First Noun Principle). (VanPatten, 2004: 14)

For the present study the first principle (P1.) together with two of its corollaries is relevant:

a) learners prefer processing lexical items to grammatical items for semantic information (The Lexical Preference Principle);

b) learners tend to process items in sentence initial position before those in final position and those in medial position (The Sentence Location Principle). (VanPatten 2004a: 14)

PI is a type of focus on form which draws on the principles of a particular input processing model (VanPatten, 1996: 2004a). This model refers to 'the initial process by which learners connect grammatical forms with their meanings' (see VanPatten 2004a: 5).

VanPatten (2004a) emphasises the primary role of input in second language acquisition assigning a less fundamental role to output. In his model of second language acquisition he suggests that:

> input provides the data, input processing makes (certain) data available for acquisition, other internal mechanisms accommodate data into the system (often triggering some kind of restructuring or a change of internally generated hypotheses), and output helps learners to become communicators and, again, may help them become better processors of input. (VanPatten, 2002: 760)

In VanPatten's view (1996) the main objective of PI is to help learners to circumvent the strategies used by them to derive intake data by making them rely exclusively on form and structure to derive meaning from input. In order to achieve this goal PI must provide learners with the following: 1) explicit information about the target form they are learning and the particular processing strategy which may affect the way they process that target form during comprehension; 2) a type of comprehension practice (structured input activities) which should force learners to process the target form in the input and to make form-meaning connections. Input refers to the fact that during the activities learners do not produce the target grammatical form, but they are engaged in actively processing input sentences.

VanPatten (1996) claimed that PI provides a more effective practice (through structured input practice) than any other form of output-based practice as it equips learners with the tools to convert input into intake. As Wong puts it: PI 'pushes learners to abandon their inefficient processing strategies for more optimal ones so that better form-meaning connections are made' Wong (2004: 35).

In contrast to traditional instruction (henceforth TI) the purpose of PI is to change the way learners attend and process input considering that acquisition is an input dependent process which takes place when learners are exposed to meaning-bearing input. TI is still a common approach to grammar instruction and consists of a paradigmatic explanation of a form or structure in a target language which is followed by mechanical drills in which learner output is manipulated and the instruction is divorced from meaning or communication.

Research evidence on the effects of processing instruction vs. meaning output-based instruction [2]

PI has been contrasted to TI in a number of studies which could be defined as conceptual replications of the first study conducted by VanPatten and Cadierno (1993) on the effects of PI on the acquisition of word order and object pronouns in Spanish with the 'The First Noun Principle' as the processing problem. Overall the findings of all the studies contrasting PI and TI (see Lee, 2004; and Benati et al., 2005 for a full review) have provided evidence for the superiority of PI over TI in different languages, on learning different linguistic features and with a focus on different processing problems.

Farley (2001a) contrasted the effects of PI and meaning output-based instruction (henceforth MOI) on the acquisition of the Spanish subjunctive. The material for the PI treatment and the MOI treatment was developed following the guidelines for structured input activities and structured output activities provided by Lee and VanPatten (1995) and VanPatten and Sanz (1995). Unlike TI, MOI contained no mechanical drills and the activities were all meaning-based. Both the PI and the MOI groups were assessed following a pre-test/post-test design which included interpretation and production tasks. Farley's results differed from the previous studies comparing PI and TI. Both the PI and MOI groups made equal and significant improvements on both the interpretation and the production tests. Farley (2001a) attributed the equal performance of the two treatments to one main factor. The MOI treatment is different from TI as it does not contain mechanical drills practice and its communicative and interactive nature might have resulted in incidental input. Farley argued that the MOI treatment used in his study was not a pure output treatment.

> MOI is not an instruction type that is entirely input free; when learners responded during the follow-up phase of each activity their utterances served as incidental input for their classmates: the incidentally focused input made the subjunctive more salient than it would be with raw, unfocused input. (Farley, 2001a: 76)

The incidental input learners received during output practice and not the output practice itself, was considered to be responsible for learners' performance. It must also be noticed that in an identical study (same structure, design and procedure) conducted by Farley (2001b) the results showed that although the

PI and MOI groups made similar gains from a pre-test to a post-test, the PI gains were maintained in a delayed post-test whereas the effects of the MOI treatment declined.

Benati (2005) conducted an experiment investigating the effects of PI, TI and MOI on the acquisition of English Past Simple Tense. The subjects involved in that study were Chinese and Greek school-age learners of English residing in their respective countries. The participants in both schools were divided into three groups. The first group received PI; the second group TI; and the third group MOI. One interpretation and one production measure were used in a pre- and post-test design (immediate effect only). The results showed that PI had positive effects on the processing and acquisition of the target feature. In this study the PI group performed better than the TI and MOI groups in the interpretation task and the three groups made equal gains in the production task.

Motivations for this study

The results of the studies briefly reviewed in the previous section have demonstrated that when PI is compared to TI superior effects for PI are obtained. However, when PI is contrasted to MOI (that is a more meaning-oriented, output-based approach to grammar instruction), conflicting results have been found. On one hand, one set of results (Farley, 2001a, 2001b) showed that MOI could have an equal effect on interpretation and production tasks when compared with PI. On the other hand, the study conducted by Benati (2005) contrasting PI and MOI has yielded overall superior effects for PI. These conflicting results generate the two questions in this study:

1. Why do the PI and MOI groups in Farley's (2001a, 2001b) studies perform similarly in the interpretation and production tasks and why do the findings from these studies differ from Benati's study (2005)?
2. Is it the particular structure (subjunctive) investigated in Farley's studies which causes the results to be different than those obtained by Benati?

As far as the first question is concerned, the positive effects of the MOI treatment in Farley's studies (2001a, 2001b) could be attributed to the nature of the MOI activities. MOI activities did not contain any mechanical or traditional practice. In Farley's studies MOI activities pushed learners to express opinions and beliefs by producing a subjunctive in utterance-initial position. As in any output-based instruction involving oral responses, when learners are giving a correct answer to a particular activity item, their answer might (as discussed above) serve as incidental input for other participants in the treatment. The structure of the incidental input provided by MOI does mirror the type of structure input practice contained in the PI treatment. Therefore, the MOI treatment might have been more similar than the PI treatment than initially planned.

As far as the second question is concerned, the difference between Farley's studies (2001a, 2001b) and Benati's study (2005) might be found in the nature of the target item. Unlike tenses where the difference between present and past is relatively clear, mood is not a clear and transparent feature. In the case of the subjunctive this feature is triggered by a variety of semantic conditions and there is no mechanical one to one correspondence.

In order to shed some light on the questions raised in this section this study explores whether or not we are bound to obtain similar or different results if we contrast the effects of PI to MOI in the acquisition of subjunctive in another romance language. In addition, the possible role of incidental input in the MOI activities is addressed. A comparison of the effects of input-free MOI, delivered via isolated computer terminals, with the effects of PI, delivered via the same medium might offer a better picture of which variables within MOI promote acquisition of subjunctive.

Research questions

The aim of the present study is to compare the effects of two instructional treatments (PI and MOI) delivered via isolated computer terminals in the acquisition of Italian subjunctive of doubt. Two specific questions were formulated:

Q1: What are the effects of PI and MOI on the acquisition of Italian subjunctive of doubt as measured on an interpretation task at sentence level?

Q2: What are the effects of PI and MOI on the acquisition of Italian subjunctive of doubt as measured on a production task at sentence level?

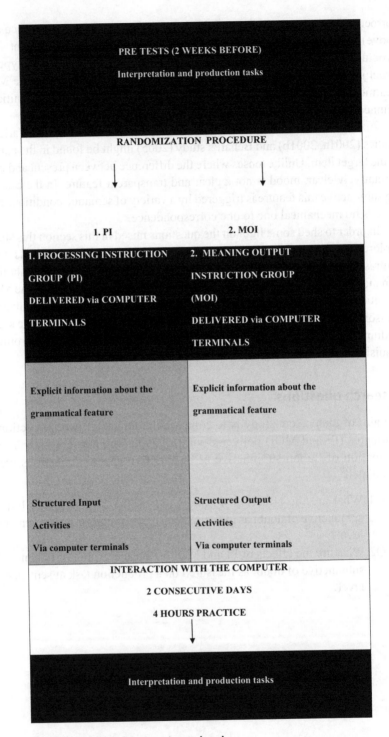

Figure 1: Overview of the experimental study

Method and procedure

Participants and procedure

A comparative study was carried out among second-semester undergraduate students in a British university (University of Greenwich). The participants were enrolled in an intermediate course in Italian as part of their language degree. In the final data pool English native-speaker students (they were all aged between 20 and 21 years, with males and females equally distributed across the two groups) were split into two groups using a randomisation procedure: PI group ($n = 14$); MOI group ($n = 14$). The initial plan was to match the two groups for various characteristics (GCSE results, sex, age and so forth) in order to enhance the comparability aspect of this study. However, it was found that the number of variables was too high for matching successfully two groups and a randomisation procedure was preferred. Despite the practical difficulty, the randomisation of sample groups obviates the need to consider individual variation and is an effective way to assure group comparability. A background questionnaire was used to collect information on the participants at the start of the study The original sample of 39 subjects was reduced to 28 (final data pool) as they went through a series of filters before the two groups were randomised: subjects who might have had some previous experience of, or practice in the target language (in this case the linguistic feature under investigation) outside classroom instruction were taken out of the experiment. Two of the criteria established for subjects to be included in the data pool were:

i)   participants' learning was limited to classroom instruction;
ii) participants who had previous experience or linguistic knowledge of the target language were excluded from the study.

At the end, only the participants who had participated in all phases of the treatment were included in the final data collection. Two main considerations were taken into account when deciding to select the second-semester students:

i)   vocabulary familiarity and level of study;
ii) no exposure to the target grammatical feature prior to the experiment.

For the final study all the subjects were English speakers. The non-English students were excluded from this experiment as a different L1 could interfere with the result of experiment. The two groups interacted with a different computer lesson for two consecutive days for a total of four hours (two hours per day) of instruction and practice on the target feature. Each group was exposed to the material of the two instructional treatments via computer terminals. The instructional materials were balanced in every way. However, the type of practice the students received varied (i.e. input vs. output practice). To examine short-term effects of instruction a pre-test and post-test procedure was adopted (see Figure 1).

Target grammar feature: Italian subjunctive

The subjunctive was selected for a number of reasons. First, the subjunctive in Italian is a very similar grammatical feature in concept and structure to the subjunctive in Spanish, thus permitting comparability with the studies conducted by Farley (2001a, 2001b) Second, the processing principles involved in the processing of this particular feature are important. According to the 'Sentence Location Principle' learners tend to process items in a sentence initial position before those in final position and those in medial position. This processing strategy has been investigated in previous studies (Farley, 2001a, 2001b). In Italian the subjunctive is located in medial position where it is least likely to be processed. In the sentence *Non penso che parli bene italiano* (I do not believe he/she speaks Italian well) the subjunctive inflection (the *-i* of *parli*) is in the middle of the sentence and the Sentence Location Principle predicts that learners will overlook the subjunctive inflection because it is not located in a more salient position. Third, another principle that might affect the processing of the acquisition of the Italian subjunctive in nominal clauses after expression of doubt is the 'Lexical Preference Principle'. In a sentence like *Non penso che canti bene* (I doubt that he/she sings) the non-affirmative phrase *non penso* expresses doubt to the learner. Therefore there is no reason for the learner to attend to the subjunctive verb ending (*-i* in *canti*) because it simply re-communicates the non-affirmation already expressed by the lexical units in the main clause.

Instructional packs

Two instructional treatments were used in both experiments. The first group received the PI treatment; the second group the MOI treatment. The two sets of materials developed for this experiment were balanced in terms of activity types, use of visuals and vocabulary which consisted of high-frequency items. An equal amount of processing practice in PI and output practice in MOI was provided. The vocabulary used in the activities was also roughly the same across the groups. The two treatments received the same amount of explicit information regarding the target feature prior to practice (see Appendix A). The students were able to complete the activities in exactly the same way as they would do if completing the exercises with pen and paper. However, the delivery of MOI and PI via computer terminals (input-free treatment) should help determine whether incidental input could have been one of the factors responsible for the performance of the MOI group in Farley's studies (2001a, 2001b). The technology used to create these exercises was Macromedia Flash and Action Script programming language. Altogether there were 20 paper activities for the Italian subjunctive (10 for each instructional treatment) to be converted into online format. Most activities involved listening to a sound file, conjugating a verb by filling in a blank or ticking a box to give an opinion about a statement.

The packet of materials used for the PI treatment contained explicit information (including information about the processing principle) and structured input activities (an equal number of referential and affective activities). In the PI treatment, all the activities were developed in order to alter the two processing strategies described. The main clause was separated from the subordinate clause to take advantage of primacy effects that cause a form in an initial position to be processed more easily than a form in a medial position. In the referential activities because the subordinate clause was separated from the main clause, participants were not able to rely on the lexical item (subjunctive triggers) to determine that doubt was expressed (see Appendix B). Participants in this group were forced to attend to the subjunctive or indicative mood forms to determine whether or not doubt or opinion was expressed by selecting the corresponding trigger. As PI aims to force learners to process form to get meaning (in this case the subjunctive), no activities were developed where learners had to produce the target grammatical item. The activities in this instructional treatment were all communicative and meaningful and were constructed in an attempt to alter the processing problem addressed in this study. Only the third person subjunctives in nominal clauses after expression of doubt or opinion was presented and practised. Participants were exposed (they were only allowed to hear the sentence once) to structured input activities through computer terminals. In referential activities, participants were required to select the correct trigger or subordinate clause to complete each sentence. Implicit feedback was provided by the computer responding 'OK' or 'correct' if the user's response was correct. 'Wrong' was displayed on the screen if a participant chose an incorrect response. Learners were told whether they were right or wrong but no explanation as to why was given. This procedure is in line with the purpose of structured input activities which is to push learners to a different processing strategy and this can only happen if the participants receive information that an interpretation is incorrect.

The packet of materials used for the MOI treatment consisted of grammatical explanation (same as the PI group) and meaning-based output practice. No mechanical activities were included in the output practice. Students were required to produce the linguistic feature (Italian subjunctive) and were always engaged in output communicative practice. As stated by Lee and VanPatten (1995: 121) structured output activities have two main characteristics: i) 'they involve the exchange of previously unknown information'; and ii) 'they require learners to access a particular form or structure in order to express meaning' (see Appendix C).

Data collection instruments

A pre-test and post-test design was used (see Figure 1). Pre-tests were administered to the subjects a few weeks before the beginning of the instructional period. The pre-test was also used to eliminate subjects from the original pool (anyone who scored 60 per cent or better on the two assessment measures were not included in the final pool). Two versions of the tests were designed, one interpretation task and one written production task, in order to form a split block design. The interpretation task consisted of 20 sentences: ten distracter items in the Present Tense (Indicative mood) expressing certainty, and ten in the Subjunctive mood expressing doubt or opinion. The participants had to listen to the sentences and indicate (interpret) whether the sentence they heard was related to a past or present action. No repetition was provided so that the test would measure real-time comprehension. In the interpretation task the raw scores were calculated as follows: incorrect response = 0 point, correct response = 1 point. The written production task was developed and used to measure learner's ability to produce correct sentences using the subjunctive. The students were required to transform ten sentences using the subjunctive form. The same scoring procedure was used in this discrete item test (correct form = 1 point; incorrect form = 0 point). The production task was not a spontaneous task and allowed learners to monitor their responses and to provide their answers in writing.

Results

The t-test statistical analysis procedure was adopted to compare the means of the two groups.

Results from the interpretation task

The t-test conducted on the pre-test for the first experiment showed no significant differences in the instructional treatment means before instruction ($F(14) = .206$, $t = .654$). The means (see Table 1) indicates that only the PI group seems to significantly improve from pre-test to post-test. The MOI group improved slightly but the gains made were not statistically significant. A t-test measure was also used on the raw scores of the interpretation data. The statistical analysis revealed that there is a significant effect for Instruction ($F(14) = 6.132$, $t = .02$).

Variable	n	Pre-test		Post-test 1	
		Mean	SD	Mean	SD
PI	14	2.3571	.63332	8.1429	1.09945
MOI	14	3.1429	.66299	3.6429	.49725

Table 1: Means and standard deviation for Interpretation task pre-test and post-test

Results are shown graphically in Figure 2.

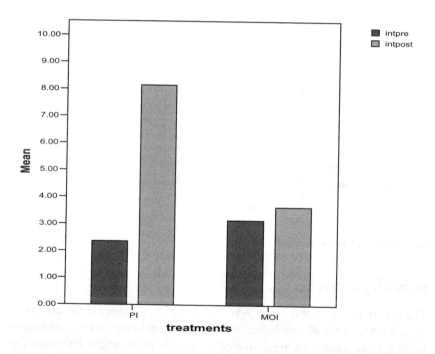

Figure 2: Bar plot for interpretation task

Results from the written production task

A t-test conducted on the pre-test showed no statistically significant difference between the groups (F 47) = .662, t = .423) before the beginning of the
instructional period. The means in Table 11.2 show that the groups improved
almost equally from the pre- to the post-test. A second t-test was used on the raw
scores of the written production task. The results from the statistical analysis
indicate that there was no significant main effect for Instruction ($F(14) = .170$,
$t = .683$). The findings from the statistical analysis suggest that the two groups
improved and made equal gains from the pre-test to the post-test. Results are
presented graphically in Figure 3.

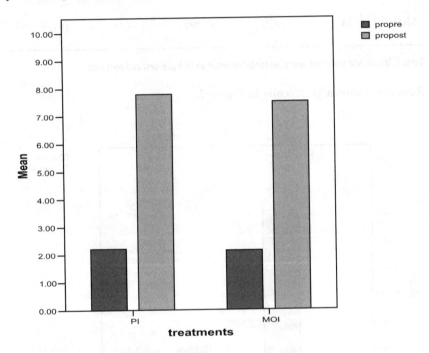

Figure 3: Bar plot for production task

Summary of results

The first question of this study was formulated to investigate the effects of
PI, and MOI on the interpretation of sentences containing the targeted feature
when the two treatments are delivered via computer terminals. The results of
the statistical analysis clearly showed that the PI made significant improvement
(from pre-test to post-test) on the interpretation task. The PI treatment delivered

via computer terminals was superior to the MOI treatment delivered by the same means in terms of helping learners to interpret utterances containing the subjunctive that expresses doubt and opinion. The findings of the interpretation sentence-level task support previous findings in PI research which indicated that PI is successful in altering learners default processing strategies (in this case the 'Sentence Location Principle' and the 'Lexical Preference Principle').

The second question of this study sought to investigate the effects of the two treatments delivered via computer terminals in the production of sentences containing the subjunctive expressing doubt and opinion. The results of the statistical analysis indicated that PI and MOI made an equal improvement (from pre-test to post-test) on the production task (sentence-level task). Even in this case the findings of the experiment support the main results of previous PI research which showed that the PI group made significant similar gains from the pre-test to the post-test compared with the TI and MOI groups in production tasks. The evidence obtained in this study on the production task suggests that the effects of PI not only have an impact on the way learners interpret sentences but also on the way learners produce sentences. PI has clearly altered the way learners processed input and this might have had an effect on their developing system and subsequently on what the subjects could access for production as the group receiving PI was not exposed to any output-based practice.

Discussion and conclusion

The overall findings of the present study support the results obtained by the majority of studies investigating the effects of PI, which show that PI is superior to output based instruction (MOI and TI). It is interesting to note that the results from the present study differ from Farley's research (2001a, 2001b) and support Benati's (2005) findings in indicating that PI is better than MOI. The results obtained in the present study confirm the consistency and effectiveness of PI in improving learners' performance in both interpretation and production tasks (sentence level).

In the attempt to understand the difference in the two sets of results contrasting PI and MOI, a possible explanation is the fact that in the present study both treatments were delivered through computer terminals. In the case of Farley's studies (2001a, 2001b), it was argued that in the MOI group, the incidental input to which learners were exposed (which occurs when there is a classroom focus on structured output), might have served as structured input and therefore explained the results. In the case of the present study, the MOI group received input free treatment and was compared to PI delivered with the same medium. The findings from this study have shown that structured input activities are the main component and the causative variable for the change in performance (see summary of the results investigating the effects of PI and its components in VanPatten, 2002; Benati, 2004a, 2004b; Benati and Lee, forthcoming). The MOI treatment which contained meaning-based activities was not successful at producing positive effects (altering the processing problem) on students' performance, as students, because of the use of computers in the delivery of this treatment, were not exposed to any incidental input. The results from the present study also suggest that PI may be a successful instructional intervention for any form or structure.

The results of the study presented in this paper make some contributions to the ongoing debate on the effects of PI when compared to MOI. The main outcome of this study has reaffirmed the positive effects of PI in altering learners' processing strategies and consequently its positive effects on learners' developing systems. The results clearly indicate that PI is a successful instructional treatment as it helps learners to make form-meaning connections which lead to language acquisition. The evidence collected in the present study has shown that PI is not only a better instructional treatment than traditional output practice, but also is superior to MOI. The MOI treatment is not successful in bringing about similar effects to those brought about by PI.

The results of this study support previous results that investigated the effects of PI versus output-based instruction and make a contribution to the view that in language teaching input practice should precede output practice. Research on PI has clearly indicated that this input-based approach (PI) offers better instructional benefits than output practice. The fact that the PI group performed better than the MOI group in the interpretation task clearly indicates that structured input activities are the causative factor in the improved performance of learners as both groups received the same amount and type of explicit information.

This study did not have a delayed post-test. This is a clear limitation in this study when comparing its results with Farley's research (2001a, 2001b) for example. In order to understand the long-term effects of the variables under investigation, a delayed post-test procedure should be considered. The findings from the present research may well have been different if delayed post-tests were included. Another limitation in the present study is the nature of the production task used: it lends itself to the use of conscious knowledge. A production test that includes time pressure (see Erlam, 2003) and does not allow students to monitor their responses might also have produced different results. The sample size of this experiment is relatively small (28 subjects), and would need to be replicated with larger populations before we can comment with more confidence on the general significance and relevance of the findings.

Despite the results obtained in the present study and in Benati's study (2005) that have shown that learners receiving PI improve their performance in both interpretation and production tasks, further research is needed in order to compare PI and MOI to ascertain whether MOI has any impact on how learners interpret other language features or different processing problems.

Acknowledgements

I would like to thank the editors for their priceless comments on a first draft of this paper. Instructional materials and tests are available on the University of Greenwich website (http//www.wilburnontheweb.co.uk/langproject/) or from the author.

Notes

1   A focus on form approach to grammar teaching involves a focus on meaning and a focus on form: learners' attention is being focused on specific linguistic properties in the course of a communicative activity.

2   PI consists of three basic components: 1) explicit information about a linguistic form/structure is provided; 2) information about a processing principle is given; 3) structured input activities are used.

MOI activities have two main characteristics: 1) they involve the exchange of previously unknown information; 2) they require learners to access a particular form or structure in order to express meaning.

References

Benati, A. (2004a) The effects of structured input and explicit information on the acquisition of Italian future tense. In B. VanPatten (ed.) *Processing Instruction. Theory, Research, and Commentary* 207–25. Mahwah, NJ: Erlbaum.

Benati, A. (2004b) The effects of processing instruction and its components on the acquisition of gender agreement in Italian. *Language Awareness* 13: 67–80.

Benati, A. (2005) The effects of PI, TI and MOI in the acquisition of English Simple Past Tense. *Language Teaching Research* 9: 67–113.

Benati A., VanPatten, B. and Wong, W. (2005) *Input Processing and Processing Instruction*. Roma: Armando.

Erlam, R. (2003) Evaluating the relative effectiveness of structured-input and output-based instruction in foreign language learning: results from an experimental study. *Studies in Second Language Acquisition* 25: 559–82.

Farley, A. P. (2001a) The effects of processing instruction and meaning-based output instruction. *Spanish Applied Linguistics* 5: 57–94.

Farley, A. P. (2001b) Authentic processing instruction and the Spanish subjunctive. *Hispania* 84: 289–99.

Lee, J. (2004) On the generalizability, limits, and potential future directions of processing instruction research. In B. VanPatten (ed.) *Processing Instruction. Theory, Research, and Commentary* 311–23. Mahwah, NJ: Erlbaum.

Lee, J. and Benati, A. (forthcoming) *On Delivering Processing Instruction in Classrooms and on Computers: research and practice*. London: Equinox.

Lee, J. and VanPatten, B. (1995) *Making Communicative Language Teaching Happen*. New York: McGraw-Hill.

VanPatten, B. (1996) *Input Processing and Grammar Instruction*. New Jersey: Ablex.

VanPatten, B. (2002) Processing instruction: an update. *Language Learning* 52: 755–803.

VanPatten, B. (2004) Input processing in second language acquisition. In B. VanPatten (ed.) *Processing Instruction. Theory, Research, and Commentary* 5–31. Mahwah, NJ: Erlbaum.

VanPatten, B. and Cadierno, T. (1993) Explicit instruction and input processing. *Studies in Second Language Acquisition* 15: 225–43.

VanPatten, B. and Sanz, C. (1995) From input to output: processing instruction and communicative tasks. In F. R. Eckman, D. Highland, P. W. Lee, J. Mileham, and R. Weber (eds) *Second Language Acquisition Theory and Pedagogy* 169–85. Mahwah, NJ: Earlbaum.

Wong, W. (2004) The nature of processing instruction. In B. VanPatten (ed.) *Processing Instruction. Theory, Research, and Commentary* 33–63. Mahwah, NJ: Erlbaum.

Appendix A: Information

EXPLICIT INFORMATION

The Italian Subjunctive of doubt and opinion

Subjunctive expresses uncertainty, doubt rather than fact. It also conveys the opinion and attitudes of the speaker.
The subjunctive verb is located either at the end of the sentence (e.g. Io non credo che parli) or in the middle of the sentence (e.g Io non credo che parli bene il francese).
The subjunctive is generally preceded by a main clause (independent) and the conjunction *che*.

ATTENZIONE

When the verb or expression in the independent clause denotes certainty, the present indicative is used in the dependent clause.

When the verb or expression in the independent clause expresses opinion, doubt or uncertainty, the present subjunctive is used

Compare these pairs of sentences :

So che Paolo non parla inglese	Penso che Parlo non parli inglese
Sono certo che Giorgio canta	Dubito che Giorgio canti

Expressions indicating opinion, doubt
Credo
Dubito
Ho l'impressione
Immagino
Penso

Expressions indicating certainty
So
Sono sicuro
Sono certo
Sono convinto

The present subjunctive is formed by adding the appropriate ending (third person singular) to the verb stem.
Lavor-i
Scriv-a
Dorm-a

Appendix B: Activity

Attività 1: « Personaggi Famosi »

You will hear the beginning part of a sentence that deals with facts and opinions about famous people. Based on what you hear, place a check mark by the phrase that best completes each statement.
1)
… … … . *è un bugiardo*
… … … . *sia un bugiardo*
2)
… … … . *è un genio della regia*
… … … . *sia un genio della regia*
3)
… … … . *è una donna attraente*
… … … . *sia una donna attraente*

4)

... ... *ha molti soldi*

... ... *.abbia molti soldi*

5)

... ... *sa cantare*

... ... *.sappia cantare*

(5 more script items of identical nature)

Transcripts

E' certo che George Bush ...

Non penso che Tarantino ... .

Non credo che Jodie Foster ...

E' sicuro che la Regina ...

Non penso che Celine Dion ...

Appendix C: Activity

Attività 1 : « George Bush, politico ideale ? »

Complete the following sentences by putting the verb in bracket at the correct tense and answer the question at the bottom.

1. **Non credo che Bush ...** a. _____ (essere) un politico intelligente.

    b. _____ (conoscere) le lingue straniere.

    c. _____ (avere) buon senso.

    d. _____ (rispettare) l'ambiente.

    e. _____ (diventare) il prossimo presidente.

2. **Sono certo che Bush ...** a. _____ (essere) disonesto.

    b. _____ (essere) un bugiardo.

    c. _____ (giocare) a tennis.

    d. _____ (essere) sposato.

    e. _____ (amare) il suo paese.

Non Pensi che Bush sia il politico ideale? Perchè ?_____

12 The conditions and consequences of professional discourse studies[1]

Srikant Sarangi

Introduction

This paper is primarily intended as a necessarily selective appraisal of two complimentary fields of research – applied linguistics and professional discourse studies – with a special reference to the healthcare setting. I am reminded of Tom Burns (1970) when he alludes to the competing foci underpinning such a task: (i) to outline a manifesto and announce departure for a new subject area; (ii) to invoke the achievement of predecessors; (iii) to offer a guided tour. Each one of these options has strengths and weaknesses. Of the last – the guided tour approach – Burns writes:

> Less striking in its appeal than the first, less elegant in manner than the second, more pedestrian by definition of course than either, the guided tour runs the twin hazards of losing half one's audience by boring them with what is already distressingly familiar stuff, and the other half by hurrying them through the more complicated or remote precincts. (Burns, 1970: 56)

As I see it, the guided tour strategy can fail miserably as it can aspire neither to 'make the strange familiar' nor 'make the familiar strange' within the space constraints, given the widely divergent applied linguistics community of researchers. Instead I will combine different aspects of the three trajectories in an eclectic fashion as a way of raising some mutually overlapping issues for further reflection.

Profiling applied linguistics and the applied linguist

At the outset let me outline four major paradigms of research: pure, applied, consultancy and consultative. Researcher motivation may be an indicator of what these different paradigms might mean, and these can be linked to issues of relationships, reflexivity and relevance (see Sarangi and Candlin, 2001; Sarangi and Candlin, 2003; Candlin and Sarangi, 2004). With regard to researcher-researched relations, we may think of a multitude of possibilities, roughly along the following lines: as outsider or insider, as invited or self-imposed, as assessor of performance; as expert and agent of change, as a resource for transfer of expert knowledge/methodology, and this list can go on. While in pure research, enlightenment may be the motivating factor, in applied research, a form of engineering and influence may be of central significance. Pure and applied are not only definable in terms of target outcomes, but also in the very ways in which the research process is constituted: in addition to the variable role-relations as outlined above, questions regarding what counts as data, and how the analyst attests his/her findings emerging from the data vis-à-vis their dissemination assume relevance.

The prefix 'applied' is the cornerstone of many scientific and social scientific disciplines, with a set of shared core values and perspectives. Let me turn briefly to Pit Corder's (1973: 10) original formulation of 'applied linguistics':

> The application of linguistic knowledge to some object – or, applied linguistics, as its name implies – is an activity. It is not a theoretical study. It makes use of the findings of theoretical studies. The applied linguist is a consumer, or user, not a producer, of theories.

Whether applied linguistics is a discipline or an activity is a rather moot point, but in the way Corder formulated the remit, applied linguists come closer to the profession of medicine which selectively uses scientific knowledge for the benefit of an individual client – what Freidson (1970) captures as 'the clinical mentality'. In this sense, professional practitioners are unlike scientific experts who are committed to knowledge-generation in a 'pure' sense, although, as Stehr (1994) observes, professionals are both 'knowledge-disseminating' and 'knowledge-bearing' agents.

Consider the application of linguistic knowledge to language teaching, which Corder uses as an exemplar:

> The linguistic approach is responsible for determining how we *describe* what we are to teach. This is not the same as saying that it *determines* what we teach. It contributes nothing to specifying how we teach. (Corder, 1973: 31, original emphasis)

Underlying this statement is a sense of modesty, a clear division of labour between description and prescription, a caution about how far one can go in professing the applicability of one's knowledge. This echoes the received wisdom in other areas of social scientific research that there is always a spatio-temporal lag between what is discovered in 'pure' terms and how it might directly or indirectly impact upon professional practice. Within the context of medical education/socialisation studies, Becker et al. (1961) even go as far as insisting that 'we do not report everything we observe'.

The final two paradigms – consultancy and consultative – are perhaps more overlapping than the pure and the applied dichotomy. For me, there is a crucial difference between the consultancy and the consultative models of research in terms of the researcher-researched relationship; the division of expert knowledge; the invited vs. self-imposed nature of the researcher involvement,[2] and more importantly, in the ways in which the research findings may be presented and disseminated for potential uptake. While the consultancy model may foreground the researcher as an expert trouble-shooter in a problem-solving ethos, the consultative model is more of a collaborative exploration of the nuances of professional practice, where the applied linguist/discourse analyst has not only to justify and problematise what constitutes the object and objective of research but also to rely heavily on the insights of the professional practitioner in making sense of the phenomena under study. A consultative research network is premised upon collaborative partnership, mutual respect and trust.

Here I am not going to debate different possible definitions of these research paradigms nor their boundaries. Instead I would like to suggest that it is possible for any one of us to participate in more than one research paradigm – simultaneously or at different points in our professional career. Very crudely, the applied linguist can be profiled along the following lines:

- Applied linguist as mediator (linguistics applied in a post-hoc mode);
- Applied linguist as problem solver (in a responsive, consultancy mode);
- Applied linguist as educator (in a proactive, futurist mode);
- Applied linguist as joint collaborator and co-researcher (in a consultative, reflexive mode).

A professional applied linguistic mentality

The application of scientific knowledge to solve 'the real world problems in which language is a central issue' (Brumfit, 2001: 169) constitutes the 'jobbing linguist' – 'someone who offers technical skills in the service of somebody else's activity' (Brumfit, 2004; Crystal, 2004). This applied, 'jobbing' linguistic mentality of 'problem solving' which implies that a given profession is aware of the salience of its language-centred practices is some guarantee for the continuing relevance of applied linguistics. With this comes the recognition that some professional contexts are more language-centred than others (e.g. law and medicine vs. architecture), and within a specific professional context, certain sub-specialities may profess different degrees of language fronts (e.g. psychotherapy vs. neurosurgery). In other words, if we were to take a problem-solving approach to language-based professions, then the frontiers of applied linguistics, to use Crystal's (2003) metaphor, can extend beyond its mainstream engagement with language education.

This mentality of 'problem solving' however needs to be kept separate from a mentality of 'joint problematisation leading to problem solving' in a consultative mode. This takes us into the heart of our professional applied linguistic practice – how we go about identifying and engaging with self-initiated and other-initiated real-world problems. Roberts (2003) makes a case for applied linguistics to become more practically relevant and reflexively grounded in not only addressing real-world concerns, but also in doing so collaboratively in a sustained way with practitioners involved (see also Roberts and Sarangi, 2003; Sarangi, 2002). Her concerns are captured in the expression 'applied linguistics applied' – which is a salutary warning about our work becoming too remote and abstract, almost bordering on non-applicability of research findings despite the original intentions/motivations. This is the opposite end of the 'problem solving spectrum' where self-imposed solutions are in need of uptake. Brumfit (2004) quite aptly captures this as a 'metaphorical pretence', i.e. 'on the one hand … you can isolate the phenomenon that you're looking at, and on the other hand the need to be embedded in real-world practice'. To minimise this pretence, I would imagine, the professional applied linguistic mentality has to harbour a long-term, collaborative action plan beyond snap-shot action research.

Let me revisit the parallel between applied linguistic mentality and clinical mentality – in terms of applying scientific knowledge in order to solve individual clients' problems. For a 'professional' applied linguist to operate effectively in another professional context, the knowledge of the discipline needs to be supplemented by the knowledge/experience of a given profession in its organisational environment vis-à-vis their clients. A sense of commitment mediated through a situated understanding of participants and their life-world becomes a necessary attribute of applied linguistic mentality.

One way of looking at professional practice is to consider it as ritualistic and predictable, and therefore easier to describe and interpret than casual conversations (Heath, 1979). However, such an approach may belie the analytic burden: the reality that a profession's knowledge base operates mainly at a tacit level. Polanyi's (1958: 49) general claim that skilful performance in the context of swimming or cycling is accomplished by 'the observance of a set of rules which are not known as such to the person following them' holds true for professional competencies. Schon (1983: viii) echoes this sentiment: 'Competent practitioners usually know more than they can say. They exhibit a kind of knowing-in-practice, most of which is tacit.' This 'knowing-in-practice' is often referred to as 'practical knowledge' which cannot be simply replaced by any set of rules or explicit rule following.

This poses an inherent paradox: as discourse/communication analysts we are more geared towards interpreting manifest performance (mainly language, but also to include visual, non-verbal and paralinguistic features), but professional knowledge and experience may not always be explicitly visible. Additionally, given the complex inter-relationship between language and context, what may be visible is not easily interpretable.

If description of language-in-use is the key applied linguistic activity, then Corder was quick to acknowledge that both the functions of language and the variability of language posed particular challenges to our descriptive enterprise. Most crucially, he draws our attention to what is now taken for granted in applied linguistics circles:

> [T]here is no one-to-one relation between a class of speech acts and the grammatical form of an utterance, and that it appears that almost any utterance can have almost any function in some context and situation. It is thus not only the *form* of the utterance which determines how we understand it, but the characteristics of the whole speech situation. *This is what makes it so difficult to categorise speech acts in a systematic and scientifically valid way, and why we have to fall back very largely on ad hoc criteria which are based on common sense.* One of the great unresolved problems in linguistics is to discover what the relations between the formal features of the utterance and the situation are which lead to a particular interpretation of that utterance as *a warning, a promise, an assertion* or an example of some other class of speech act. (Corder, 1973: 42, original and added emphases)

The language-context inter-relationship has been central to Levinson's (1979) notion of activity type (for an overview, see Sarangi, 2000). In a more recent paper, Levinson points to the apparent paradox that utterances can create their own contexts:

> The paradox would be: if it takes a context to map an interpretation onto an utterance, how can we extract a context from an utterance before interpreting? The idea that utterances might carry with them their own contexts like a snail carries its home along with it is indeed a peculiar idea if one subscribes to a definition of context that excludes message content, as for example in information theory. (Levinson, 1997: 26)

The nuances of language-context relationship are most evident in professional discourse settings and this can pose a key interpretive challenge for applied linguists. It is not enough for us as applied linguists to carry our own context-based linguistic repertoire to interpret and understand situated professional practice. We need the time and space to socialise into professional ways of seeing and doing, and recognition of this requirement is a necessary condition for our intervention.

I have elsewhere referred to this challenge as the analyst's paradox (Sarangi, 2002) – which can be minimised, if not overcome, by orienting to the practitioners' insights as a way of enriching our interpretive practice. A 'thick description' of professional practice, in Geertz's (1973) sense, can only be premised upon what I would call 'thick participation'. The notion of participation has to be taken broadly to include continuity of involvement in a research setting, including maintenance of relationships with participants in temporal and spatial terms – or what Levi-Strauss (1967) would see as a form of 'saturation of experience'. Long-term immersion in the research setting becomes a necessary condition, which is synonymous with learning a foreign or second language in a bilingual or multilingual community for purposes of survival. Cicourel (1992, 2003) quite rightly emphasises the need for ethnographic insights as a way of supplementing one's discourse analytic stance. Ethnographic studies in the cultural anthropological tradition have highlighted the importance of such extended participation in the life of a community and their everyday practices. 'Thick participation', for me, extends beyond data gathering and data interpretation – it also includes the provision of feedback and the facilitation of conditions for potential uptake of discourse analytic findings (Roberts and Sarangi, 2003; Sarangi, 2004).

Thick participation constitutes a form of socialisation and it should not be equated with becoming a professional expert. There is more to expertise than a familiarisation with experience from the periphery. What I have in mind here is more of an acquisition of professional/organisational literacy that would provide a threshold for interpretive understanding. Without an adequate level of literacy, it is difficult to imagine how a researcher can understand and interpret professional conduct in a meaningful way. In the context of social studies of science, Collins and Evans (2002: 254) offer a distinction between interactional expertise and contributory expertise: while interactional expertise 'means enough expertise to interact interestingly with participants and carry out a sociological analysis', contributory expertise 'means enough expertise to contribute to the science of the field being analysed'. I shall return to this later in relation to 'discriminatory expertise', but it is suffice to say that thick participation is not an either/or matter and that there are degrees of participation at stake. Understanding and interpreting others' practices are dependent on such a participatory stance, which amounts to a reconfigured fusion of ethnomethodology, praxiology and ethnography. As Malinowski (1935: 320) points out, one cannot 'understand the rules of the game without a knowledge of the game itself'. It is the knowledge of the game that becomes accessible via 'thick participation'.

Professional vision and categorisation of professional practice

My argument in favour of thick participation comes with some disclaimers. In addition to inevitable biases – observer-related as well as more systematic ones – there are limits to what we can have access to and are able to interpret, although we accept that professional practice is constituted in discourse. As Goodwin points out:

> Professional settings provide a perspicuous site for the investigation of how objects of knowledge, controlled by and relevant to the defining work of a specific community, are socially constructed from within the settings that make up the lifeworld of that community – that is, endogeneously, through systematic discursive procedures. (Goodwin, 1994: 630)

Goodwin (1994) goes on to draw our attention to how 'professional vision' is constituted in specific discursive practices, e.g. coding, which transforms phenomena observed in a specific setting into the objects of knowledge that animate the discourse of a profession; highlighting, which makes specific phenomena in a complex perceptual field salient by marking them in some fashion; and the production and articulation of material representations.

Our role as applied linguists and discourse analysts is double-edged: the professional groups we study use language to categorise events and our task is one of (re)categorising and (re)interpreting what professionals categorise in their everyday practice. In other words, professional discourse, for us, is both the object of study and the process through which we study professional practice. As Lee (1992: 16) points out, 'Language [is] a classificatory instrument ... categories are not objective, ready-made, inherent properties of the external world but are subject to processes of perception and interpretation'. So, like the professionals under study, what we as analysts do with language is bound to be biased and ideologically framed, because our analytic tools are inherently theory-laden.

The main challenge facing an outside researcher is one of interpreting professional knowledge and practice in a competent manner (Sarangi, 2002). As I have already indicated, professional conduct is informed by tacit 'scientific' knowledge, practical experience as well as organisational procedures – all of which are not necessarily available at the explicit discoursal level for applied linguistic description and intervention, even with sustained ethnographic involvement. Following Wilson (1963), the business of (applied) linguistic analysis cannot deal with scientific facts and their truth status, but is better equipped to examine their discoursal realisation and usage. Questions of fact – e.g. 'Is a whale able to sink a 15,000 ton liner?' – are beyond the remit of language/discourse researchers. Questions of concept – such as 'Is a whale a fish?' – are certainly within the purview of our interpretive expertise, as we can discuss how the categorisation of whale as a fish may vary across different language users, e.g. biologists, fishermen, the bureaucrats and politicians representing the Ministry of Agriculture and Fisheries. Such categorisation will have consequences – not so much for the whale – but for those fishermen who depend on whales for a livelihood. It also proves that categorisation is always evaluative in nature, although the point of view of the categoriser may remain implicit.

The limitation of our interpretive circumference is brought out clearly by Gilbert and Mulkay's analytic positioning in the study of scientists' discourse:

> [It] does not seek to go beyond scientists' accounts in order to describe and explain actions and beliefs as such. It focuses rather on describing how scientists' accounts are organised to portray their actions and beliefs in contextually appropriate ways. Thus, discourse analysis does not answer traditional questions about the nature of scientific action and belief. What it may be able to do instead is to provide closely documented descriptions of the recurrent interpretative practices employed by scientists and embodied in their discourse; and show how these interpretative procedures vary in accordance with variations in social context. (Gilbert and Mulkay, 1984: 14)

It follows then that discourse analysis, as a methodological toolbox, should be aimed at recovering evidence (at the levels of the said and the unsaid) rather than assessing professional knowledge and its truth status.

Towards an applied linguistics of professions

Notwithstanding the limitations of our interpretive expertise in the wider professional contexts, in what follows I would like to move away from a narrow characterisation of the applied linguistics task vis-à-vis language education. Corder observed in 1973 that 'foreign language teaching is often taken as being synonymous with that task', and it is perhaps still the case 30 years later. A precise question would be to see what is it that the FLT task accomplishes which makes applied linguistics tick. In institutional and sociocultural terms, 'thick participation' must count towards the continued survival of this applied linguistic venture. I would like to suggest that applied linguistics has other relevant tasks to take on board across a wide range of professions. Examples include: language and the legal profession (under the brand name of forensic linguistics), translation and interpreting, healthcare, and workplace/organisation studies more generally. The bigger question before us is: under what conditions can 'applied linguistics' become 'effective linguistics'?

If by 'effective' we mean guaranteed uptake of our intervention, i.e. the positive consequences resulting from our research, then we need to consider carefully not only what we discover but also how we communicate our discovery. As I shall elaborate later, professionals are not very good at communicating explicitly to their clients what they do, although their actions are informed by expert knowledge. Applied linguists as professionals are not outside of this characterisation: we rarely analyse and reflect upon our engagement with practitioners whose conduct we observe and analyse even though our output is meant to be client-/other-oriented.

The key point of my proposal here is to expand the boundaries of applied linguistic themes and sites as a way of recognising the emerging interest in language-focused activities in professions. I would like to suggest a broadening of the scholarly enterprise devoted to 'language/discourse of professions' (as is the case within the field of Language for Specific Purposes drawing on genre analysis), which can be labelled as 'Applied Linguistics of Professions' along the lines of cognate social scientific approaches to professions (e.g. Sociology of Professions, Anthropology of Professions). This transition can be characterised as a shift in focus from 'professional discourse as a register' to 'professional discourse as an expert system', while accommodating a more involved fieldwork-based collaborative enterprise.

More than 25 years ago, in 1979, when commissioned to contribute a chapter titled 'The context of professional languages: an historical overview' for an edited book, Shirely Brice Heath opened her chapter thus: 'In a volume entitled *Language in Public Life*, it is somewhat ironic to include the language of professions, since many professionals are today charged with making special efforts to keep their language apart from the public' (1979: 102). She underlines her position with the following argument:

> First, the language of the professional set him apart from the client or patient. His language was a mark of the special province of knowledge which was the basis of what it was the patient was told, though the knowledge itself could not be transmitted to the patient. […]

> A second feature of the language of the professional was his articulated knowledge of ways to obtain information from patients while restricting the amount and types of information transmitted to the patient. […]

> Professionals have, therefore, been socialised to have certain perceptions of their role in communicative tasks, and they have been trained to use language as an instrument to maintain that role and to accomplish ends often known only to them in interchanges.

(Heath, 1979: 108)

Heath's observations echo the points I have already made about the tacit basis of expert knowledge and practice, especially in relation to the healthcare profession. In the context of the book, Heath (1979) offers a useful historical overview of the characteristics of professionalism (in the USA context, between 1840s and 1960s) which can be summarised as follows:

1. Access to 'knowledge of abstract theories and working definitions of concepts basic to their fields'.

2. High degree of internal organisation through professional associations to monitor rule of conduct, recruitment etc.

3. A special concern for the public interest ... to rid society of quacks, amateurs etc.

4. Nationalistic drive: strong inclinations to select English materials, preferably written by American professionals.

5. 'The conscious development of a specialised vocabulary and special formats for the presentation of knowledge'. Agreement on standard methods of labelling and describing symptoms. A good doctor means how to talk like a doctor – how to use words in appropriate ways:
   a) Allow discussion of only certain topics.
   b) Restrict the choice of conversational partners ('elicit from the patient both 'subjective' and 'objective' views of illness').
   c) Use a detailed procedure for interviewing patients ('it was the task of the physician, not the patient, to ask questions; in the words of one doctor: "The wisest [patients] ask the fewest questions"').
   d) Avoid the truth, and also discourage elaboration of their information from other sources (the assumption being the patient will not understand the truth about their condition; so, he should be told what is good for him, what he should do, etc.).
   e) Assure the patient he is ultimately responsible for his own improvement.

Points 1-4 above are applicable to any professional community and they no doubt characterise us as applied linguists and discourse analysts. It is the last point (5), with its detailed application to the healthcare context, which is directly relevant for my purposes. It shows how the medical profession routinely goes through the rites of communicative socialisation, and may as a result come to believe that 'good' communication is an embedded part of their professional competence, while at the same time suggesting that their specialised communicative repertoire is not necessarily transparent to the untutored eye of either the patient or the outsider analyst.

The body of work in professional discourse studies over the last 30 years or so can be generally grouped under three categories[3]: (i) the descriptive, genre-based studies focusing on specialised registers, mainly involving written texts, chiefly from the academy; (ii) the interpretive studies of talk and interaction in professional settings, sometimes involving critical sites such as team meetings, cross-examination in the courtroom, and delivery of bad news in healthcare contexts; and (iii) problem-centred, interventionist studies in the spirit of applied linguistics, often involving close collaboration between discourse analysts and members of various professions. A quick glance at the early days suggests that researchers relied on naturalistic data that could be analysed within a rigorous descriptive framework. There have been very few instances of thick participation in the research site or joint collaboration with professionals themselves: one exception is Labov and Fanshel's (1977) study of therapeutic discourse, although it is difficult to see in this highly descriptive study – what one might call a 'thick description' – of a therapeutic encounter lasting about 15 minutes, what could be of interest to the professional group. This is not to undermine the research findings of various interaction-based studies that have contributed significantly to our knowledge of professional-client encounters without reducing them to interactional orthodoxies.

Communication skills training in healthcare settings: the UK experience

Let me now reflect on the communicative turn in the healthcare setting and suggest how this communicative turn can be seized upon further by linking the applied linguistic and discourse analytic studies of communicative competence and situated performance. Over the last few years in the UK the General Medical Council (GMC) has emphasised the need for better communication abilities for the doctors (*Tomorrow's Doctors*, GMC, 2002). The same holds for in-service training (*Good Medical Practice*, GMC, 2001). This is a recognition of the fact that healthcare professionals may be proficient in their medical/scientific knowledge but not in the communicative dimension. This is borne out by the scale of litigation settlements arising out of communication failure. The number of complaints to ombudsmen and to various health complaints commissions proves that many professionals fail to communicate adequately. We are however far from knowing the exact scope and nature of this communication failure: Is it overload of information? Is it lack of adequate information provision? Is it collusion between healthcare providers and patients with regard to not telling the 'hard' truth? Is it overuse of professional jargon? Or is it simply a matter of professionals not listening to the patient? The 'official' response to this crisis is the move towards 'patient-centred' healthcare, which includes communication skills training as a necessary part of the curricula for medical education.

A second possible reason for putting the spotlight on communication may be that many of the new emergent illnesses demand communicative sophistication in dealing with uncertainties associated with diagnosis and prognosis. A third dimension is the increased level of patient literacy with ease of access to the health-related websites. The deficit model of healthcare delivery now gives way to health providers reinterpreting what patients already know and in distilling relevant knowings from irrelevant information overload.

In general, many healthcare professionals have welcomed this communicative turn in medical education and continuous professional development, although some tend to believe that a good doctor is by default a good communicator. No doubt there are some professionals who are both good doctors and good communicators. But it is risky to assume this correspondence as a given, especially when the patient population remains infinitely diverse, with varied experiential trajectories and expectations. Moreover, the notion of the 'good doctor' is itself problematic as it implies competent performance at an individualistic level. It is commonplace that doctors often work in teams, as much of healthcare delivery is organised along multiprofessional division of labour. What may come across as good doctoring to the patient may not always be good for the team members. For example, a nurse may feel his/her tasks have been impeded or surpassed, that there was not a fair division of expert labour. This suggests how as language and communication researchers we are not in a position to evaluate professional practice without giving due consideration to the organisational ethos.

We can look at these communication-centred developments in two ways: from practitioner-training perspective and from professional research perspective. From practitioner training and medical education perspective, one may reluctantly concede that healthcare professionals can manage their business without any help from communication training and research. However, this conceals the fact that there has hardly been a channel of communication between applied linguists and those who are in charge of practitioner training and education. Communication skills training and assessment (as in the Objective Structured Clinical Examination) has mainly developed outside of the discipline of language and communication (here applied linguistics). Some early examples of descriptive work include Candlin et al. (1976, 1981, 1982), which are responsive to problems, with the potential opportunity for intervention and empowerment of clients and/or professionals both within the mainstream healthcare encounters as well as those involving allied professionals. The collaborative work I have been involved in with Celia Roberts over the last seven years is an attempt to build a bridge across our professional boundaries, both in analytical and educational terms (see e.g. Roberts and Sarangi, 1999, 2002, 2003, 2005; Sarangi and Roberts, 2002).

When we consider the current provision in medical education and professional training, we see that, independent of the research developments in applied linguistics and discourse studies, communication is seen as a recipe-style skill that can be learnt with the help of a DIY guide (Peräkylä and Vehviläinen, 2003). Moreover, communicative competence in these highly specialised settings is viewed as a separate layer of ability vis-à-vis professional, scientific expertise. There is an overall sense of fragmentation of expertise in order to manage and assess learning output, which is not helped by a reductionist view of language-in-use. It necessarily overlooks the gap between displaying communication as a set of learned skills and their overall integration into professional practice.

When applied linguists become involved in the delivery of training programmes of healthcare professionals, especially in a multicultural, multilinguistic environment, one may begin to smell professional success in terms of potential intervention informed by robust theories of language-in-use. However, this is far from being the case as the outsider language specialists may shy away from 'thick participation' in their belief that an extra dose of context-free language/communication awareness will fix the communication problem. There may be the lack of motivation to develop a critical perspective towards professional communication as a specialised activity, comprising many differentiated sub-specialities. For example, giving bad news in a primary care clinic and in an oncology clinic should not be approached in the same manner.

A further point relates to the healthcare profession's natural inclination to look for evidence. Has training in communication skills made a difference to practice? Williams and Lau (2004) claim that this is not the case and characterise the communication skills training as an exercise in evangelism – trying to convert doctors to become good communicators. According to them, the medical curriculum is becoming a crowded space, with pressure from ethics, psychology, religion, etc., and we may be in danger of producing doctors who are good at everything except in knowledge of medicine. This makes one think of the excesses associated with the alternative position – good communicators are good doctors! The assumption here is that patients want good communication at the expense of everything else. In a recent study, however, Burkitt Wright et al. (2004) suggest that breast cancer patients may not be primarily concerned with doctor's communication skills, but with their technical expertise.

A final point relates to the growing area of health communication skills research. One is intrigued to find naïve categorisation systems which ignore the 'non-correspondence principle' (that is, there is no one-to-one correspondence between linguistic form and function), and urge that the category systems allow for a context-independent universal description of professional communicative practice (see e.g. Stewart and Roter, 1989). The quantitatively robust findings these studies generate are scientifically respected, but their practical, applied relevance remains questionable, especially from a qualitative discourse analytic perspective. By a similar token, we can anticipate professionals asking the 'so what' question when faced with very sophisticated analysis of specific interactional sequences. Elsewhere (Sarangi, forthcoming) I have argued in favour of activity analysis, which aligns with a theme-oriented discourse analysis (Roberts and Sarangi, 2005), to become a central commitment of professional discourse studies. In a nutshell, activity analysis responds to two major concerns raised by professionals themselves (Candlin, 2003; Clarke, 2003). In the words of Clarke:

> Studies of talk-in-interaction, whether labelled as CA or DA, would align more readily with the perspective of professionals if they could examine episodes of interaction as long as the whole consultation ... Professionals will perhaps be more enthusiastic about collaboration if the lens used to study their activities could be switched to even a slightly lower power, so that the give and take of discussion over a longer period – perhaps even during the whole of a consultation – could be examined. (Clarke, 2005: 191)

The two main concerns voiced by Clarke have to deal with context-embed-dedness and the part-whole dynamics of interpretation, both of which require the analytic means of mapping as part of activity analysis. Rethinking the microscope metaphor, Clarke continues:

> The analyst must steer between the Scylla of decontextualisation and the Charybdis of over-generalisation. A microscopist would remind us of the need to use a lens of appropriate magnification – neither too high power (removing essential context) nor too low power (revealing insufficient detail). (Clarke, 2005: 189)

Methodologically speaking, the above remark aligns with Cicourel's call for 'ecological validity'.[4] Any analysis of professional practice needs to steer a midway between 'constructionism' and 'radical situationalism' as a way of avoiding, on the one hand, 'micro-analytic myopia' (Wilson, 1986, cited in Mehan, 1991) and on the other, 'the fallacy of abstractionism' (Douglas, 1971).[5] While embracing the analytical and methodological sophistication, one needs to identify a range of topics and sites for future investigation. Here is an indicative list:

1. Study of professional practices beyond the mainstream doctor-patient communication as a way of understanding how professional knowledge is constituted – which will no doubt inform our interpretation of doctor-patient encounters. This is a call for studying the backstage activities (briefing sessions, case presentations, medical records, corridor talk etc.).

2. Extend our work into other healthcare settings: nursing, pharmacy, health visiting, midwifery and other areas of language and communication linked disorders: autism, deafness, schizophrenia, dementia etc.

3. Identify sites where language and communication issues play an even more significant role. These are settings such as genetic counselling, chronic fatigue syndrome, epileptology and palliative medicine, where medical knowledge is stretched to its limit. For instance, in end-of-life consultations, medical failure and futility have to be negotiated interactionally, as Barton et al. (2005) show, in the shifts from curative treatment to palliative care. In genetic counselling, where cure is not an option, risks of knowing overshadow risks of disease and prognosis, which require delicate communicative participant structures.

4. Other mediated healthcare settings such as NHS Direct provide another opportunity, where professional expertise has to be reconfigured in order to deal with 'patients at a distance' in an interactional environment made complex through the use of algorithms, telephone systems and computer technology.

5. Areas of assessment, e.g. in gatekeeping settings, including validation of assessment tools. This provides an opportunity for the interface between language assessment and testing research and professional education.

6. The intercultural dimension, as in interpreter-mediated consultations, given the potential consequences that might follow if doctors and patients bring different cultural and linguistic assumptions to the interaction. The differences in the affective and epistemological domains may lead to differential symptoms presentations and potentially different treatment regimes (Roberts et al., 2004).

7. Towards developing a paradigm of communication ethics: communication has undoubtedly an ethical dimension which includes, in the genetic counselling setting for instance, what is communicated or not communicated; how decisions about diagnostic and predictive testing, and disclosure of test results are accounted for; how the 'need to communicate'/'know' may be used as a reason for testing; how communication/talk itself may lead to decision about testing and disclosure; how (consequences of) communication might be seen as problematic, and hence avoided.

Concluding remarks: reflexivity, relevance, and discriminatory expertise

In this concluding part, I draw attention to professional communication researchers as an expert community of practice and raise a number of questions for us to reflect on. I have elaborated many of these elsewhere (Sarangi, 2002, 2004), and as a way of characterising the interface between applied linguistics and professional discourse studies, I pose them as follows:

a) What knowledge do communication researchers bring to bear on their understanding of other professional practices? How can the discourse practices of communication researchers be informed by the personal knowledge of professional practitioners – i.e. what constitutes under-standing, belief, experience, practice and action? To what extent are communication researchers able to access the knowledge/belief systems of professional practitioners through a study of their communicative ecologies? How does one avoid extreme reductionism in the interpretation of local practices?

b) In what ways can communication researchers claim practical relevance for their interpretive and interventionist work? Will a utilitarian research goal require one to go beyond the description of surface-level discourse and to acknowledge the problem of providing an evidential link between observable communicative practices and tacit knowledge systems?

c) What can be learnt by making the communication researcher a part of the process of our inquiry? In other words, what does it mean to move from language as action/activity to language/discourse analysis as action/activ-ity/activism?

Effective applied linguistics, of the kind I have been alluding to, can be seen in the experience we have had in publishing work outside of our mainstream journals. During the peer review process, one of the referees for the *Journal of Genetic Counselling* remarked (perhaps as a direct response to a standard question from the editor) that 'this paper would not change my counselling practice, but while reading it, it made me think about my practice'. Following the acceptance and publication of our research (Sarangi et al., 2004, 2005), there was an editorial request to come up with a set of questions which could be used for the purposes of Continuing Professional Development. This was no mean exercise, and it did make us reflect on our writing by drawing attention to our analytic practices in categorisation of discoursal patterns and in claims-making (see also Roberts and Sarangi, 2003; Sarangi et al., 2003).

This leads me to suggest that as applied linguists we need constantly to reflect upon the nature of our analytic expertise. Following Collins and Evans

(2002), it is the discriminatory expertise which concerns me here. As I see it, discriminatory expertise should involve the following:

a) discriminating between discovery and usefulness (Rampton, 1997);
b) discriminating between different traditions of discourse analysis (conversation analysis, critical discourse analysis, interactional sociolinguistics etc.) in relation to their analytic focus and usefulness (i.e. to go beyond the idea that by applying our analytic framework we make our work relevant); more generally, I feel that researchers of professional discourse will have to remain committed to a research site rather than to a narrow analytic tradition, so that they understand professional practice through 'thick participation';
c) discriminating between variations of professional practice (here interactional trajectories) and accounting for such differences in terms of discoursal evidence, although not always going as far as labelling instances of professional practice as good or bad.

With a commitment to making our work reflexive and visible, we have to form a collaborative partnership with our professional practitioners. In a self-reflective mode, Firth (1978) wrote about anthropologists and physicians sharing a common curiosity about 'the human condition'. This led Heath (1979) to speculate how (applied) linguists and professionals in human services delivery systems may come to share a curiosity about communication. We certainly have reached the point where 'the human communication condition' can bind us all together in the healthcare domain. However, this is no guarantee that our analytic mentalities will unproblematically converge. My proposal to connect professional discourse studies with applied linguistics echoes what Palmer and Redman said ages ago:

> Medical science is built up on a study of diseases; cases of disease have been collected and classified. The doctor's capacity to diagnose and ultimately to prescribe is based on the collection of cases of abnormality that he has known directly through personal experience, and indirectly through study. Linguistic science is, alas, not so far developed as medical science, and we can rely less on reported abnormalities as a basis for diagnosis. We have to rely mainly on the cases we can observe ourselves. What we really want is a good collection of cases. (Palmer and Redman, 1932: 54)

This amounts to 'breaking the individual mould' and make an attempt to establish a collective 'discriminatory expertise' which prioritises cumulative evidence, based on clusters of comparable projects/findings. There is thus the need to go beyond the practice of 'noticing' and to avoid reporting findings that (i) either lack newsworthiness as knowledge or (ii) are clothed in an alien discourse. In the process, we will have to consider 'breaking the sequential mould' – first find and then recommend. Instead we have to opt for joint problematisation and provision of 'hot' feedback as well as negotiation of educational/training programmes, all of which involves ongoing dialogues with our professional practitioners. As we know, much applied linguistics work, especially in the interaction/discourse-based studies, is oriented to answering the Goffmanian question: 'what's it that's going on here'. But this is also the question that practitioners whose conduct we make our business to study may increasingly ask of us. And this is more so in the case of professional discourse studies, thus compelling us to think what is or is not applied or applicable in what we do.

Notes

1   An extended version of this paper was delivered as The Pit Corder Lecture at the BAAL Annual Conference in Bristol, September 2005.

2   When the researcher is an 'invited guest' as opposed to 'an uninvited intruder' in a professional/workplace setting, the role-relationships work differently, with differential expectations of usefulness (Bosk, 1992). As Bosk illustrates, even when invited, one has to balance between informants' expectations of usefulness and the researcher's methodological determination to remain detached and objective.

3   Some key book-length studies include Atkinson and Drew (1979); Candlin (2002); Drew and Heritage (1992); Di Pietro (1982); Fisher and Todd (1983, 1986); Gunnarsson et al. (1997), Labov and Fanshel (1977); Mishler (1984); O'Barr (1982). For a general overview, see Sarangi and Roberts, (1999) and for a more specific treatment of the healthcare setting, see Candlin and Candlin (2003), Sarangi (2004) and Sarangi (forthcoming).

4   Ecological validity (Cicourel, 1992, forthcoming) focuses on how we seek to convince others of the viability and authenticity of our claims and can be understood by our use of primary and secondary data sources. Ecological validity can only be approximated in the social and behavioural sciences.

5   *'Any scientific understanding of human action, at whatever level of ordering or generality, must begin with and be built upon an understanding of the everyday life of the members performing those actions.* (To fail to see this and to act in accord with it is to commit what we might call the *fallacy of abstractionsim,* that is, the fallacy of believing that you can know in a more abstract form what you do not know in the particular form.)' (Douglas, 1971: 11)

References

Atkinson, J. M. and Drew, P. (1979) *Order in Court: the organization of verbal interaction in judicial settings*. London: Macmillan.

Barton, E., Aldridge, M., Trimble, T. and Vidovic, J. (2005) Structure and variation in end-of-life discussions in the surgical intensive care unit. *Communication and Medicine* 2(1): 3–20.

Becker, H., Geer, E., Hughes, E. C. and Strauss, A. L. (1961) *Boys in White: student culture in medical school*. Chicago: University of Chicago Press.

Bosk, C. (1992) *All God's Mistakes*. Chicago: University of Chicago Press.

Brumfit, C. (2001) *Individual Freedom in Language Teaching: helping learners to develop a dialect of their own*. Oxford: Oxford University Press.

Brumfit, C. (2004) Coping with change in applied linguistics. *Journal of Applied Linguistics* 1(3): 387–98.

Burkitt Wright, E., Holcombe, C. and Salmon, P. (2004) Doctors' communication of trust, care, and respect in breast cancer: qualitative study. *British Medical Journal* doi: 10.1136/bmj.38046.771308.7C.

Burns, T. (1970) Sociological explanation. In D. Emmet and A. MacIntyre (eds) *Sociological Theory and Philosophical Analysis*. New York: Macmillan.

Candlin, C. N. (ed.) (2002) *Research and Practice in Professional Discourse*. Hong Kong: City University of Hong Kong Press.

Candlin, C. N. and Candlin, S. (2003) Healthcare communication: a problematic site for applied linguistics research. *Annual Review of Applied Linguistics* 23: 134–54.

Candlin, C. N. and Sarangi, S. (2004) Making applied linguistics matter. *Journal of Applied Linguistics* 1(1): 1–8.

Candlin, C. N., Bruton, C. and Leather, J. (1976) Doctors in casualty: applying components of communicative competence to specialist course design. *International Journal of Applied Linguistics* 3: 245–72.

Candlin, C. N., Bruton, C., Leather, J. and Woods, E. (1981) Designing modular materials for communicative language learning, an example: doctor-patient communication skills. In L. Selinker et al. (eds) *Papers in Honour of Louis Trimble* 105–33. Rowley: Newbury House.

Candlin, C. N., Coleman, H. and Bruton, J. (1982) Dentist-patient communication: communicating complaint. In N. Wolfson and E. Judd (eds) *TESOL and Sociolinguistic Research* 56–81. Rowley: Newbury House.

Candlin, S. (2003) Issues arising when the professional workplace is the site of applied linguistic research. *Applied Linguistics* 24(3): 386–94.

Cicourel, A. V. (1992) The interpenetration of communicative contexts: examples from medical encounters. In A. Duranti and C. Goodwin (eds) *Rethinking Context: language as an interactive phenomenon* 291–310. Cambridge: Cambridge University Press.

Cicourel, A. V. (2003) On contextualising applied linguistic research in the workplace. *Applied Linguistics* 24(3): 360–73.

Cicourel, A. V. (forthcoming) A personal, retrospective view of ecological validity. To appear in *Text and Talk*.

Clarke, A. (2003) On being an object of research: reflections from a professional perspective. *Applied Linguistics* 24(3): 374–85.

Clarke, A. (2005) Commentary 1: professional theories and institutional interaction. *Communication and Medicine* 2(2): 189–91.

Collins, H. and Evans, R. (2002) The third wave of science studies: studies of expertise and experience. *Social Studies of Science* 32(2): 235–96.

Corder, P. S. (1973) *Introducing Applied Linguistics*. Harmondsworth: Penguin Books.

Crystal, D. (2003) Final frontiers in applied linguistics? In S. Sarangi and T. van Leeuwen (ed.) *Applied Linguistics and Communities of Practice* 9–24. London: Continuum.

Crystal, D. (2004) Coping with change in applied linguistics. *Journal of Applied Linguistics* 1(3): 387–98.

Di Pietro, R. J (ed.) (1982) Linguistics and the Professions. Norwood, NJ: Ablex.

Douglas, J (ed.) (1971) *Understanding Everyday Life: toward the reconstruction of sociological knowledge*. London: Routledge and Kegan Paul.

Drew, P. and Heritage, J. (eds) (1992) *Talk at Work: interaction in institutional settings*. Cambridge: Cambridge University Press.

Firth, R. (1978) Social anthropology and medicine – a personal perspective. *Social Science and Medicine* 12: 237–45.

Fisher, S. and Todd, A. D. (eds) (1983) *The Social Organisation of Doctor-Patient Communication*. Washington DC: Centre for Applied Linguistics.

Fisher, S. and Todd, A. D. (eds) (1986) *Discourse and Institutional Authority: medicine, education and law*. Norwood, NJ: Ablex.

Freidson, E. (1970) *Profession of Medicine: a study of the sociology of applied knowledge*. New York: Dodd, Mead and Company.

Geertz, C. (1973) *The Interpretation of Cultures*. New York: Basic Books.

General Medical Council (2001) *Good Medical Practice*. London: General Medical Council.

General Medical Council (2002) *Tomorrow's Doctors*. London: General Medical Council.

Gilbert, G. N. and Mulkay, M. (1984) *Opening Pandora's Box: a sociological analysis of scientists' discourse*. Cambridge: Cambridge University Press.

Goodwin, C. (1994) Professional vision. *American Anthropologist* 96(3): 606–33.

Gunnarsson, B-L, Linell, P. and Nordberg, B. (eds) (1997) *The Construction of Professional Discourse*. London: Longman.

Heath, S. B. (1979) The context of professional languages: an historical overview. In J. Alatis and G. Tucker (eds) *Language in Public Life* 101–18. Washington, DC: Georgetown University Press.

Labov, W. and Fanshel, D. (1977) *Therapeutic Discourse: psychotherapy as conversation*. New York: Academic Press.

Lee, D. (1992) *Competing Discourses*. London: Longman.

Levinson, S. (1979) Activity types and language. *Linguistics* 17: 365–99.

Levinson, S. (1997) Conextualizing 'contextualization cues'. In S. Eerdmans, C. Prevignano and P. Thibault (eds) *Discussing Communication Analysis 1: John J. Gumperz* 24–30. Lausanne: Beta Press.

Lévi-Strauss, C. (1967) *Structural Anthropology*. Garden City, New York: Anchor Books.

Malinowski, B. (1935) *Coral Gardens and Their Magic*. Vols 1 and 2. London: George Allen and Unwin.

Mehan, H. (1991) The school's work of sorting children. In D. Boden and D. Zimmerman (eds) *Talk and Social Structure: studies in ethnomethodology and conversation analysis* 71–90. Cambridge: Polity Press.

Mishler, E. G. (1984) *The Discourse of Medicine: dialectics of medical interviews*. Norwood, NJ: Ablex.

O'Barr, W. (1982) *Linguistic Evidence: language, power and strategy in the courtroom*. New York: Academic Press.

Palmer, H. and Redman, V. H. (1932) *This Language Learning Business*. London: Harrap.

Peräkylä, A. and Vehviläinen, S. (2003) Conversation analysis and the professional stocks of interactional knowledge. *Discourse & Society* 14(6): 727–50.

Polanyi, M. (1958) *Personal Knowledge: toward a post-critical philosophy*. London: Routledge and Kegan Paul.

Rampton, B. (1997) Retuning in applied linguistics. *International Journal of Applied Linguistics* 7(1): 3–25.

Roberts, C. (2003) Applied linguistics applied. In S. Sarangi and T. van Leeuwen (eds) *Applied Linguistics and Communities of Practice* 132–49. London: Continuum.

Roberts, C. and Sarangi, S. (1999) Hybridity in gatekeeping discourse: issues of practical relevance for the researcher. In S. Sarangi and C. Roberts (eds) 473–503.

Roberts, C. and Sarangi, S. (2002) Mapping and assessing medical students' interactional involvement styles with patients. In K. Spellman-Miller and P. Thompson (eds) *Unity and Diversity in Language Use. British Studies in Applied Linguistics* 17: 99–117. London: Continuum.

Roberts, C. and Sarangi, S. (2003) Uptake of discourse research in interprofessional settings: reporting from medical consultancy. *Applied Linguistics* 24(3): 338–59.

Roberts, C. and Sarangi, S. (2005) Theme-oriented discourse analysis of medical encounters. *Medical Education* 39: 632–40.

Roberts, C., Sarangi, S. and Moss, R. (2004) Presentation of self and symptom in primary care consultations involving patients from non-English speaking backgrounds. *Communication and Medicine* 1(2): 159–69.

Sarangi, S. (2000) Activity types, discourse types and interactional hybridity: the case of genetic counselling. In S. Sarangi and M. Coulthard (eds) *Discourse and Social Life* 1–27. London: Pearson.

Sarangi, S. (2002) Discourse practitioners as a community of interprofessional practice: some insights from health communication research. In C. N. Candlin (ed.) *Research and Practice in Professional Discourse* 95–135. Hong Kong: City University of Hong Kong Press.

Sarangi, S. (2004) Towards a communicative mentality in medical and health-care practice. *Communication and Medicine* 1(1): 1–11.

Sarangi, S. (forthcoming) Healthcare interaction as an expert communicative system: an activity analysis perspective. In C. Prevignano and P. Thibault (eds) *Language and Interaction: discussing the state-of-the-art.* Amsterdam: Benjamins.

Sarangi, S. and Candlin, C. N. (2001) Motivational relevancies: some methodological reflections on sociolinguistic practice. In N. Coupland, S. Sarangi and C. N. Candlin (eds) *Sociolinguistics and Social Theory* 350–88. London: Pearson.

Sarangi, S. and Candlin, C. N. (2003) Trading between reflexivity and relevance: new challenges for applied linguistics. *Applied Linguistics* 24(3): 271–85.

Sarangi, S. and Roberts, C. (eds) (1999) *Talk, Work and Institutional Order: discourse in medical, mediation and management settings.* Berlin: Mouton de Gruyter.

Sarangi, S. and Roberts, C. (2002) Discoursal (mis)alignments in professional gatekeeping encounters. In C. Kramsch (ed.) *Language Acquisition and Language Socialisation: ecological perspectives* 197–227. London: Continuum.

Sarangi, S., Clarke, A., Bennert, K. and Howell, L. (2003) Categorisation practices across professional boundaries: some analytic insights from genetic counselling. In S. Sarangi and T. van Leeuwen (eds) *Applied Linguistics and Communities of Practice* 150–68. London: Continuum.

Sarangi, S., Bennert, K., Howell, L., Clarke, A., Harper, P. and Gray, J. (2004) Initiation of reflective frames in counselling for Huntington's Disease predictive testing. *Journal of Genetic Counseling* 13(2): 135–55.

Sarangi, S., Bennert, K., Howell, L., Clarke, A., Harper, P. and Gray, J. (2005) (Mis)alignments in clients' response to reflective frames in counselling for Huntington's disease predictive testing. *Journal of Genetic Counseling* 14(1): 29–42.

Schon, D. (1983) *The Reflective Practitioner: how professionals think in action.* New York: Basic Books.

Stehr, N. (1994) *Knowledge Societies.* London: Sage.

Stewart, M. and Roter, D. (eds) (1989) *Communicating with Medical Patients.* Newbury Park, CA: Sage.

Williams, G. and Lau, A. (2004) Reform of undergraduate medical teaching in the United Kingdom: a triumph of evangelism over common sense. *British Medical Journal* 329: 92–4.

Wilson, J. (1963) *Thinking with Concepts.* Cambridge: Cambridge University Press.

Contributors

Alessandro Benati is Head of Department of the Department of Languages and International Studies at the University of Greenwich in the UK. He has researched and taught in the area of second language acquisition and processing instruction. He has authored numerous book chapters and books and his research has appeared in journals such as *Language Teaching Research*, *Language Awareness*, *Rivista di Psicolinguistica Applicata* and *Rassegna di Linguistica Applicata*.

Maggie Charles is a Tutor in English for Academic Purposes at Oxford University Language Centre, where she teaches academic writing to postgraduates. Her research interests are in the study of evaluation, phraseology, discipline-specific EAP and the application of insights from corpus linguistics to the teaching of academic writing. She has recently published papers which take a corpus approach to the analysis of stance and the use of citation in theses.

Maeve Conrick is Statutory Lecturer and former Head of the Department of French, UCC, National University of Ireland Cork. She set up the MA in Applied Linguistics programme at UCC, with colleagues in the Department of English. She has published widely in international journals and edited collections in the areas of sociolinguistics (French in Canada, language and gender), applied linguistics (French as a second language) and Canadian Studies. She is author of *Womanspeak* (Mercier Press, 1999) and co-author with Vera Regan of *French in Canada: Language Issues* (Peter Lang, 2006, forthcoming).

Doris Dippold is currently a PhD student and tutor for German at the University of Southampton. She is interested in Second Language Acquisition, Interlanguage Pragmatics, Pragmatic and Sociolinguistics. In her PhD project, she researches the construction of identity by L2 German learners from a developmental perspective. Furthermore, she is also interested in e-learning, in particular how learning technologies can contribute to the development of learners' reflexive skills.

Hannele Dufva is a Professor at the Department of Languages, University of Jyväskylä. She is currently involved in applying the dialogical theory of language to the research of applied language studies, particularly language learning and language education. Her recent publications include papers on beliefs about language learning, children's metalinguistic awareness and the dialogical psychology of language. She has also a co-edited (with Pietikäinen and Laihiala-Kankainen) collection of papers on multilingualism and multi-voiced identity.

Sue Fraser is a Doctorate in Education student at the University of Durham. She is currently conducting research into the communicative competence of learners of English in high schools in Japan. She has taught at the Institute for Applied Language Studies, University of Edinburgh, where she was involved in teacher-training and materials writing. Her research interests include phonology, discourse analysis, and the use of literature and drama in ELT.

Sheena Gardner is a Senior Lecturer in the Centre for English Language Teacher Education at the University of Warwick, and is coordinator of the MA in English Language Teaching for Specific Purposes. Her research in educational linguistics centres on the analysis of spoken and written discourse from systemic functional perspectives.

Lynda Griffin is an Associate Lecturer with the Faculty of Education and Language Studies at the Open University and an English tutor at a Sixth Form College. Her research interests are in the area of academic writing practices and academic literacy in higher education, audience construction and identity in writing, discourse analysis and the discoursal construction of writer/reader relationships in student academic writing.

Roz Ivanič is Professor of Linguistics in Education and Associate Director of the Lancaster Literacy Research Centre. Her research interests include writer identity, intertextuality, multimodal communication, writing practices in both academic and non-academic settings and adult literacy. Her publications include *Writing and Identity: the discoursal construction of identity in academic writing* and, with Romy Clark, *The Politics of Writing*. She is co-editor with David Barton and Mary Hamilton of *Worlds of Literacy* and *Situated Literacies*.

Hilary Nesi is a Reader in the Centre for English Language Teacher Education at the University of Warwick, and is project director for the BASE and the BAWE corpora. Her research interests include the analysis of academic genres, corpus linguistics, learner dictionary design and EAP materials development.

Bojana Petrić teaches at the Department of Applied Linguistics at Eötvös Loránd University in Budapest, Hungary. Her doctoral dissertation was a study of citation practices in student academic writing. She has published in journals such as *English for Specific Purposes, The Writing Center Journal, Novelty, System,* and *International Textbook Research.* She is a contributing editor of *Misao,* an educational review in Serbia.

Sari Pietikäinen works as a researcher in the Department of Communication, University of Jyväskylä. Her research interests lie in critical discourse analysis, multilingualism in Sami language contexts and revitalising language practices. She has published articles on critical discourse analysis, media representations of ethnic minorities and discursive construction of Sami identity. She is currently working on a project focusing on the empowerment potential of Sami language media.

Srikant Sarangi is Professor and Director of the Health Communication Research Centre at Cardiff University. His research interests are in discourse analysis and applied linguistics; language and identity in public life and institutional/professional discourse studies (e.g. healthcare, social welfare, bureaucracy, education etc.). He currently holds several project grants (Funding bodies include The Wellcome Trust, The Leverhulme Trust, ESRC) to study various aspects of health communication, e.g. genetic counselling, Quality of Life in HIV/AIDS and Telemedicine. The other areas of healthcare research include communication in primary care, palliative care, with particular reference to the assessment of consulting and communication skills. He is author and editor of six books, guest-editor of five journal special issues and has published over one hundred journal articles and book chapters. He is the editor of *Text & Talk: an interdisciplinary journal of language, discourse and communication studies* as well as the founding editor of *Communication & Medicine* and with (C. N. Candlin) of the *Journal of Applied Linguistics.* He is also general editor (with C. N. Candlin) of two book series[es]: *Studies in Applied Linguistics* and *Studies in Language and Communication.*

Andry Sophocleous is Lecturer in the Department of Languages at Intercollege, Nicosia. Her teaching covers the areas of Linguistics and English as a Second Language. Her present research is concerned with the language attitudes of young Greek-Cypriots towards the Greek-Cypriot Dialect. Her research interests include diglossia, code-switching, majority-minority language relations and language and national identity.